Dancing With Shadows

A Mystic's Guide to Enlightenment

NIRVANA

Dancing with Shadows

ALSO BY NIRVANA

The Silent Path
The Greatest Love Story Never Told
In Search of I
The Ocean in a Drop
The Whirling Dervish
Where the Hell Are You Going?
Storm Before the Calm

Dancing with Shadows

Copyright © 2024 Nirvana Foundation
All rights reserved.

ISBN: 978-1-962685-06-1

No part of this publication may be reproduced, distributed, or transmitted in any form or by any means, including photocopying, recording, or other electronic or mechanical methods, without the prior written permission of the publisher, except as permitted by U.S. copyright law.

For permission requests, contact
Nirvana Foundation
Email: info@nirvana.foundation
Website: www.nirvana.foundation

Acknowledgment

The whole universe has to come together to move a single blade of grass. This book would not have been possible without the support of everything that has ever happened. I am especially grateful to my students, who record, transcribe, edit, and publish my talks.

Dancing with Shadows

Table of Contents

Introduction	11
Introduction to Meditation	13
Meditation is a Journey	15
Perfect Posture	19
Sthira Sukha Asana	23
The Flame Within	29
The Ultimate Reality	32
A New Body	35
The Technique	37
Someone Else is Watching	39
You are the Creator	47
Eternity is Within	50
Jumping the Religious Hurdle	52
The Rhythm of Life	57
Understanding Destruction	58
Perception and Creation	61
Just Begin Dancing	63
When Dancing Becomes Meditation	66
Stop What You're Doing	73
You Have to be There	74
Going Deeper	76
Karma	80
The Technique	85
Feel the Body	95
Nature of the Body	96
Sleep and Sex	100
The Technique	107
The Fleeting Flower	113

The Technique	114
Buddha's Philosophy	116
Mind is Momentary	118
Heart of the Matter	**121**
Mind is Not the Brain	122
Politics and Religion	129
The World of Ideas	132
Journey to the Heart	135
Inner Voice	**143**
Irresponsible Mind	146
Survival Instinct	151
Mind, Meet Silence	154
Watching the Noise	159
Embellishing Silence	**163**
The World of Senses	164
Between Notes	167
No Words	170
Music for Sattva	172
Where is Music Happening?	176
Laughter is Sunshine	**181**
The Ultimate Joke	182
Postponing Happiness	189
We are All Connected	194
Mirror, Mirror	**199**
Am I Real?	200
The Technique	208
Consciousness and Awareness	215
Mother Nature	**221**
Change	223
The Technique	225

Half Awake, Half Asleep	228
Watching Pain	231
Why Pain?	232
Watching Pain	238
Experiencing Bliss	244
Transcending Pain	245
Just for Fun	251
Life is a Play	252
Getting to the Center	254
Bright Light Meditation	257
Remove the Mind from Meditation	260
Fear of Losing Ourselves	264
Breaking the Rules	269
Path of Knowledge	272
Disturbing the Body	276
Mind is time	278
The Technique	282
Read Yourself to Enlightenment	291
Language	292
Recorded Knowledge	296
The Technique	298
Shiva's Third-Eye Meditation	305
Transcending the Head	305
Shiva	311
The Technique	313
Shavasana	319
Contemplation on Death	320
Nothingness	324
Knowing That You Don't Know	327
Imaginations Gone Wild	330

The Technique	333
Sit Down and be Quiet	339
Mind is a Filter	340
Stillness of the Mind	344
Sound of Silence	349
Missing Silence	350
Emptiness	353
Madness of the Mind	358
Whirling Your Way to Bliss	369
Rumi	370
Music and Language	373
Whirling	381
The Technique	385
Tantric Sex	387
Orgasm	389
Marriage	394
Sex on the Mind	401
Taranga Meditation	407
Don't Compromise on Truth	408
Playing with Stillness	410
The Technique	416
Vipassana	421
Pranayama	423
The Technique	427
Watching the Dream	437
You're Always Dreaming	439
You have to Wake Up	445
Conscious Watching	449
The Technique	453
About Nirvana	465

Introduction

In the quiet spaces of the mind, where light meets the dark, lies the realm of meditation. "Dancing with Shadows" is an invitation to explore this realm, a comprehensive guide designed to illuminate the path for both the beginner and the experienced meditator. This book is not merely a collection of meditation techniques; it is a journey through the myriad ways in which we can connect with ourselves and the universe.

Filled with insights, practices, and stories, "Dancing with Shadows" dives deep into the art and science of meditation. Each chapter, dedicated to a unique form of meditation - from the physicality of Asana to the tranquil silence of Vipassana - offers not just the method but also the rich tapestry of history and personal narratives that surround each practice. It is a reminder of the diverse ways in which we can achieve mindfulness and inner peace, acknowledging that there is no one-size-fits-all approach to meditation.

The techniques presented in this book, ranging from Candle Meditation to Tantric Sexual Meditation, and from the joyful abandon of Laughter Meditation to the profound tranquility of Silence Meditation, are gateways to different aspects of our consciousness. They are tools to help us dance with our shadows, to embrace the light and the dark within us, and to find harmony in their coexistence. To fully experience the effectiveness of a technique, practice it for at least thirty days to see if it's a fit for your path.

"Dancing with Shadows" is more than just a book; it is a companion for your meditation journey. It seeks to demystify the practices of meditation, making them accessible and relatable, while preserving their depth and significance. Each chapter is a stepping stone that invites you to experience meditation not just as a practice, but as a celebration of life.

This book is for those who seek to understand the why and the how of meditation, for those who wish to deepen their practice, and for those who are just beginning to explore this ancient path to self-discovery. Let "Dancing with Shadows" guide you through the landscape of your inner world, as you discover the beauty and the transformative power of meditation.

Welcome to your journey. Let the dance begin.

Introduction to Meditation

Meditation is complete by itself and is separate from all other activities. It stands apart from your normal waking consciousness, your dreaming, your sleep, and all your mental activities. It must be approached as a distinct and separate entity. Only after progressing far enough on the path can you realize how everything is meditation, and how every other aspect of life is connected to meditation. When you're just beginning, you need to make a clear distinction. You have to identify the right posture, the correct technique, and all the subtle nuances of meditation. Additionally, you must learn how to avoid common pitfalls in meditation.

So, let us start with asana or posture. We are familiar with the term "asana" in yoga. "Yoga" is union, and "asana" is the posture you take to unify your mind, body, and spirit. Yoga and meditation are a unification process. What has separated you into multiple entities? Why do you need a unification process? Are you not already one? When you pay closer attention, you will see you're not one entity, but multiple.

There's your mind, which operates independently. It has a mind of its own. Then there's your body, with its own memories and desires. Lastly, there's the silent witness, your self, which desires only to be itself. You want to be you. When you're not you, that yearning for you manifests as a desire. So, you have three distinct entities pulling you in different directions. Your mind and body want to pull you away from the present moment, but the self wants to bring you back. This creates a conflict. Meditation serves as a means to resolve this internal conflict.

The starting point of resolving this conflict is making a conscious decision to align these three elements. That is what happens when you assume the meditation posture or asana. Patanjali talks about the best asana for meditation - he calls it "sthira sukha asana." "Sthira" is firm, "sukha" is pleasant, and "asana" is posture. This is very important to understand. He gives the most simple of postures that you can take to go deep into meditation. He gives direct access to taking the perfect posture in meditation. At the same time, he does not make it rigid. He does not give you the exact posture but he gives you a framework on which every posture is built. He gives you the blueprint of what a posture should be in meditation.

His structure is so simple and so natural. The farther you move away from his structure, the more disturbing your meditation becomes. Why does he talk about "sthira" or firm? Because he understands that your body loves movement, your mind loves movement, and that is what takes you away from the present moment. Firmness means your body has to be firm, as close as possible, to the present moment.

Meditation is a Journey

What is the actual purpose of meditation? Meditation is a journey from the now to the now. It is not about going somewhere, imagination, or a sense pleasure. It is none of these things the mind and body are familiar with. It is a unique journey with its own destination, pathways, and sensations. What you experience in meditation is unique to all other experiences of life. There is not even a comparison, and you can never know what you're going to experience. The unknown is the most important aspect of meditation.

When you start with the assumption that you know what you're looking for, then you start doing too much with your mind and body. That is what a desiring process is. When your mind is consumed by a desire, it has some conception of that desire, and it knows what to do to work toward that desire. Hence, it starts doing things, imagining things, and creating things.

Similarly, the body - once the body identifies certain ways of experiencing pleasure, it starts moving toward that pleasure and aligning itself with those pleasures. In meditation, you don't know what you're going to find. You cannot assume you know what you're going to find. The moment you drop the assumption that you know the sensation, feeling, or experience you're looking for, then mind and body, and all their activities, become mere distractions. Then you realize, "Meditation is just a word. I don't know what meditation is. No one knows what meditation is. It is a pure mystery, and that mystery can be explored only from the now because the journey is from the now to the deeper now. So, I cannot go from the now to the deeper now if I'm moving around too much physically, and I cannot get there if I'm moving around too much mentally."

This is where the posture of sthira sukha asana comes from. That is why Patanjali says you need to be firm. And then he says it has to be pleasant. The posture has to be comfortable. It's the same in meditation. Sukhasana is when your body is put in such a comfortable position that your meditation journey becomes easy - it's not bumpy. You are allowing yourself to forget the body so that you can go deeper. The whole objective of meditation is to move away from the body - not outward, but inward. Now, this is where Patanjali's description of yogasana has been totally misunderstood. It is not even Patanjali's description. Patanjali explains asana in the most simplistic terms. He does not go into elaborating on it. But even before him, the words "yoga" and "yogasana" were popular enough. Without this clear understanding that the purpose of yoga asana is to go deeper into meditation, people turned yoga into pure gymnastics. It is not just a modern phenomenon.

There has always been a dominant branch of yoga more concerned with the body's movements - exploring its capabilities, the extent of twisting, and creating discomfort. This branch of yoga focuses on inflicting pain through bodily actions. What we witness as modern yoga is merely a small subset of this approach. It still involves experiencing pain and contorting the body, although less extreme than the original practices.

The initial forms of contortion were highly extreme, practiced by sages and yogic practitioners who pushed it to the furthest limits, such as lying on beds of nails. The aim was to induce maximum discomfort to the body, believing that enduring such extreme discomfort while remaining relaxed indicated an achievement of relaxation. This notion is fundamentally flawed; torturing the body isn't a prerequisite for meditation. Much of these physical gymnastics stemmed from the male perspective. Men, as in their other pursuits, perceived yoga as an accomplishment. They interpreted yoga's language of conquering the mind and body as a physical conquest, overlooking its subtleties. While the language appears worldly - conquering the body - it doesn't endorse bodily torture.

There have been instances of yogis who meditated while standing at the edge of a cliff. They aimed to prevent falling asleep, understanding that sleep hampers meditation. Taking this practice to an extreme, they used the risk of falling off the cliff if they dozed off. Meditating outdoors in the heat and sun contradicted the body's needs. Mahavira practiced this form of meditation, earning him the title 'Mahavira,' meaning the great warrior. However, he possessed a deeper understanding, comprehending the concept of surrender.

Many stories attributing extreme yogic practices to Mahavira might be exaggerated, yet they depict real scenarios where yogis pushed the simple idea of sukhasana, a meditative posture, to extreme levels. Patanjali emphasizes that the posture must provide comfort and pleasantness. He dismisses all yogic gymnastics as mere distractions, asserting that a firm and comfortable body is crucial. All other aspects are inconsequential for yoga and meditation.

Perfect Posture

Now, let us try to understand how to attain this posture. What are some ways in which we can observe our posture to align it toward being firm and comfortable? In this regard, a slight distinction has to be made between men and women because inherently, the minds of men and women differ. Their approach to life, philosophy, and consequently, meditation, varies. Even though both seek the same experience in meditation, their inherent differences lead to distinct approaches. Therefore, posture also needs to be approached uniquely for males and females.

For men, firmness comes naturally. If you were to instruct a man to sit, close his eyes, and not move an inch - resist the urge to scratch an itch or adjust to a comfortable position, to be as still as a statue, to conquer his body - he would easily grasp that concept. Firmness is something a man comprehends effortlessly. However, what's challenging for him is understanding a comfortable, pleasurable posture. This is something he needs to learn. In meditation, he tends to stiffen his body more, engaging in a battle with his body due to his inherent warrior-like nature of the mind. He needs to recognize when the battle with the body becomes torture and relax into a more comfortable position. Overthinking about the body and posture detracts from deeper meditation. Relaxation becomes crucial for a man. While firmness naturally aligns with his posture, paying attention to relaxation is crucial.

For a woman, it's the other way around. Comfort comes more naturally to her. If you were to tell a woman, "Just sit comfortably," there's no difficulty in understanding what is comfortable; she knows what is comfortable. But the problem lies in understanding firmness because if she's not firm, she becomes a little too comfortable and falls asleep. The firmness in meditation is basically to counter sleep. So, look at the beauty of these two terms Patanjali has used: firm and comfortable. If you become too firm, you start agitating your mind and body. If you become too comfortable, you will fall asleep. So, you have to be right in the middle of firmness and comfort because we know what absolute firmness is. It's like having to assume this posture with no deviation. It's an obligation you have taken upon yourself. We understand what absolute firmness is when we make a decision and want to hold on to it. We also know what absolute comfort is - where your body is completely at rest, not moving, your spine, head, and legs in comfortable positions, with natural blood circulation happening. You don't even have to think about the body, which happens when you go to sleep. So, we know what a comfortable posture is, and we also know what firmness is. Meditation is about finding a balance between the two.

So for a woman, firmness is what she has to work on. Comfort is easy for her to understand because she does not try to fight the mind or challenge the body too much. It's there - it's her mind, it's her body. She's developed a comfortable relationship with her body. Again, there are exceptions. Some males are more female; some females are more male. Male and female are not just the physical form; it's also how much you connect with yourself, and how you understand yourself. The general understanding is a male is a male because he is a male, both inside and outside; similarly, a female. But depending on how much you have journeyed in understanding yourself, you can connect with your feminine self if you are a male, and you can connect with your masculine self if you are a woman. In meditation, both are needed.

One of the reasons it has been a little difficult for women to pursue the direct meditative path is because of this firmness. Meditation requires a certain level of firmness, a certain level of resolve that says, "Yes, I want to be still, and I want to stay awake. When my mind is taking me away, when I'm drifting into thoughts, I need to forcefully bring it back." That has been a challenging aspect for women. For men, the challenging aspect of meditation has been the lack of challenge. After spending some time meditating, they keep fighting and fighting, and once they become comfortable enough, they lose interest. They reach a point where there's not much of a challenge. That's why you can see many people have tried meditation. They've attained a comfortable posture, they know what a meditative posture is, but they have not become enlightened.

Somewhere in the middle of the meditative journey, you have to drop the man in you and embrace the woman in you. You have to drop conquering and achieving, and embrace acceptance, allowing things to happen. For women, it's exactly the opposite. Initially, they have to start with a little more of the male elements. "I want to conquer this meditation. I want to understand this. I want to get to my true self." In a way, these are manly qualities - achievement, the desire to get to it - but in a different qualitative way, in an inner dimension. But once they start journeying, once they get to that middle path, a woman has no trouble going deeper. That's why if a woman has passed through the initial layers of difficulties in meditation, she has gone all the way. There aren't many examples of women who have dropped their meditation journeys in the middle, mainly because they have touched a zone that is their own, which they are very familiar with, and they realize, "Oh, I'm becoming more and more of myself. More natural and simpler. I like what I'm experiencing, and I'm going to continue to pursue it."

For a man, it's slightly different because of the qualities and changes it brings in him - the way he moves changes, and the way he speaks changes. If he wants to be an absolute man, the subtlety, the feminine movements, and the feminine qualities will disturb him: "I do not like what meditation is doing to me. It's making me soft. It's turning me in a different direction." All those men who have reached the ultimate have embraced, in the middle of the journey, that they're willing to let go of their masculine nature. Patanjali gives us the right way - sthira, which is in a way a male quality, and sukha, which is a feminine quality. He says bring both together, sthira sukha asana.

Sthira Sukha Asana

There are three ways in which you can attain this meditation posture for different types of meditation. One is the sitting posture. You can sit cross-legged, the way traditional Buddhist or Hindu meditators sit, because that is their natural way of sitting. It's not even a meditation posture; that's how Hindus have learned to sit. They sit on the floor. Chairs, cushions, and recliners are all modern phenomena. There was a time when they didn't have any of these things. So sitting on the floor, cross-legged, gives the maximum possible comfort because you are distributing the weight much more evenly throughout your lower body. It's not only your back that is taking on the weight; your legs are also involved. It's just like any building - the wider the foundation, the firmer it is. So when you sit cross-legged, you're basically expanding your foundation, and it's a natural posture. But this doesn't mean that it is comfortable for everyone or that it is the only comfortable posture.

If you are used to sitting on a chair - as long as your alignment is centered, your lower body is comfortable where you're not cutting off blood circulation, the upper body is firm where your head and shoulders are not drooping, and you have good support for your back or have learned how to keep your back erect - sitting on a chair is fine. So, one of the simplest meditation postures is just sitting either cross-legged or on a chair with eyes closed, facing ahead. Although your eyes are closed, you should imagine that you're looking straight and slightly up. Why slightly up? To counter sleep. If you make a conscious decision to look slightly up, it's difficult to fall asleep. Your body has a memory of what a sleeping posture is, so when it wants to go to sleep, it naturally moves the body in a certain way, towards a certain posture. But if you try to keep it firm and not allow yourself to move into those postures, indirectly you're countering sleep.

The majority of meditation practices around the world have adopted this posture. It has been scientifically proven that it's the easiest and simplest of meditation postures: sit still, keep your body firm, look slightly upwards, rest your hands gently on your lap or toward the side. You don't have to assume any specific mudras, which is another deviation from what you can do with your hands. There are many different mudras you can adapt, which have nothing to do with meditation. It doesn't matter, as long as you are just keeping your hands comfortable, going back to Patanjali's "sthira sukha asana."

You can also do standing meditation. If you are meditating for an extended period and feel that sitting for a prolonged time is causing discomfort or hurting your back, you can choose to alternate. For instance, if you're sitting for one hour, you can stand for one hour. However, standing meditation requires a little more effort and support. At least you need to have some kind of back support, like a wall or something to lean on, and you need to be more wakeful when standing and meditating; otherwise, discomfort and the chances of your head drooping increase. So, standing meditation is not the most preferred, but it is an alternative that allows you to meditate for longer periods without disturbing your body too much.

A slight variation of standing meditation could be walking meditation, often referred to as mindfulness.

You can be in a meditative state and draw a simple boundary, then move around that boundary, like walking in a small circle, without losing your centeredness. This is comfortable for the body because the body is comfortable walking. However, the challenge with walking and meditating is the tendency to deviate too much from the present moment. If you start imagining your walk or what you're doing, you deviate. So, while it's a technique you can follow and a posture to consider, it might not be the most advisable meditation technique.

And then there is the lying-down posture - known as Shavasana - where you put your body completely at rest. You're lying flat on your back, looking up, closing your eyes, keeping your spine, back, head, and shoulders just like when you're going to sleep or watching your breath. Again, the challenge with Shavasana - where it's almost like lying down like a dead body, but you are awake and trying to meditate - is sleep. It's very difficult to avoid drifting into sleep during Shavasana.

You can almost see your meditative journey as starting with sitting meditation. Once you've developed your meditative faculties enough and understand what meditation is - how to meditate, how to connect with your inner silence and stillness - then you can transition from the sitting posture to the standing posture or even lying down. Lying down becomes a useful meditation posture when you have exerted the body. Some meditation techniques involve exerting your body, like intense dancing or movements. Then, when you lie down, that becomes the perfect posture because it is the exact opposite of movement.

The important thing to remember in meditation posture is not to wander off into yogic gymnastics or torture the body; it's about keeping it comfortable and firm so that you don't have to constantly think about it. The best posture is the one you can forget once you've assumed it. This allows you to freely explore the realms of meditation. That's the ideal posture for meditation.

Dancing with Shadows

THE FLAME WITHIN

The Candle Flame Meditation is a very different kind of meditation when compared to traditional practices. Traditionally, meditation involves sitting still, closing your eyes, and focusing on something within - your breath, heartbeat, or keeping your focus on a bodily sensation. Watching the candle deviates from this traditional approach by breaking one of the cardinal rules of meditation: closing your eyes. Instead, in candle meditation, you keep your eyes open, actually focusing on the flame.

This brings its own beautiful dynamic to the practice. One aspect is that it helps you relax a bit. Since you're not closing your eyes, it removes that initial fear often associated with meditation. When you first sit in meditation, it's natural to feel apprehensive because you're witnessing the mind in all its glorious and disturbing patterns, watching it move right in front of you. With the mind's tendency to exaggerate everything, it can naturally induce a state of fear. With eyes open, you feel a little more at ease because you're aware of your surroundings. You're looking at the candle flame but also aware of what's around you, easing the tension of solely watching. However, having your eyes open can also bring more distractions. Your awareness might shift from the candle flame to the candle itself, and you might start imagining what's happening around you. Since your eyes are open, any tiny movements or changes can easily draw your mind's attention, leading to drifting into imagination. There are benefits and things to be mindful of in candle flame meditation. This meditation mirrors the nature of life very closely. Let's try to understand this further.

There is a beautiful story from the life of Buddha: One of the disciples comes to him and asks, "What happens to me? What happens to my body after I die?" Buddha shows him a candle flame, blows it out, and says, "What happened to the flame?"

If there's one reaction I would have loved to watch and enjoy, it would be the reaction on the face of the individual who asked this question. To see his face when Buddha blew out the candle and asked, "What happened to the flame?" If you think about it, he would have come with a lot of expectations. He was looking for a philosophical explanation. Buddha spoke to Hindus, most of whom already had deep-rooted preconceptions of what a self is, what a past life is, and what happens after death. Hindu ideology is filled with detailed explanations of rebirth - reincarnation is one of the pillars of Hindu philosophy. The self, the soul, and the immortality of the soul are the foundations on which the whole doctrine is built: The belief is that there is something inside you - your spirit, your soul, your self - that is immortal. Your body will die, your mind will die, but your soul cannot die; it continues.

The idea of the immortal self, reincarnation, the transmigration of the soul, past life, future life - these are very important ideas in Hindu philosophy. So naturally, this guy would have come with a lot of expectations, trying to get some justification for his beliefs. He asks, "What happens to my body after I die?" expecting something like, "Your body dies, your soul moves, and depending on your tendencies, habits, and past karma, you will take birth as another human being or as an animal. Then your search begins again." - that's what he would have expected. But he's come to an awakened man. He's not come to a Hindu priest, a philosopher, a theologian, or a hypocrite who has no experience of what he's talking about.

THE ULTIMATE REALITY

Buddha knows the impermanent nature of the self. For Buddha, the self was not the immortal self. He did not use the word "self" in the same sense as Hindus did. This is the single biggest conflict between Buddhism and Hinduism. The single biggest difference is that Buddha did not believe in the existence of an immortal soul, an immortal self. For a Hindu mind, that is sacrilege. Then what is the point of spirituality? What is the point of meditation? What is the point of enlightenment? But experientially, Buddha is saying something very significant. He is referring to the self as the individual identity, while Hindu philosophy refers to the self as the ultimate self devoid of all qualities, devoid of all properties. It's the same word but used in two completely different contexts.

For Buddha, that ultimate reality can never be spoken about. He did not utter a single word about the ultimate nature of being, the self, or consciousness. He only spoke from the point of view of the body because he knew that it led to all kinds of misunderstandings. Trying to define in human language the ultimate nature of reality - whatever you call it - the human mind will understand it in its limited sense. So, he refused to speak about the ultimate reality. For him, the self was you - your mind, your body, your thoughts, your separate existence.

For the Hindus, the ultimate self, the true self, the Brahman, was the ultimate state you attain after you've dropped all your individual identification with the ego. Even that supreme reality was the self for them. So, Buddha is referring to the self as the human body, and he shows him the candle, saying, "Look at the candle flame. There is nothing permanent here. This candle flame isn't a continuous flame. Every moment, some conditions are coming together to create the flame. It needs the fuel, the burning of the wax, the wick, and air - all these things are coming together to support that candle flame. Although you are looking at the candle flame and thinking it is one flame, the flame you looked at was long gone. Every time you look at the flame, it's actually a new flame that is being created. But your mind holds on to the permanent nature of the flame. So if you were to light the candle and come back after five minutes, would you be able to say that is the flame that I lit? No. The flame that you lit gave birth to another flame and it disappeared. That's what is happening every moment. One flame is lighting another flame, and it has done its job, and it's gone. And the next flame is doing the same thing. As long as all the conditions are there, the flame continues to burn. When one of the conditions - not even all - when one of the conditions changes, it is no longer conducive for the flame to exist; the flame goes away."

The body is exactly like that. Your individual self is exactly like that. Certain conditions are keeping it alive - the air you breathe, the food you eat, the earth on which you stand. Existence is holding the candle flame of your body alive. For whatever reason, if one of the conditions is not met, suddenly, if the air is sucked out of the room that you're in or the ground gives away, what happens to that permanent nature of the self that you're holding on to? It's gone. And then the question, "What happens to it after you die?" Now, that question is irrelevant because what happened to the flame after I blew it out? Where did it go? It never went anywhere because it was never there in the first place. For it to go somewhere, you have to assume some level of reality. And because you hold on to that idea that the body is real, you keep on thinking about it even after death.

This is a very hard concept for Hindus to understand because you are looking for an answer. Yes, my body is gone, but I'm still there. My soul migrates. But Buddha is talking about something else altogether. Buddha is so scientific, so precise, and so reluctant to drag people into any philosophical discussion. He just wants to shut your mind. He wants to shut that part of you that goes on thinking about the permanent nature of the body, the permanent nature of the self, when it isn't permanent; it is just a coming together of the conditions. The candle flame was never there.

A NEW BODY

Every moment, our body is manifesting itself in our consciousness based on certain conditions, but it's not just one body. Every moment, the image of the body gives rise to another image before the old image disappears. Every moment, you are taking birth and you're dying. Because you hold on to one permanent nature of your body, you believe that "This is me, I cannot be changing every moment." You don't see the changes that are happening every moment. But every few months, every few years when you go back and look at how you were, you will see there is a difference. You're not the same person - something has changed. And you tend to think, "Oh, that is growing old. It is still me." You still hold on to the same idea, although existence is telling you that you are something totally different now.

Look at how you were when you were five. And look at now when you are fifty. You are completely different. Everything is different. With very few exceptions, nothing in your body has stayed the same. Your whole body is different. You don't need a philosopher or an enlightened person to tell you this. Even scientists will tell you this. The body has gone through a complete recycling process. But what is the only thing that is giving it its sense of permanence? It is your holding on to the image. You see that child and yourself as one because there is a resemblance in form. You look at the face and you can see the resemblance. You can see the resemblance in the body. Although so much has changed, there's that deep desire to hold on to that permanent nature of the body because that's your only identity. You don't know anything else other than that. You hold on to it, although every moment you are taking birth and you're dying.

Death is not something that happens at the end of an experience of life. Death is an eternal, constant reality of life. You can see that impermanence in the candle flame. When you are meditating on the candle flame, you are meditating on the impermanence of life. Initially, you will start with a fixed image: "This is the candle. This is the wick. This is the light. This is where I'm sitting. This is the room I'm in." You start watching. Initially, it is impossible to shake off the idea that none of this is real. It has to be real for you. The candle flame has to be real. Your body has to be real because that is where you're starting from. And to realize that none of this is real is the ultimate objective of meditation. What you will eventually experience - awakening, enlightenment - cannot be put into words. You can call it the ultimate experience of the self where your perception of the body and mind disappears and your self expands to engulf the whole universe, and you become everything. Or in Buddha's terms, you attain to nothingness. It's just words, but both are saying the same thing. Something happens. Something fundamentally changes.

The Technique

When you're starting, you have to assume that all this is real, and you start watching the candle. You start watching the flame. Initially, there is a disturbance - the mind keeps drifting while watching the candle flame. Sometimes it moves to the outermost layer of the flame and sometimes it tries to focus on the center because even the candle flame is a complex mechanism for the mind. It's not just a fixed thing that is sitting there. It is moving. It is changing, there are multiple colors, and you can identify both the center and the outside of the flame. The size and shape of the flame are constantly changing, and you are watching all this.

Although you want to simply keep your focus on one object - which is the candle flame - multiple things are happening there. This is where it takes a little bit of practice to keep your awareness on the flame in totality. Everything that is happening inside and outside that flame is your point of observation. You have to be a little gentle with your observation. You cannot focus too intently like the way you would in a third-eye meditation. Third-eye meditation is all about focus. Watching the candle flame is all about awareness. There's got to be gentleness because the flame is very gentle. The way it's moving is very gentle. There's no force, and it is not straining to draw your attention. It is so beautiful, so serene, so glowing, and moving. You can watch it, being relaxed. You don't have to force yourself to watch it. Sometimes the attention shifts to the wick, sometimes it shifts to the candle, and it's fine. Anytime your awareness shifts away, bring it back to the flame. Sometimes it might shift even outside the candle, and it can start visualizing what's happening around it. Just bring it back to the flame. Continue to watch it.

Every day, spend a couple of hours meditating on the candle flame. A minimum of one hour is recommended, but ideally, aim for about two hours - perhaps one in the morning and another in the evening. Avoid exceeding a couple of hours in a day for candlelight meditation to prevent straining your eyes. When you sit to observe the candle flame, your eyes might begin to burn, and tears may form. Keep your eyes open as much as possible, though this may naturally cause irritation and watering. It's perfectly normal for your eyes to become watery during candle flame meditation. It's acceptable to blink occasionally, yet try not to do so continuously.

At the end of about a month of practicing this meditation, during one of the sessions, just keep watching the flame. When you think you are watching the flame without too much disturbance, your focus and awareness have improved, and you're not thinking about anything else, gently close your eyes, and something magical happens. You will close your eyes, but the flame will still be there. You will still be looking at the flame. That is when you'll realize, "Oh, I'm actually seeing the flame inside. My eyes are closed, but I'm seeing the flame inside." Stop there. Take that experience in. Let that experience sink in. Don't bring in your mind. Don't bring in your philosophy. Don't bring in all kinds of explanations. "Oh, it's because my retina was focused on the light, and when I closed it, the image was still in my retina, and that is what I'm seeing." All that is a nonsensical explanation. Your eyes are closed, my dear; you are looking at nothing. There is no light penetrating. Your eyelids are shut. How can you still be looking at the candle? If the eye were capturing the light, and if the eye is the mechanism through which you were observing the light, the moment you close your eyes, the candle flame should disappear.

Someone Else is Watching

The reason the candle flame did not disappear is that you were not only using your eyes to watch. There is some other watcher inside you. It should send a chill up your spine when you see that light while your eyes are closed. Your whole world - the physical world that you have created, all your explanations, all your theories, all your scientific and philosophical discussions of what life is - should shatter right there because your experience is telling you something different. It is telling you that you can see without light. Your imagination can be so powerful that you don't need anything external to see it. Your imagination alone is enough. What else is happening when your eyes are closed? No light particles are entering your eyes, but you're still seeing the candle flame exactly as you are seeing it with your eyes open. So whether your eyes are open or closed makes no difference to your experience of watching the candle flame. That should shatter all preconceived notions of what life is, of what an eye is. The starting point of your journey is when you discard all borrowed knowledge. Then you open your eyes. You might even cry. The experience is so beautiful, so magical, but it's just the first step.

If there are a hundred steps on the ladder of enlightenment, the bliss, the joy that you're experiencing is just the joy of having climbed the first step. Take that first step and you're off the ground. You're off the fixed ideas people have given you. You're off dogmatic belief systems. Now, you're on a journey to know the truth through your own experience. That first step is the most significant. It is also the hardest because that is the step where your preconceived notions are so strong. Your ideas of life are so strong, and that is what you keep fighting when you initially sit in meditation. What is it that you're really fighting? You're fighting the mind which has been seeped in all these ideas. Otherwise, meditation is gentle. You're sitting, just watching the flame. You close your eyes and the flame is inside because there is someone else watching, and he's watching through your body. Once he's learned how to watch enough, he'll discard your body. He'll say, "Okay. Do you want me to watch the candle light? I will watch it. I don't need you." That's why, whether you keep your eyes closed or open, it doesn't matter to him. He's continuing to watch. It's a magical experience, but that's the first step, and then continue to watch.

Let a few more months pass, and then something else happens. You're sitting and watching the flame, and a moment comes when the flame disappears - it's no longer there. Not only the flame but the candle wick and the candle are gone. Everything is gone. Your eyes are open. You're supposed to be seeing things. That is the definition of eyes open. But everything is dark. There's no difference at all between eyes open and eyes closed. Your eyes are perfectly open. You know it. You know the sensation of eyes open, but everything has gone dark. You're not seeing anything. You're not seeing the candle flame. You're not seeing the light. You're not seeing the candle. Nothing. You are scared. You don't know what's happening. And then you close your eyes, and there is the flame inside.

Why does this happen? It's because you have been watching the candle flame with so much focus, so much awareness, and for such a long time, that after a while, the one who's watching loses interest in the candle. Initially, he's excited. He wants to see how the candle moves. He wants to practice this meditation. He wants to prove to himself that he can focus. All these ideas are there, keeping him fixed on the candle. But he's done this day in and day out. He's traveled enough around and inside the candle. He's explored the entire dynamics of watching the candle, and slowly his awareness is being withdrawn. Although his body is there, his mind is there, and he's trying to watch the candle, there's someone deep down inside who's the least bit bothered about the candle. He wants to be inside. And in a single moment, he chooses not to watch the candle.

What is it telling you? There is someone else watching. And he is the one who chooses whether to watch the candle or not. "Whether I want to watch the candle or not is immaterial. Up until now, my entire life, whatever I thought was me - my body, my mind - was only a tiny part of me. My eyes are open, and if I am a mechanism, if my body is just a mechanism, then why am I unable to see? I'm giving it all the conditions to perceive the light. But if someone inside chooses not to watch the light, he need not. What does that mean? It means there is something inside me that can remain independent of the body. If something can remain independent of the body, then that something has to be beyond death because death can happen only to the body. Death can only happen to something physical." For the first time, you will know there is something permanent there. You've touched the zone of immortality, but you've only glimpsed it. It's not your experience yet. That's why when you finish your meditation and engage in something else, you'll forget all about it. But during that experience, all these thoughts start racing in your mind. And as you're watching, the fundamental reality shifts. It has to generate that new way of looking, and it will generate.

What is happening here? I'm supposed to be sitting and watching the candle flame, and I'm doing it, but where is the candle flame? When I keep my eyes open, it's not there. When I keep my eyes closed, I can watch it inside. Why am I behaving differently from how I'm supposed to behave? It's because you're meditating. That's what meditation is. Meditation is to break that pattern you have built for yourself. Nothing is real there. Your body is not real. Your mind is not real. Your idea of yourself is not real. The room you're sitting in is not real. The candle flame is not real. The candle is not real. Everything is imagined in your consciousness. The only thing that is real is that aliveness, that consciousness, that being, that self. Apart from that, everything is imagined, and meditation has just revealed that to you. It has just given you a glimpse of the other. Because your mind was so clouded with all these concepts and ideas of life, it was keeping you bound to it. For the first time, a simple practice of watching the candle has awakened something inside you. You've taken the next step on the ladder of awakening. But that is just a glimpse of the glimpse of the glimpse when compared to the ultimate that you're going to experience because your body is still there. It is only one sense, which is the sense of seeing, that has turned inward, and that too, only momentarily.

You need to continue meditating to turn every sense inward, and not just for a single moment but for as long as you desire. Then a day will come, just like that. While you were sitting and watching the candle, the candle flame disappeared, and everything disappeared. Similarly, a day will come when you are sitting in meditation, all your senses will withdraw inside, and everything you know about yourself, everything that you think you are, will vanish in the snap of a finger. In a single moment, just like that candle flame, your body is gone, your mind is gone. You cannot even explain how it happened, just like you couldn't explain where the candle flame went. You cannot make it happen, but it will happen.

Once that moment happens, when you realize it doesn't matter whether you keep your eyes open or closed, and it also does not matter what you are watching - you have gotten a sense of the watcher. You have connected with the watcher. Then automatically, your desire to watch the candle flame disappears. It should happen naturally. It can happen at the end of two months or three months, but you don't do candle flame meditation forever. It is a beautiful meditation to start with, but after a while, you will naturally drop it. You will just close your eyes because it feels a little more comfortable now, your eyes are not irritated, and it's not making too much of a difference. When it's not making too much of a difference whether your eyes are open or closed, that means your fear is gone. The initial fear of keeping your eyes closed is gone. Now you can just close your eyes, go inside, and continue to meditate. Then you can shift to watching the breath.

If you think you've still not found that solid space that you can watch clearly, pick a technique, but let that technique be inward, something you can practice with your eyes closed. The next time you go and sit there, yes, you're sitting in the same room, in the same place, but there's no candle, no watching the flame. But this has to happen naturally. As long as there is the desire to watch the candle flame, watch it; that means your attention is still drawn outward. But once that turning happens, when you see there is no necessity to watch the candle, just drop it.

Dancing with Shadows

You are the Creator

Creative meditation is about watching the creator. Every moment, you are creating. You're watching the breath. Watch who's creating the breath. There is someone - something is creating the breath. At that very moment, thoughts are running in your mind. Who is creating these thoughts? There are your body sensations. Who's creating these sensations? For a moment, try to watch these sensations and try to drift away from those sensations. Try to move your awareness to something else. Now, what happens to these sensations when you move your awareness away from them? They disappear. What happens to a thought when you don't watch it? It is gone. You have to be there to add fuel to this creative process. If you're not watching, what is the use of creation?

What is the use of creativity? If you let things happen without your conscious awareness, without watching, then you are not watching the creator.

That is where confusion comes from. That is where uncertainty arises. There's so much creation happening inside you, and so little of it is being watched. When you decide to watch, there's too much to take in, and that is the world that you are seeing. You created all this in your unconsciousness, in your sleep. Every day you go to sleep, and in your dream, you're creating things, you're creating worlds, you're creating experiences. But because you are unconscious, when you wake up, it's all too overwhelming. So you restrict yourself just to the body and to the mind. "Let me try and understand this. I don't know who created all this. Look at this. There's no way I can create all these things. How can I create all these things? I'm just a tiny creature." Well, you are a tiny creature in the body, maybe tiny even in the mind, but what if there's something else to you? What if you are at the very center of life? What if you are consciousness itself? What if you are aliveness itself? What if you are creating without knowing it? What if all this is being created in your dream? What if this life is your dream?

Naturally, it's overwhelming to think like this - it's a very big responsibility. Then you need to take responsibility for pain and suffering in the world, and you have to take responsibility for suffering in your own life. But Buddha did it beautifully. He took responsibility. He saw the suffering in the world. He took responsibility for that suffering but he did not take it as a burden. He did not try to end the suffering in the world. He went one step further and said, "If there is suffering in the world, why am I experiencing suffering inside me? How can there be suffering outside and not inside? When I experience suffering, I'm experiencing it inside. When I see pain in the world, I'm experiencing the pain inside me." He turned the whole game around. And he said, "Leave your God, leave your creator, and all that nonsense, I am experiencing all these things inside me. I am creating thoughts. I am creating anger. I am creating jealousy. I am creating uncertainty. I have to be the creator."

After a few years of learning from various teachers and gaining insights from his own experiences, Buddha encountered some challenges. However, through these trials, he ultimately discovered the true nature of his being. He emerged as the Buddha, the awakened one, the enlightened one. Long after the concept of God has faded, along with notions of divine judgment, heaven, and hell - long after the nonsense of religious dogma is gone, Buddha will remain relevant. His refusal to accept a creation outside of himself distinguishes him. He pursued self-discovery wholeheartedly, declaring, "I will discover it for myself." Every moment, you shape your reality through your thoughts, imagination, preferences, and conscious actions, thereby creating your life.

ETERNITY IS WITHIN

There is no external entity. Drop that burden. Drop that responsibility. Drop trying to satisfy an external entity. That is simply a deviation that has kept Man far away from his true search. When you drop that, you have to start watching your creation; otherwise, life will be chaotic. That is why humanity has lived in so much chaos and so much pain. That is why there is so much violence, so many wars, and so much injustice - we put the responsibility outside us. Then we said God is going to judge us, but as long as we can carefully and artfully use words to define our experience so that we're satisfying God, we can go ahead and do whatever nonsense we want to do in this world.

Think about it: God tells Abraham, "To show your loyalty to me, I want you to burn your son on the altar. I want you to offer him as a burnt sacrifice." Abraham takes his son to the hilltop, ties him up, and is about to kill him. Then it is said that God interferes and says, "Now you have proved your allegiance to me. Now you have proved you're loyal to me; you don't have to kill him." What a stupid story! These are the stories that have dominated the human mind. And what is the definition of the word "holocaust"? It means a burnt offering. Where do you think that idiot Hitler got the idea of sacrifice? Where do you think he had the vision and the guts to imagine that he could sacrifice a group of people and be closer to God? Because of these stupid ideas - if God can sacrifice, if God can ask for your son as a burnt offering, then maybe He'll be more pleased if I offer all these Jews to Him. Not just one, but millions of burnt offerings. That is literally what the word "holocaust" means.

Religion has caused so much destruction both inside and outside. It has divided humanity. It has severed the connection between Man and nature. It has placed him in a completely different space where he can act against the will of nature, against the will of life, and merely articulate his life cleverly to appease God - thinking that's enough. Then one can continue doing whatever they want. There's no need to monitor the mind, the body, or consider the impact on others or animals - nothing. Just artfully phrase yourself. Sprinkle some water; that's sufficient. Confess your sins. And if the person sitting in that confessional booth tells you, "Yes, your sins are forgiven. Now, you are ready for heaven," off you go. Maybe a little donation helps too.

All that nonsense is what has kept humanity in this state. One look at the world, and we know what has happened to the human race. Where did we falter? The first step. We faltered on the first step of self-inquiry. We put a step, and we called it God, and we became afraid to step on it. Self-inquiry ended right there. How can I step on God? It's just a step. You have to step on it; you have to step on Him to go ahead and discover the true nature of your being. And people have been afraid. Meditation, going deeper, realizing the truth - my God. What is all this? How? It's not in the Bible. It's not in the Quran. It's not in my Gita. All they are telling me is just to believe. And if I can believe, it's enough. Why the hell do I have to worry about meditation? If I can simply believe, I don't have to take responsibility.

Jumping the Religious Hurdle

Creativity, creation, creative meditation - it's all about taking responsibility and watching every moment of what you're creating because you are the creator. Anything and everything you do can be turned into a creative meditation provided you step on that stone. Look at it. "God" is written on it. "Creation" is written on it. Step on it, and you'll see there are several more steps to go. That's only the first step. After that, there's your breath, your mind, your emotions, and consciousness. There's light, there's alignment - there's so much, but God is the first hurdle. Break through that, and the whole universe is waiting there. The universe has always been waiting; it wants to reveal itself through you. That's why it keeps pushing you.

For thousands of years, it hasn't stopped, and it will never stop. It's looking for that individual, for that one person who can reject all this, sit under the shade of a tree, under the sky, and watch life happening inside and outside. That's it - no scriptures, no logic, no reasoning, nothing required. Just a pure scientific attitude. Because even with logic and reasoning, we've applied too much to religion, too much to theology. It may make logical sense, but at the end of the day, it's all nonsense.

Perhaps science is the only thing that remains pure because it inquires. It isn't dogmatism; it isn't belief. Meditation is pure science, the ultimate in science. There can't be science above meditation because you're sitting and watching. You are the experimenter - you are the experiencer. Everything is right there - the inquiry is happening right there. All you have to do is step away from the constructed prison walls of religious dogmatism and venture into the open sky. Go to nature, go to life, and ask them: "What is it that you want me to be? Why are you so beautiful? Why is there so much joy? When I wake up in the morning, why do you sing to me? Why do you use birds? Why are you so intoxicating?" Ask nature, and she'll give you the answer. You will see the beauty in nature, and you will see the beauty inside. The ultimate expression of beauty is your own true self. When you go deeper and connect with your true self, you'll know why nature is so beautiful - because you are beautiful. Why nature is so pure - because you are pure. Why there is so much joy, so much bliss in existence - because you are joyful, you are blissful. Your mind has been hijacked by religion, by God - not your body, not your spirit. You are still fully you inside. You just need to make a small turnaround.

It's not enough to simply drop the idea of God. You have to drop the whole process. Many people have abandoned the idea of God, but they haven't engaged in self-inquiry. Dropping the idea of God implies taking responsibility for understanding life from within. Just choosing to be an atheist isn't enough because you're still within the same mindset. You're only choosing atheism as a reaction against belief in God. It's merely a response. It cannot be a response. The rejection has to arise from within, not merely an ideological or theological response. For instance, "People who believe in God are stupid. I don't believe in God, so I must be smart." It's not that kind of belief. It's something that surges from within, leading you to reject the idea of an external creator so completely that you have to accept the fact that you are the creator and you have to observe your life.

Creative meditation involves turning every moment of creation, every moment of your creative energies' outflow, into a meditation.

Dancing with Shadows

The Rhythm of Life

Shiva is the king of dancers. He is the one who dances existence into being. He's the one who creates, sustains, and destroys all through his dancing. In Hindu mythology, his dance is what creates the universe. Of course, it's a symbolic way of saying that the whole universe is a dance. It is not a structured, purposeful creation. It is an unstructured, flowing, changing dance and we can see it - dance is how nature creates. There is a rhythm to creation, there is beauty in creation, and there is the cyclical nature of how things come and go, with all the characteristics of a dance - rhythm, movement, change, and cycles. And how can we forget music? Nature is filled with music. When she's dancing, she's also singing. She's dancing to her own beats.

Shiva, apart from being a yogi or an enlightened man, is the primary mover in Hindu mythology, and he occupies a unique place among all the other deities. Of course, he is the destroyer, one of the trinities alongside Brahma and Vishnu. Shiva is identified as the destroyer, Brahma as the creator, and Vishnu as the sustainer. However, Shiva is sometimes referred to as all three: the creator, the sustainer, and the destroyer. It is his dance that we experience as reality. Now, more than the creator and sustainer, Shiva occupies a unique place as the destroyer. That is unusual. Why would you worship a destroyer? You can worship a creator or a sustainer. Almost all major religions worship the creator, but there are hardly any cultures where you hear about the destroyer being worshipped.

Understanding Destruction

The nature of destruction is not understood. What is being destroyed? Destruction by itself is not bad. Destruction also implies creation. At that very moment of destruction, something is being created. For example, during a forest fire, while the forest fire is burning, the loss of existing plant life and sometimes animal life might be seen as pure destruction. However, if you come back after a while and look at the place where the fire has been, you will see fresh, new growth. After some time, you can observe that it's growing more lush than those regions that were not touched by fire. In a way, the fire provided the necessary space for new growth to happen. Shiva is the destroyer of the mind. Shiva is the destroyer of the ego. And Shiva is also the destroyer of sexual passions. He's primarily identified as the destroyer of all that you're not. If you were to go to Shiva and ask him a question, he'd metaphorically dismiss it. He won't answer or engage in discussion. He'd simply say, "Watch your breath and enter into bliss. Keep your focus on your third eye and become the ultimate." He gives you one sutra at a time, and that's it. He does not encourage conversations or discussions because he understands that it's all about the mind. He's identified as the one who overcame sexual desires, symbolized through the act of burning sex with his third eye. This is a symbolic, mythical way of expressing that through meditation, he conquered bodily and mental desires. Sex is just a representation of the ultimate desire.

If you can go beyond even the desire for sex, then you have almost conquered all your desires. In a way, most other desires are subsets of that ultimate desire - to experience bliss, to transcend. He's not against sex, but he offers a way through which you can conquer and transcend it. He does this not through a structure, not through a method, but through his dance. It is said that when he dances, the whole universe dances. The ferocity with which Shiva moves causes streams to change their direction of movement, mountains to tremble, and oceans to swell up because when he dances, it's not just him dancing - it's the whole universe dancing with him. Why? Because he is the universe.

An individual is not a simple phenomenon. He is very deep, the beating heart of existence. He's just unaware of it most of the time. Because he's unaware of it, he moves in his sleep. He creates when he wants to. He sleeps when he wants to. He eats when he wants to. He lives and dies. But when he realizes the true nature of his being, he cannot help but dance. He cannot help but see the whole of existence as his expression of dancing. He can see the movement. He can see the rhythm in everything. In a way, it is befitting that where the particle collision experiments are being conducted in Geneva, there is a statue of Nataraja, a statue of Shiva. It was donated by India as a symbol of the destruction of ignorance and the birth of knowledge. Shiva is a representation of wisdom, a representation of knowledge - but the way I see it is Shiva is the destroyer. The destroyer of everything old, of everything past, and all that has happened. He wants you to be here now. He wants you to participate in the cosmic dance. He wants you to see yourself as a part of the dance. In a way, Shiva is the one who destroys all theories and concepts of life so that you can experience the truth of the present moment.

PERCEPTION AND CREATION

The latest discoveries science has been making have, in a way, destroyed the classical idea of physics. All the ongoing quantum mechanical experiments have completely turned classical physics on its head to a point where scientists now unanimously agree, without any exception, that there is no objective reality outside human perception. Because we perceive it, it's human perception. They say that an electron, one of the fundamental particles, has neither a specific position nor a specific path until someone observes it. Only when you begin to observe it can you either see it at a certain position or see it follow a certain path. Just imagine the significance of this statement. Up until now, we had thought the world was out there and I was here. And even if I'm not there, the world will go on by itself. I am just a tiny part of life. But here, the scientists are saying something totally different. They're saying that if you don't participate in creation, if you don't perceive, if you don't observe, then there is no creation happening there.

Literally, they are talking about the point of creation. When I perceive it, the electron comes into existence.

It comes into being. Otherwise, it isn't even there. Of course, we are reluctantly beginning to accept this concept because that almost marks the end of all objective science. And as Einstein says, "Science is nothing but a true, strong, firm belief that there is an objective world above and beyond my perception." That is why he refused to accept the new information, new evidence that was coming through the quantum mechanical studies. He still firmly believed until his death that there was an objective world outside. He could not even imagine trying to understand the nature of reality using science if there was no objective world outside. It's literally the end of science itself.

But what Einstein didn't know is that science need not always be about the outside. There can also be science about the inside. That is what Shiva represents. In a way, it's beautiful, it's befitting that Shiva sits there outside, indicating that all your old science is done. "I've destroyed it," he seems to say. This new invention of man, the particle collider, and all the experiments happening here will mark a new beginning in science, eventually turning us inward. The experimentations have to become inward. But you cannot go on experimenting. True science begins where experimentation stops and experiencing begins. The approach has to be completely different. In dancing, there is no experimentation, no analysis, no thinking - there is just chaos. And out of that chaos, something new will take birth.

Friedrich Nietzsche says, "Unless there is chaos inside you, you cannot give birth to a dancing star." He's right. Ultimately, we don't know how things are created. Many things are happening inside us, but we do know there is chaos inside, tremendous chaos. This chaos is not negative - it's creative chaos. There is a deep yearning inside to create, a profound thirst within us to connect, merge, and become one with existence. Yearning is a pure expression of that thirst; it's not something artificially added to the creature - we are born with it. Every single creature in existence is born with that innate ability to dance. Why? Because deep down, we have the desire to transcend the body. When you dance, when you move, you are, in a way, forgetting your restrictions, forgetting the limitations of the body, and trying to connect with the spirit that is moving you.

JUST BEGIN DANCING

Dancing meditation isn't about you dancing; it's about letting your spirit move you. It's about surrendering to the process of dance. You can listen to music and start moving. You can simply close your eyes and begin moving around, slowly and rhythmically, like a wave. There are various ways to approach dancing meditation. You can start slowly, just as you observe in nature. Nothing in nature is abrupt - there's a rhythm to it. Before something happens, if you know how to watch for it, there are signs in nature. You can see the waves swelling up, indicating a possible hurricane or storm. Now, I see clouds gathering in the sky. There might be lightning, there might be thunder - there are always signs. You can start with waving and moving to the music. You can use any music for this practice.

There is not an indigenous culture in the world that has not used music and dance as a form of self-expression and connection with existence. You cannot find an ancient culture that does not have dance and music as a central form of what we now call entertainment - for them, it was a way of connecting with life. You can use music from any of those cultures and adopt the dance moves from them, whether it's from the native Indian culture, African culture, Hindu culture, Japanese, Chinese, Sufi, or countless other types of movements, along with music that complements those movements. So pick your music and start moving. Begin waving. Drop your self-consciousness. Forget that you are moving.

It is better to do it alone if you're too self-conscious, but after a while, you should be able to drop that self-consciousness and dance wherever you feel like dancing. It doesn't matter. You can dance on the streets, in front of people. Dropping self-consciousness is the objective of dancing. It's about realizing that when you dance, everything has to stop. If others aren't stopping to dance and continuing with their lives, then you shouldn't be concerned about them. The only way you can entertain people or draw them into your dance is if they want to be spectators. Alternatively, your dance has to be so infectious that it prompts them to start dancing too. Because in that moment, you are the universe. Nothing else exists - no people, no places, nothing. Just move - just wave. Let the music penetrate you, let it flow through you. Move like a child.

It's interesting when you watch a group of people dancing, and if children happen to be there, it's amazing to observe the dance. The moves may be the same, but the way children interpret those moves, the way they move to the dance, is different. They add their twists and turns, and there's a sense of joy when they do it. Dance cannot be taught. Yes, you can learn some steps, but the rhythm of dance, the movement, has to come from within. That's why some of the best dancers develop their skills when they're young. You can't suddenly become a great dancer when you are, let's say, forty or fifty and decide, "Now I want to learn how to dance." Yes, you can learn to dance, but unless you go deep into meditation and become childlike, your dance will have that adult quality to it. It'll have structure but won't capture that rhythm. So, move like a child. Just let your body do what it wants to do.

When Dancing Becomes Meditation

This is where one condition has to be added for your dancing to become a meditation. Everything else remains the same. Your connection with the universe, your connection with yourself, your deep desire to forget yourself - it's all the same. But here, as a meditator, you want to experience the stillness amidst all this movement. You should not forget the one who's dancing. You can dance however you want with just one condition: hold on to the dancer. Because ultimately, that stillness - the one who's not dancing, the one who dances without dancing, the one who's dancing in their stillness, in their silence - that ultimate being is right there, is you. But because you're identified with the body, it's easy to forget the one who's dancing and just become attached to the dancing. Keep your awareness on the one who's dancing.

Now, how do you know you're aware of the one who's dancing? You're watching your dancing without focusing on any specific part of your dancing. You are fully aware of your dancing - not any specific moves or body movements, but there's a certain quality to dancing. You can feel that vibration, that connection. As long as you are connected to that, as long as you're aware of that, you can be certain that you are aware of the one who's dancing.

Slowly, from waving, move into rhythmic movements. Create your own steps, your own movements. Slowly intensify your movements and then start shaking your body, vibrating your body. Again, you don't have to do this in a structured way - it will naturally happen. The deeper your abandon is, the more rhythmic and vibrational your body becomes. Because once the body understands that it is trying to connect with stillness, it starts to move in a certain way that allows you to experience that stillness.

If you observe some African or Native American dancers, watch how the dance progresses. Initially, there's a structure to it. They're wearing their costumes, making sounds of animals, and moving rhythmically. But after a while, something completely takes over them, and they forget that they are dancing. You cannot even stop them. Something inside takes over that makes them completely forget they are moving. Almost every indigenous culture has spoken about this effect. In deeper states of dancing, the dancer disappears. There is only the dancing. How is that possible? It's possible because the dancer was never there. You were living your life in such a structured way, such a planned way - carefully, without doing anything other than what your mind is familiar with.

Here, for the first time, your mind is going crazy because you're moving in a way the mind is not familiar with. It doesn't know what to make of that movement. Fifteen minutes after your dance, it retires and goes away somewhere because there's no necessity for the mind to be there. It's the dance of the body. It's the dance of the universe. The mind is a flimsy coward. It cannot face dancing; it just runs away after a while. Here, there's vibration, rhythm, movement - this all happens. Naturally, you connect with that part of you where there is nobody there. Something takes over. Native Americans call it the Great Spirit. It is the Great Spirit that moves, that has put things inside you, and it is the Great Spirit that is dancing, not you. The same in African culture. It is literally the spirit that moves.

If you watch some of these African dancers, it's amazing how, without their awareness, the body is both still and moving at the same time. If you were to sit and watch, you'd see they can keep their upper body still and just move their lower body. It's almost as if the upper body is solidified - nothing is moving, but the lower body is fully rhythmic, dancing everywhere. Then they shift this to the upper body - the lower body becomes still, and the upper body moves. It almost feels like magic. How can a human body do this - when you're dancing, your whole body has to move. But when you're dancing with awareness, when you're dancing in connection to that stillness, automatically, some parts of your body become still.

Even without your awareness, while you're moving one part of the body, there's more enjoyment in keeping another part of the body still. That's what dancing is. Dancing isn't totally chaotic. Somewhere, there's a conversation happening between stillness and movement, an exchange occurring. And there's so much more happening in dance. You don't have to analyze it; you just have to forget yourself and move - move as intensely as you can. Take your intensity to its peak. Let's say you've designated one hour for your dancing. After at least about thirty to forty minutes, you'll know when to intensify. If you've been practicing dancing meditation regularly, the first time you do it, of course, you'll be fully self-conscious, concerned about the time and how you're doing it. But after a while, you'll get into the rhythm. As you approach the end of your dancing, you can intensify as much as you want, reaching a point where you completely forget that you're dancing. And at the peak, when you know you've touched a certain zone, a certain peak, suddenly drop and lie down on the floor. Enter into meditative silence. Connect with your stillness. Don't walk away immediately after your dance. For dancing to become meditation, immediately after the dance, it has to be followed by absolute surrender of the body. Almost imagine that you're gone, the dance has taken you. Your head is clear of thoughts. Just lie down and become that stillness. Do this enough times, and you'll know how to connect with your inner stillness.

You can do the dancing meditation alone, or you can form a group and do it. You can create a structure for the dancing, with simple steps on how to start, progress, and finally surrender, all with one ultimate objective: to dance yourself into realization, into ecstasy, into awakening. Don't doubt if dance can lead you to enlightenment. Just because Buddha didn't dance doesn't mean you should not. Buddha attained through sitting quietly, but Shiva danced and reached. There are various examples of individuals who have attained in their unique rhythmic way. Ultimately, remember what you're searching for need not be created; it is already there. It just has to be realized. Any restriction imposed from outside - saying "No, you cannot do this" or "You should not move like this" - all stems from the past.

Dancing meditation aims to remove the conditioning of your past. Where is the conditioning of your past most solid, most rigid? In your body. The way you move, how you move, how you experience your body - all are direct consequences of your conditioning. There are certain things you will not do with your body. Just observe yourself. When you're taking a walk or among people, there are things you'll never do in public that you might do alone. Even simple movements, simple things done without fear or shame when alone, might not be done in public. Why? Because it's deeply conditioned. When we're outside, when we're with people, it's almost like we're wearing a mask. There's always something restricting us, some rule holding us back. Dancing meditation is a way to break all those rules.

An Islamic couple preparing for a religious wedding meets with their Mullah who asks if they have any final questions. The man inquires, "We understand it's a tradition in Islam for men to dance with men and women to dance with women. However, at our wedding, we would like your permission to dance together." The Mullah responds firmly, "Absolutely not. It's considered immoral and forbidden in Islam. Men and women should always dance separately."

The man continues, "What about intimacy?" The Mullah affirms, "Of course, intimacy is permitted within marriage." The man further queries, "What about different positions?" The Mullah responds, "That's acceptable. Women on top?" The man pushes, "Can it be on the kitchen table?" To which the Mullah responds, "Yes, that's permissible."

The man persists, "Can we engage with all four of my wives together?" The Mullah replies, "You may indeed." The man then asks, "Can we do it while standing up?" The Mullah firmly denies, "No, that's not permissible."

"Why not?" questions the man. The Mullah responds, "Because that could lead to dancing."

STOP WHAT YOU'RE DOING

Some meditations start with the mind, while others start with the body. Movement meditation initiates with the body and eventually leads to stillness. The entire purpose of this meditation is to use the movements of your body to connect with your inner stillness. It uses the contrast between the still part of you and the agitated, disturbed part - your outer body - to bring about a sudden realization that you're not just the body. Movement and stillness meditation aims for a sudden awakening. It's a method, a technique. From the outside, it appears chaotic, making it challenging to comprehend how such movement can lead to stillness. It might seem contradictory, but there's a pure science supporting this meditation.

You Have to be There

If you want to understand how it works, you can dive in. Theoretically, you can understand it. You can get a clear scientific explanation as to how the contrast between movement and stillness can lead to enlightenment. If you don't want to get into the explanation, you can practice this meditation for the sheer joy of it. Movement is fun; the body enjoys movement. In fact, the body is movement. The mind is also movement. When everything is still, we get to certain fundamental questions of life. What is life? If nothing is moving, then how do we recognize life? What would that life be like?

One day, while sitting by his fire, René Descartes came up with this maxim. He said, "I think, therefore I am." He believed that this statement was self-evident. You don't need anything external to prove this statement: "I think, therefore I am."

I disagree with him from an existential point of view because, for me, you have to be there to think. But that "you" is not the "you" that you recognize in your waking consciousness. That you is somewhere deep down. You get in touch with it once in a while, and that is what you're searching for in your meditations. It is that "you" that is giving rise to everything, giving rise to your thinking. But if you look at a statement from a purely human perspective, from the perspective of the mind and the body, there is some truth to the statement "I think, therefore I am," which means you know you are only because of your thinking. If you're not thinking, there is no way to know that you are because what you are is purely a reflection of what your mind is doing and what your body is doing. And if you were to accept that to be true at a certain level of consciousness, you can go one step further and say, "I move therefore I am," because that is also self-evident. Only in movement do you recognize yourself. When your body moves, you know you are. The sensations of the body, the changes your mind records of the body, the pleasure and the pain you experience in the body - every time you learn something new, when the memory seeps into the body - all this is a part of your moving self. When your body is absolutely still, what are you doing? You're asleep. You're not even conscious of the body. You're not even conscious of the "I am." So, in a way, when you're not moving there is something taking you away from this non-moving body, removing the awareness of the self.

The mind is also movement. What happens when the mind is not moving? What happens when you're not transitioning from one thought to another? In moments of absolute stillness of the mind and the body, you disappear. The conception of "I" disappears. With the "I" goes the ego, and with the "I" goes all mentation because you need to be there to even say, "I am thinking. I am moving, I am living." "I move, therefore I am" seems to be more fundamental as a reality than even, "I think, therefore I am," because there are moments when you can arrest your thinking. Something can captivate your attention, and your mind, for a moment, can become still. You've experienced moments when there is no thought there, just a momentary stillness, but you don't disappear. Why? Because the body is still there, and the movement is still happening in the body.

Going Deeper

Nirvana is absolute. That word knows no other meaning except for total disappearing. If there's anything present, you are still there. This is one thing a meditator struggles with. "I have spent so much time meditating. Yes, there are moments when I'm unable to control my thoughts. It's a raging storm, but there are moments I experience deep stillness. Thoughts are not pushing me. Thoughts are not disturbing me, and yet I have not experienced that explosion of bliss that I hear about. What is it that I'm missing?" You're not missing anything. There is another movement that you have to go beyond. You've gone beyond the movement of the mind. You have touched zones of the stillness of the mind. But you still have to go beyond the movement of the body. Now, what is the movement of the body when you're sitting still? You're not moving. You can, for all practical purposes, say, "Stillness of the body comes first, and then comes the stillness of the mind." But when you observe closely, you will see that just keeping the body still on the outside does not constitute stillness. True stillness of the body means you've touched a zone where the sensations of the body are unable to enter.

You've touched pure emptiness, pure stillness. Pure stillness is always blissful. It's like the stillness of the ocean: there is great depth to it, great calmness to it, and it is an extension of your being. When you touch that level of stillness, you know that it is something different from the body. But this stillness is hard to experience without the contrast of movement. It takes longer, it takes more conscious watching, and it takes deep intellectual understanding. First, you need to understand the mind - you need to still the mind and then go deeper and find the stillness of the body.

Movement meditation bypasses some of these processes. The first thing movement does is shift your focus and awareness away from your mind to your body. It acts as an immediate release from the stress and strain of your mind. You could be disturbed in your mind, worried about something, and when you sit in meditation, the same disturbance continues for a while before you're able to still the mind. That is what takes effort and practice in traditional meditation. In an active, intense meditation like dancing and stillness, you don't even care about all that. You are, in a way, forcing your awareness to forget all about the mind. When your body is moving, your awareness has to be on the body with one condition: none of those movements should be automatic. They should not be rehearsed or practiced movements - they have to be spontaneous. Your body should be allowed to move naturally. In fact, you should not move the body; you should let the body move to whatever is moving it, whether it's the music, an emotion stirring inside you, or even a thought. Sometimes your body moves in pain, recollecting a bad memory. But there is a significant difference between sitting quietly and recollecting a bad memory and moving while recollecting something. When you're moving, the recollection feels almost distant. You can recognize the feeling is not that great, but it won't disturb you because your awareness is on the body, and your body reflects that.

Let your body do what it wants to do. Don't impose restrictions on the movement. Don't be self-conscious - self-conscious in the sense that you're worried too much about how it's going to look. It doesn't matter. Let your body do what it wants to do. Let it find its own rhythm, its own zones of movement and stillness. If you were to just watch a dancer from far away, you would know nothing about dancing. One thing you can say with absolute certainty is that after a while, there is no effort in dancing. Maybe initially, when the dance is beginning, you can see the dancer fidgeting a little, being a little nervous, conscious of what's happening around her, ensuring everything is fine, and making sure she does her steps well. This involves the mind. But somewhere in the middle of their dancing, if you pay attention, you will see that there is pure joy in dancing, pure joy in movement. Why? Because all that self-consciousness is gone. They've moved from the mind to a more existential zone. That is why dance is natural in existence. Almost every culture has found its emotional and psychological release through dancing. You cannot imagine a single culture without dance, music, and singing. You cannot even imagine. Why? Because it comes naturally to us.

When you move, you are touching the memory zones in your body and breaking through them. Just as your mind is a reservoir of all your mentation, all your thinking, your body is a memory of all the physical experiences it has had in the world. Your body remembers everything, just like if you have a burn, it leaves a scar, a mark. You could have forgotten all about it, going about your life as if it never happened, but your body remembers it. It's a memory for the body. Similarly, with every strain, every stress, everything you wanted the body to learn, you put the body through that grind - the body remembers. And the body also remembers abuse. If someone has not treated the body rightly, given it pain, the body never forgets it. How does it remember this? It doesn't remember through thinking. It remembers when you touch those zones in the body. Your whole body is, in a way, a karmic body, if you have to use the spiritual word "karma." What is karma? Karma is the accumulation of all your actions. Your body is a karmic body because that is where all that accumulation is. And eventually, that is what you're trying to transcend - you're looking for that karmic release where all your accumulated karma disappears in a single moment.

Karma

Karma is a very practical and simple philosophy. The body has memory, so in this lifetime, whatever you're doing, your body is accumulating memories. There are two ways of going beyond your karma: One is consciously transcending the body through meditation. That's what religiousness is, what spirituality is, what awakening is - consciously releasing your karmic bonds. The other way is through dying. When you die, the karmic accumulation of the body goes away, but the karmic accumulation in your mind doesn't disappear. Your fears, guilt, likes, dislikes - all that remains in the mind and carries forward to your next life. So, truly, if you want to go beyond all that you've accumulated, all that is weighing you down, quite literally, physically, you have to do it consciously.

This idea of karmic release has been misunderstood due to a lack of simple understanding that karma is nothing but an accumulation of your actions on the body. For example, in Jainism, this idea was taken quite literally. Karma, to Jains, is the dust accumulated on your being through your actions. They took this idea to such an extreme level that they believe all living forms - every creature, small or big - have been trapped by their karmic action.

Instead of looking at themselves, examining their bodies, and trying to find a way out of this karmic accumulation, they started developing deep guilt for hurting another creature, for harming another creature, because every creature is trapped at a certain level due to this karmic accumulation. So, some Jains went to the extremes of not even moving - they remained totally immobile because they didn't want to inadvertently step on a living creature.

On one hand, this looks like an act of compassion and carefulness not to hurt another creature. However, if you look at it in the same breath where they believe they are compassionate, they're being extremely cruel to themselves. Some of them refused to eat, refused to wash, and subjected their bodies to harsh environments - as harsh as possible. The whole purpose was to torture the body, exposing themselves to extreme heat and extreme cold because they misunderstood the idea of karma. They looked at karma as something negative, almost equating it with sin, instead of considering it as a natural accumulation process of the mind and the body that can be transcended through conscious watching.

Of course, when Vardhamana Jnatiputra Mahavira (the father of Jainism) was alive and going through these processes and practices, he understood what he was doing. Inside, he had a sense that he was trying to find a release. However, it took him seven years. In the first four years, he completely self-tortured himself because he was not following any teacher or reading any scripture. He simply went into the forest, wanting to rid himself of his body. So, he subjected his body to extremes. Yet, like Buddha, he realized that transcendence comes not from self-torture but from experiencing inner stillness, and inner silence. That's how he eventually found his realization.

However, for the Jains, there's no way to understand all these things because Mahavira never spoke, never gave his teachings, and never explained what happened to him on the inside, but his people wanted to emulate him, to follow him. There were no guidelines to follow him. So, whatever they could see on the outside, they started following.

In a way, they started imitating him. Mahavira went naked, so let's go naked. Most Jain monks are naked, and when they come for their talks, when they interact with people, they're absolutely naked, but they wear a cloth around their mouth. Why? Because they might breathe in a creature, or harm something while exhaling. It's a neurosis. This is not spirituality; this is a total misunderstanding of a simple idea.

In a way, if you look at it, every time you move, you are permanently altering the universe in some way. Your movement causes an irreplaceable change. Something changes - the physical landscape, a few life forms get destroyed, and certain memory accumulations in your body are altered. Something physical, something real, happens when you move. When you don't move, where are you accumulating karma?

This is the idea that most Jains completely misunderstood because karma is movement - let us not move so that we don't accumulate new karma. But the real understanding is if karma is movement, being still is not how you go beyond your karma but by understanding stillness - getting to the still part of your being that is inside. Just stilling your body doesn't mean anything because your body could be still, but your mind could still be moving. You could still be experiencing movement in your body sensations. Even a person who's perfectly still is breathing. So, by that definition, a Jain monk should even stop breathing. If being immobile is the ultimate purpose, why is he breathing? Why is he blinking his eyes? Why is he swallowing? Why is he eating? Why is he drinking? All these constitute a movement. A small shift in understanding puts things in perspective.

Yes, movement is the accumulation of all the memories of all your actions, and that is what is weighing you down. So why not use that movement to connect with stillness? Why not turn that movement itself into meditation? Let's see how you can do it. Start with a basic preparation for your dancing/stillness meditation. More than dancing, it is rhythmic movement. Dancing can take many forms with varying levels of intensity. In an elegant movement meditation, your dance should be rhythmic; it should flow. The purpose is to let the body move naturally. When the body moves naturally, it attains a certain level of intensity, occupying a middle space in the level of intensity. If you have to raise the level of intensity of the movement, you have to do it consciously. But if the body is allowed to do what it wants to do, it always stays in the middle ground of intensity and picks up its own rhythm.

The Technique

What you can do to help with this is to choose the kind of music that supports the rhythmic, natural, waving movement of the body. Don't pick music that is too stimulating or high intensity; there are different meditations for that. Select music that starts slowly and gradually builds the intensity. First, stand still. Ensure you have enough space to move around. If you are practicing this meditation in a group, make sure there's sufficient distance so you don't bump into each other; otherwise, it won't be elegant movement meditation, it would be chaotic bumping meditation - a different kind of meditation. In elegant movement, you have to be left alone. You're not interacting with others. Of course, you can practice this meditation in a group, but you're essentially alone because you're closing your eyes and connecting with the stillness inside. You're not concerned about what's happening on the outside.

Once you've ensured you have enough space and the music is playing, start by taking about ten to fifteen deep breaths. Stand still with your legs slightly apart and take these deep breaths to clear out the mental noise and connect with your body. As you're usually in your mind, it might take a while for you to become aware of your dancing if you suddenly start moving. By taking these breaths, you're aligning your mind and body with the present moment. Inhale deeply and exhale fully, repeating this process around ten to fifteen times. Afterward, engage in some stretching to prepare your body for the upcoming movement. You can stretch however you want - upper body, lower body, or even do push-ups - just to get your muscles ready for the movement ahead.

While you're doing this, use this quiet period to bring your awareness and attention to the body. While stretching, focus on feeling the sensations within your body - feel the muscles moving, sense your joints, perceive the blood pumping from your heart, observe the sensations along your nerves, and notice the sensations on your skin. Slowly withdraw yourself from the external world, detaching from thoughts like "I am here meditating with these people, I'm going to enjoy this dancing meditation." All that thinking must cease. Immerse yourself in the body to a point where you are solely attentive to your body. Quiet your mind entirely; your mind is ineffective in this meditation. Just stretch and, in that process, become fully aware of your body. Afterward, the music you've chosen should gradually intensify in a rhythmic, beautiful, waving fashion, and then you can start moving to the music.

By now, you should have come so close to the body that you're ready to let the body do what it wants to do. You let the body move the way it wants to move. It's amazing when you let the body move in its own way; it always moves rhythmically. It's only when you try to do something that dance looks awkward - there is self-consciousness, there is awareness. Otherwise, elegance is natural for the body for most people. So, you watch the body move from inside, not outside. There is a tendency to watch it from the outside. When you're watching it from the outside, know that you're imagining the movements.

This is the fundamental difference between meditation and just dancing. In dancing, you don't care where you're watching from. You don't even care if you're watching; you are just dancing because you're enjoying it - the body is moving. But in movement meditation, you have to make a conscious effort to watch the sensations of movement from inside. That is where you start touching certain zones of stillness because your experience of stillness has to come from inside, not outside. When you touch certain zones of stillness, you should be able to hold onto those zones. You should be able to extend that one momentary stillness for as long as you can. That is the objective of the meditation. So, start moving and move with the body inside. When you don't imagine the body, notice how the body becomes a very simple phenomenon, just a bundle of sensations.

When you're not imagining the body, when you're not imagining being there, when you're inside, something gives way, and you feel lighter. You feel a sense of lifting. You can almost feel like you're lifting off the ground a bit. When you're allowing the body to move by itself, you don't feel the weight of the body. You don't feel the strain of the body. It's almost like you were always weightless, and you're just realizing those moments of weightlessness for the first time.

It is a fact that you are weightless. The entire perception of weight comes because of your deep attachment to the body, your deep attachment to the sensations of the body. Where is the weight of the body when you're running and thinking about something else? You're not even aware of the weight of the body; the body is doing its own thing. Throughout the day when you're moving, how often do you reflect on the weight of the body? It is only when you sit quietly, when you're in a strain, or when a sensation becomes sharp that you feel the weight of the body. Otherwise, the body is as light as air. In elegant movement, you can connect with the weightless nature of your body. Your eyes are also closed, so there's not much to see. You could be waving your hands, moving your upper body or lower body, even rolling on the ground - doing whatever you want. You're letting the body do what it wants naturally, without a care in the world, without worrying about who is looking at you.

What's happening? If something is restricting your movement, you can remove all those restrictions. If you're wearing bracelets, anklets, chains, or anything else, you can remove them. This is where the kind of clothing you choose for your meditation is also important. You don't want to pick something that restricts your movement. What is the natural state of the body? The natural state of the body is nakedness. No animal wears clothes. Inside nakedness is what allows for the free movement of the body. So, your clothing should, as much as possible, allow for that interior nakedness. As loose and thin as possible - whatever you can wear. Just let your body be natural.

Your consciousness and your awareness should not be on what is on the body. It should be on the sensations of the body. As much as possible, you should be getting in touch with the sensations inside. So, if you're wearing something that is constantly irritating you, rubbing against your body, and you're worried about tearing your clothes or whatever, then it will disturb your meditation. You have to be in a state of deep surrender, deep release. You can take care of this before you get into meditation. Anything that helps you to be naked inside - where you can, choose to be naked outside, if you're comfortable. But being naked inside is more than enough. However, if you're compelled or want to be completely free, without any restriction, you can take off your clothes. Nobody is going to bother. It's how you feel inside that matters. In fact, you might feel more self-conscious without clothes. Your meditation will be more disturbing if you're not used to that idea and if you're not in a group where everybody is naked. Forget about all that, and go deeper into meditation. The objective is not to worry too much about the outer form, how you look, or that fixed image you have about yourself. That is what you're trying to go beyond.

Just go straight into the dance. Just go in and watch the movement. Do this for about ten minutes - move naturally. Have some kind of timer or set the music in such a way that at the end of ten minutes, the music changes to something very soft, like just a simple chanting or just a single instrument - something that tells you that it's time to be still. So, for ten minutes, move your body.

When you get the cue from the music, just lie down fully flat in Shavasana and connect with your inner stillness. Become the stillness. If you have been moving with total self-abandonment, if you have been fully aware of the body moving, then something shifts when you go into stillness. The stillness you would be experiencing will be deeper than what you would experience in a normal sitting meditation.

Now, here is the scientific explanation of why this meditation works. Because what you're trying to experience is a realization, stillness need not be cultivated; it is already your nature. You are only trying to realize it and stay with it for as long as you can. Because it is a matter of realization, all that movement aids you in connecting with your inner stillness. That contrast throws you into deeper levels of stillness. Also, because you've exerted your body a bit, it is tired. When you lie down, it tends to relax a little more than if you were simply sitting still. The most important thing is that, in all this exercise, your awareness is completely on the body. All the disturbance you would experience in meditation because of the mind is gone.

This is a perfect meditation for those who cannot sit still because their mind is too disturbed, or they have too many things to worry about and too many problems. In a way, this meditation can be a gentle catharsis, a way to release certain emotional and mental blocks - not by solving those problems but by stepping away from them. Sometimes, stepping away is more important than solving a problem because you're completely forgetting the problem, and after a while, it disappears with no attention. Scientifically, something is happening there. You are being aware of your body sensations. You've turned inward and moved for about ten minutes. And now, when you go into absolute stillness, naturally without your wanting, your body wants to sink deeper, so allow it. For the next five minutes, don't restrict the body - let it go as deep as it wants to. If you start experiencing tingling sensations, a sensation of joy, bliss, or even pain, it doesn't matter. Just experience all that. Then, make sure you have a cue in the music that tells you to get up after five minutes. If you're moving for ten minutes, five minutes of stillness is something you can hold onto. Five minutes is still a long time in meditation. Then, before you start drifting into thoughts, get up and prepare yourself for the next round. Again, take ten to fifteen deep breaths, slowly get in touch with your inner movements, stretch a bit, and then begin the cycle again. Now, you can repeat this meditation with ten-minute movements and five minutes of stillness - ten minutes of movement, five minutes of stillness, four times in an hour.

The final release is when you finish the fourth round of movement, and then you rest - rest for as long as you can. Stretch that five minutes to ten minutes, even fifteen or twenty minutes. Be there for as long as you can connect with that inner stillness and blissfulness. Don't disturb it. Get up only when you realize, "Oh, now I'm drifting into my mind," or if you're falling asleep. If you fall asleep, someone will wake you up.

The whole objective of this meditation is to erase thinking and allow the body to come into your consciousness. As long as you are aware of the body, aware of the stillness, be there. This is the last step. Then, slowly, you start becoming aware of what's happening around you. If you notice a disturbance, then you can get up, marking the end of that meditation session. This is a beautiful, much more active, much more involved, and much simpler meditation. You can do it once in the morning and once in the evening. It's best to be done in a group where you get that surge of energy. Everyone is moving synchronously to the music, in a state of surrender - no self-consciousness, no awareness of the body. You're just going deeper. Of course, you can do this alone as well, but in a group, coordinating with the music and having an ideal setup helps. There's emotional support when you're doing it together in a group, and something deepens in a group setup. Your meditation deepens because there's a part of you that relaxes more naturally when you're in a group. Of course, it is still your meditation, done to connect with yourself, but that psychological feeling of being in a group, all aiming to connect with the same center, adds a dimension.

Remember, when you connect with your inner stillness and another person connects with their inner stillness, you both are connecting to the same stillness. In that stillness, your minds, bodies, and personalities have disappeared. You have touched the same zone of aliveness, the same zone of stillness. Just knowing that you are all different points of light trying to reach the same source gives you immense satisfaction in being part of the group. When you're alone, yes, you can entertain your mind a little too much. You can feel a bit lonely and experience a sense of confusion, wondering if you're doing it right or if this is the way to do it. All that, to a certain extent, is alleviated in a group. That's why deep, intense, active meditations have always been group activities. Most people who meditate on their own simply sit quietly, watching their breath and thoughts, starting with a simple traditional meditation. But in a group, you can push the boundaries a bit and expedite the process through which you connect with your inner stillness. Ultimately, all that movement, all that rhythmic waving will become the ideal backdrop against which to connect with your pure inner stillness.

Feel the Body

Let's move from the mind to the body, from the world of seeing to the world of feeling - from the visual to the kinesthetic. The world of seeing, although we use the word "watching," has nothing to do with meditative watching. In meditation, the word "watch" signifies something entirely different. It has nothing to do with your eyes; it's more about awareness. It's about being here and now. Watchfulness is your nature. You don't have to do anything additional to watch; you only have to stop doing all the things you're doing and allow the watching to happen.

What is the definition of meditative watching? It is to be aware, to be in the present moment. Awareness cannot be created or added to you, it is not a phenomenon - it's an existential reality, a part of you. Once you understand this, watchfulness becomes your nature. Then you can explore what is stopping you from being watchful - Why do I need a method? Why do I need a meditation technique?

We've been exploring meditation techniques that start with the outside, everything that the eyes can perceive - the visual senses - and then move inward. In all these meditation techniques, the mind is involved because you see through the mind. Even though you use your eyes to look at the object, your mind is there to register that experience and articulate it. The mind is an eternal companion in your meditation, especially in any meditation where seeing is involved.

NATURE OF THE BODY

To understand this, it's important to grasp a little about the body. What is the body? What is its nature? How does it differ from the mind? While the body is an extension of the mind, existentially, the body and mind aren't separate entities. There's no brick wall dividing them. In language, when we refer to the body, it seems distinct from thoughts, imaginations, and desires. Yet, there's a connection between the mind and the body. Existentially, there's a profound connection, but experientially, we can perceive either the body or the mind as if they're entirely distinct. Something delineates the experiences of the mind from those of the body. If you've found it challenging to observe this, it's because you've primarily been engrossed in the experiences of the mind, not the body. Your mind scarcely allows you to experience the body; it constantly endeavors to draw you away from it. Whose desire is it to move away from the body?

We know from experience that we don't like being with the body, watching the body. We prefer to be as far away from the body as possible. Whose desire is this? Is it the desire of the mind, or is it the desire of the body? Understanding this is crucial because it's about identifying who pushes you away from the present moment. We're getting into something fundamentally significant. Something is urging you to move away from the here and now. Is it the mind or the body? When you examine how you move away from the body, what actually takes you away from it, you can observe that it's not the mind leading you away from the body; it's the body itself. However, the mind often gets blamed for this movement.

There's something in the inherent nature of your body that resists being watched. This observation is rarely made because we're so absorbed in thinking. Any drifting or movement away, we naturally assume it's due to the mind. However, two things are at play here: the triggering point for you to move away from the body and the process of that movement. We're familiar with the process of daydreaming, which always unfolds in the mind. We often take notice after the train has already started moving. We observe it and conclude that this train doesn't want to stay in the present moment; it always wants to go somewhere. But we never ask: who started the train? The train cannot initiate itself. Something external must give it that primary instruction: "I don't want you to be here, just go."

Imagine if the mind were being instructed by something else to drift away - you would never know who is giving that instruction because, by the time you become aware, you're already drifting. To become aware of who is pushing you away from the present moment, you must be watchful and mindful. When you start observing your body and its sensations, it becomes abundantly clear: the culprit is the body. The mind merely follows suit; the body is the one issuing the instruction, urging the mind away.

Now, how do we know this? What does the body enjoy doing? More importantly, what is the primary desire of the body? The body's greatest desire isn't the body itself; it's the exact opposite of the body. Whatever the body experiences, it desires to rid itself of it. The body's entire purpose is to experience its polar opposite, which we encounter in our daily lives as pleasure-seeking. We use the body to seek something other than bodily experiences, labeling those moments as bliss, joy, or pleasure.

When we are aligned with the body, we don't term those moments as joy, pleasure, or bliss. We might call it contemplation, mindfulness, suffering, or self-consciousness, but we never refer to watching the body as bliss or joy. For the body, joy is when you forget the body, and bliss is when you've completely forgotten the body. So, in every way possible, the body is trying to push you away from the present moment. The body does not want you to watch it. Why? Because the body is the seat of discomfort. The body is the seat of pain. The body is not the seat of pleasure. Pleasure is somewhere deep within. Or, as far as the body is concerned, it is somewhere other than the body. Where is the pleasure in the body? If pleasure were to be in the body, then what is the necessity to go in search of it outside or in some other activity?

One of the greatest, most pleasurable, joyful, blissful moments for the body happens when it is asleep. If pleasure were to be in the body, why would it crave sleep? The body loves to sleep. At any given opportunity, it wants to go to sleep. What is it trying to do? It is trying to forget itself. It is trying to go as far away as possible because it knows that there is no pleasure here. There are only sensations, discomfort, and pain. Every small change in temperature causes discomfort. The wind blows too hard, it causes discomfort. There's not enough wind, it causes discomfort. If you walk too fast, you exhaust yourself, and your body is in discomfort. If you sit in one position for too long, the body is in discomfort.

How easy is it for the body to be in discomfort? It is very easy. The body itself is in a state of dis-ease. And when that dis-ease accumulates to a certain point, that is what we recognize and categorize as disease. The body is always prone to disease. Or, in simpler terms, it is the seat of dis-ease. What are those two things the body is constantly looking for? It is either looking for some pleasure where it can forget the body or it wants to drift away from the body and simply forget it. So the body is either trying to forget itself or seek pleasure. In a way, in both these activities, the ultimate objective is to go as far away from the body as possible.

Sleep and Sex

Which are those moments in our human experience where we can say with absolute certainty that these are the moments when we are farthest away from the body? There are only two experiences. One is when we are asleep. We are as far away from the body as we can be. We are deep somewhere lost in dreaming, but we are so unaware - we don't know how we got there. You have to be asleep to go deep enough to go far away from the body. So, in sleep, you are far away from the body, but you don't recollect that experience as pleasurable as something that you can pursue. The craving for sleep is there. Somewhere deep down, you know that when you sleep, you experience that bliss. When you wake up you cannot relive that bliss, but you have a memory of it.

The other activity in which we are farthest from the body is sex - when we experience the ultimate bliss, that one moment that we call orgasm, what we call ecstasy. That is the moment when we are farthest away from the body. We have forgotten the body at that moment, and that is what we register as bliss. Now, the important thing to remember is forgetting the body doesn't mean not seeing it in your mind's eye. That is not forgetting. Forgetting means not experiencing any sensation of the body. That is a much more difficult task. You can sit here, close your eyes, start thinking about something, and forget the body as an image. But still, you are feeling the pain of the body. You're feeling the pressure of the body. You're feeling the sensation of the body. You could be sitting and daydreaming, but if somebody comes and touches you, immediately you will know because you're still very much in the body, only trying to forget. There are only two times when forgetfulness is deep: deep sleep and sex. We are addicted to sleep and sex because these are two moments when we are farthest away from the body.

How do we understand this process of moving away from the body consciously? When you move away from the body consciously, you're not moving away from the present moment. Your consciousness, your awareness, takes care of being in the present moment. Your conscious moving away takes care of drifting away from the pain center, which is the body. One way of approaching it is through suppression. Is it possible to suppress the bodily desires and move away from the body? Is it possible to suppress sleep? Is it possible to suppress sex? Yes, it is possible, but it does not lead to the transformation that you're looking for. It does not take you to bliss in a conscious way. Because suppression only builds up over time, it will eventually find its outlet.

For the past two thousand years, this is what religion has been preaching. Look at how well it has worked. We have turned the whole world sexual. The whole mind of Man is sexual now - he's thinking about sex all the time. From just being in the body, from just being a bodily desire to experience bliss, it has become a preoccupation of the mind. It's because people have never been offered a method or a technique to understand sex and eventually transcend it. They have only been told to hate the body, to suppress sexual desires. They only condemned the body by calling it sin. And with one look at the world, we know it has not worked at all. In fact, it has had the opposite effect. It has divided Man right down the middle. When he has thoughts of sex, he's feeling guilty. When he tries to suppress it, it leads to depression, and that energy finds its outlet in different ways. This divide is the main problem.

This is the contribution of religion. Because you have been denying sex, condemning it so much, and pushing it to the corner, it has occupied a fascinating place in the human mind. The modern mind regards sex as something mysterious and fascinating when it is nothing but simple bodily release, just like sleep. We don't sensationalize sleep, dream about sleeping, write poetry about sleeping, or make movies about sleeping. When you're sleeping, you're unaware; you don't know how you got there. But sex is no different from sleep. It is a momentary sleep - a deep sleep where you are unaware of the body and all its pain for one moment. There is nothing sensational or spectacular about this. The orgasm that you experience is simply a momentary shift from the pain body to your blissful self, where you get a glimpse of your true nature. You've not experienced something totally different.

What you experience in sex is not limited to sex. There is a way to experience that same bliss. There are hundreds of ways, direct paths, to that bliss, but because religions have condemned sex, Man is not interested in all those other direct means. He's become obsessed with sex because that is how he wants to experience that bliss. There are other ways to experience bliss - alcohol, smoking weed, and drugs. But still, his fascination with sex has not disappeared because it has occupied his mind. If you think about it, the bliss you experience when you smoke pot or take drugs is not very different from the bliss you experience in orgasm. It's the same forgetfulness of the body. Yes, the quality is a little different, your consciousness is a little different, and your awareness is a little different, but the bliss is the same. Yet, he cannot forget sex because it's a part of his mind.

When you bridge this divide between the body and your true nature, between the body and the mind, between your transcendental self and the limited body, when you accept the totality of the body, the totality of the mind, the totality of life, all the energies as belonging to the same divine self, you won't be able to understand any of it. Unless you look at all these things in totality, there will be that divide, and somebody is going to feed into that divide. Man has identified the divide. He knows that in that moment of sexual ecstasy, he's something totally different. He's forgotten his family problems, his health problems, his money problems, his name, fame, everything. He's forgotten all the toil and hard work of the day. In that one momentary release, he is the king of his universe. And the next moment, he's crawling on the floor. He feels that. He knows that immediately after sex, he feels pathetic. There's not a single individual who doesn't feel a sense of "Where has this gone?" and "What am I going to do now?" But you don't verbalize it like that; you just feel a certain low. Just as you experience the high of sex, you also experience the low.

So, the divide is there, and religions have wonderfully taken advantage of this. They have tried to widen this divide as much as possible. To understand the body, to watch the body, to use the body as an anchor to go deeper into meditation, to experience ultimate bliss, uninterrupted meditative bliss, you have to understand sex. You also have to understand sleep, and you have to understand them while they are happening. You cannot think about them; you cannot conceptualize them. Only the experiential taste of sleep, the experiential taste of that moment of orgasm, and your experiential expansion of those moments will help you transcend them. So, you need to understand sleep while you're asleep; you need to understand sex while the desire for sex is taking over you. And when are these things happening? It is happening during your wakeful state. Before you go to sleep, the process of sleeping starts. Sleeping is not just completely forgetting the body. Any time you choose to forget the body and you drift into the mind, that is also a form of sleep. Forgetfulness is more common than anything else. We are never with the body, and it is not only during normal ordinary day-to-day living experiences.

Extraordinary individuals, great scientists, for example, Newton - it is said that he was so forgetful. Of course, they attribute it to how smart he was. He was thinking all the time, and he was forgetting things. But in reality, he was just forgetful. There were times when he used to come to the cafeteria to have lunch, and he completely forgot why he was there. He would come to the cafeteria, then turn around and walk to the street. Suddenly, he would stop in the middle and recollect, "What am I doing here in the middle of the street?" Then he'd turn around and come back to the cafeteria. What's happening there? You can see a total disconnection between the body and the mind. This disconnection has haunted even the greatest of scientists. Only an awakened mind is not haunted by this disconnection because when it becomes aware of the separation, it knows how to bring them back together. It's just a matter of choice for an awakened mind to reunite the mind and body. But for an unawakened mind, without a method, without a practice, it seems like an almost impossible task to keep the mind where the body is.

The Technique

This is where the technique of watching the body sensations comes in. Just sit and observe the pain and discomfort of the body. Just behind that pain, just behind the discomfort, is silence, stillness, and bliss. The bliss you're searching for in sleep, the bliss you're searching for in sex, is right there within you, but it is not in your body. You cannot use your body to reach it. If you try to use your body to access it, you will always be dependent. When I say the bliss of sex is inside you, I'm not suggesting finding it in your own body instead of pursuing it in another body. No. People have tried that as well, and it only creates dependency. I mean, masturbation is trying to find pleasure using your own body, but you're still dependent on the process. You're still dependent on the body, whether it's yours or somebody else's - it doesn't matter. Dependency is still there. You still don't know how to reach that bliss directly. You still have to use your body. What I'm talking about is a way to experience the bliss that is within the dimension of your body, inside the dimension, not just inside the body, but within the dimension of the body.

First, you start with the sensations. You sit and watch them. Yes, it'll be discomforting. You'll have to sit and observe the tiny sensations, changes in temperature, changes in pressure, everything happening on the surface of the body. Sometimes you can even move inside. You can listen to your heartbeat, and watch your breath. The only thing not allowed is thinking and dreaming. If you start dreaming, it means your body is instructing the mind to take you away because it does not want you to watch the body. Why? Because the body's ultimate desire is to put you in the most comfortable place. It wants you to be comfortable, knowing that by its nature, it isn't comfortable. So, it tries to push you away. But when you insist and start closely observing the body - every sensation, every sensation of pain - and if you're able to resist the body's desire to push you away, if you're able to stay in the present moment, slowly the body begins to listen. It starts to understand that there's no way to escape this discomfort other than going inward because you've blocked the door to the outside.

Up until now, every time there was discomfort, it found an outlet through the other doors it had created on the outside. Sometimes it went to sleep. It knows all these doors: There's a door that says "sleep," a door that says "sex," a door that says "go hiking," whatever. Now, you've shut all those doors. How have you shut those doors? You are sitting still, watching the body. You're introducing the body's pain to the mind, but you're saying, "Don't find an outlet. Don't escape. I want to know. I want to understand this pain." Again, it's not even unbearable pain; it's discomfort that you're observing. Of course, when the pain is unbearable, you don't have to watch it; - that's fine. I'm not talking about self-inflicting pain. So, just because there's no pain, don't start creating pain to watch it. By using the word "pain," I'm referring to the sensation of discomfort already present in the body. You don't have to create it, just watch it. As you continue to watch it, because you've shut all the outlets, sooner or later, the energy starts moving inward. It begins with finding an outlet in a different direction, the direction you want to go. It starts to move in the direction of your self, closer to your true nature.

That's when you notice that your physical discomfort is subsiding. On the first day when you sat in meditation watching your body, you could not sit for ten minutes. That one hour of meditation was absolute torture. And who was torturing you? Your own body. It was trying to itch, scratch, move - experiencing all kinds of sensations and exaggerating those sensations using the mind. But at the end of one month, you were able to sit for an hour. That right there should tell you that you have tamed the body a bit. You didn't do anything to take away its pain or discomfort; you just moved a little inside. Now, for the first time, you see a way. "Oh, there is a way to bliss. There is a way to ecstasy. There is a way to go beyond all the pain and discomfort of the body. Up until now, I've been doing it on the outside, running away from the body, when all I had to do was go inward."

Anything you find on the outside, you are dependent on because the outside does not belong to you alone - it belongs to others as well. So, if you want something from the outside, you are competing with others, fighting with others. You have to spend months and years working for it. At the center of all these desires - pursuing name, fame, and wealth - is the desire to escape the pain of the body. Man might be thinking, "I am accomplishing these things. I want to be someone important. I want to prove to the world that I am someone important." Once you understand that the same bliss can be found inside, and the inside belongs to you and you alone, there is no competition there. You don't have to fight with anybody, and nobody can stop you from going inside. Once you discover the method, once you acquire the habit, the technique of going inward, you have found the way to limitless bliss. And you have found a way to distance yourself from the discomfort of the body.

Now, that bliss you experience, that you can experience by your own conscious choice, just by choosing to sit and go deep inside and connect with this inner bliss - if you can do that, what else in the universe can be compared to that bliss? How can you even compare that experience to anything else? Everything people are running after, struggling to attain, and fighting with each other to obtain, you are traversing that entire landscape in a matter of a few minutes. You are crossing the endless desire of Man, the endless suffering of humanity, all those broken, shattered pathways in a matter of a few minutes. That is what meditation can do for you. It's not as simple as finding relaxation or getting rid of your stress and anxiety. Meditation is to experience that ultimate bliss. And what is bliss? It is freedom from the pain and discomfort of the body. That is what bliss is. Bliss is your own nature. Because you are fully attached to the body, you are unable to experience it. The beauty of watching your body is, that by observing the pain, discomfort, and sensations, you can go inward and transcend it.

Dancing with Shadows

THE FLEETING FLOWER

Watching the flower meditation is a simple, visual meditation that starts from the outside, appreciating the beauty of the flower, and contemplating the nature of beauty, and the impermanence of life. Watching the flower is more emotional than the third-eye meditation or watching the breath for the simple reason that the flower will inevitably invoke certain emotions inside you - provided you're using a real flower. It has to be a real flower. Don't use a plastic flower because meditation is deeply connected to life, and there's nothing fake in life. A flower represents an authentic expression of life. In fact, the flower is one of the most beautiful ways in which existence reminds us that it is happy, joyful, content, and brimming with life.

Imagine a world without flowers. Not a single flower. You could automatically conclude that we are living in a dry, mechanical, purposeless existence with no insight into it. Flowers remind us that existence has an insight - we're not living in a mere physical world. Physical is what we see. Physical is what our senses bring to us. It's the outermost layer of life. Existence is deep, just like an emotion, just like aliveness, just like consciousness. Existence also has depth to it. Existence is not just space, time, and energy. Otherwise, what is the necessity for flowers? And so many of them, in so many different shapes, so many different colors with fragrance. Flowers remind us that intrinsically, existence is beautiful. Beauty is an inherent quality of nature, and we are an expression of that beauty. That is why it is natural to appreciate beauty. When the human mind is not clouded by the ego, it is searching for beauty. It is searching for ways of connecting with the beauty. It is searching for a way to bridge the gap between the inner beauty and the outer beauty.

THE TECHNIQUE

Sit in your comfortable meditation posture. Keep a beautiful flower - it could be a rose or a bouquet of flowers - it doesn't matter - keep it at about an arm's length from you. Don't keep it too close; it will obstruct your vision. At the same time, don't keep it too far away. Just keep it where you can see it and at a height that is comfortable for you. You should not be drooping down trying to look at the flowers. Your head should be straight or slightly tilted upwards, so it's better to keep the flowers on a pedestal where you can see them straight. Settle into your regular meditation posture, either cross-legged or on a chair, however you're comfortable. Remember the firmness and the comfort of the posture, and then begin to watch the flower. Contemplate the nature of beauty. What is it that is beautiful in the flower? Is it the petals? Is it the color? Is it the shape, the texture, or is it something altogether different? Where is this whole idea of beauty coming from? Is it coming from the flower? Is it coming from the mind? Or is it coming from someplace altogether different from the mind and the flower?

You are trying to understand the nature of life because if you're able to get to the source of beauty, you will have also gotten to the source of life. Beauty cannot be just replicated on the outside. Real beauty has to emanate from the inside. A flower is not created from the outside. It is created from the inside, and you can observe it. As the flower begins to grow, as it begins to blossom, you can see there's a beautiful natural rhythm to how it happens, and the process is beautiful from the beginning until it blossoms. The process is also beautiful when it begins to wilt. There is beauty in life as well as in death. When you're watching the flower, you will see a change every day - because it's a real flower. One day it is filled with beauty. The colors are vibrant. You can see the petals. You can see the entire structure of the flower, and then it slowly begins to change. Observe it. What is changing? It seems like because it is no longer connected to the plant, something is slowly disappearing from the flower. Watch it. What is it? And why is it happening slowly? If death were to be sudden and absolute, why didn't the flower dry up immediately? What was still sustaining that flower? Does it mean that in some way it's still connected to life? Is physical severing the absolute severance, or is there something more to it? Does the flower have a mind? Does its mind linger longer? Contemplate anything as long as you are around the flower, and contemplate the beauty of the flower. Pay attention to the one who's observing the flower. Your eyes are open, you're watching the flower, but your meditation is about watching the watcher.

Buddha's Philosophy

There is an interesting philosophical debate between Hindu philosophy and the Buddhist school of thought, which beautifully describes the true nature of the self, how it is transcendent, and how meditation can help you to get to it. When Buddha spoke about nothingness, about enlightenment, he also had a philosophy. Although he was not a philosopher, invariably, his understanding of life stood in stark contrast to the well-established Hindu philosophy of life. Buddha was born a Hindu. He grew up a Hindu. He studied Hindu scriptures, so he knew all the terminologies and prevalent belief systems. But his realization had taken him on a completely different path. His realization had given him a different way of looking at life. Invariably, when he spoke, his philosophy of life was very different from the established Hindu philosophy. To sum up Buddha's core philosophy, he says, "You are nothing but your thoughts." So for him, you are nothing but a collection of your thoughts, which is nothing but the mind. He accepted the existence of the mind.

Buddha also said that everything in existence, everything you're experiencing, lasts only for a single moment. Nothing lasts beyond a moment. If you perceive something to be existing for more than a moment, that is happening because of your mind. Your mind is drawing the connection between one moment and the other, creating a perception of continuity. For instance, when you look at a flame, although the flame is new every moment, your mind gives it continuity. He said that everything lasts only for one moment, and it disappears. An experience arises one moment, and then it's gone. Then, a new experience arises.

He also said that there is no self, and the ultimate experience is nothingness - there is no individual self. If you were to sum up his teachings, these are the three most important. By Buddha's time, Hindu philosophy was deeply entrenched in its ideologies and understanding. There were innumerable schools of thought, most of them being philosophical rather than meditation schools, debating on different ideas of reality. They had accepted the Hindu philosophy wherein the self is the supreme being.

Here's a counterargument a Hindu philosopher presents to dismiss Buddha's understanding of life, and it is very beautiful. Not that he succeeds in dismissing Buddha's understanding, but he succeeds in dismissing the terminologies Buddha used in the context of Hinduism. If one were to use the words Buddha used and try to understand Hindu philosophy, then Buddhist philosophy might seem to not be standing on firm ground because Buddha used those words in a completely different sense. In fact, for him, nothingness, the experience of nothingness itself, was the experience of the ultimate self. But he never used the word "self."

MIND IS MOMENTARY

Let's look at it from the Hindu philosophical point of view. The argument is, that if there is no self, then according to Buddha, there are only two entities: the mind and what the mind is observing for no more than a moment, including the mind. When Buddha says everything is momentary, he does not make an exception. He's also referring to your mind. So there is no continuous mind sitting somewhere observing things. The mind is also momentary.

Let's say you're sitting and watching the flower. In one moment, you are watching the flower. So, it requires a minimum of one moment to perceive the flower, and it also requires one moment to perceive that you are perceiving the flower. The mind requires two moments if it has to give us the perception of watching. It is such a simple idea, and yet it is so profound if you think about it. With the self, the mind uses up that one moment it has in being self-aware because first, it has to be self-aware to watch the flower. Without self-awareness, who is instructing the mind to watch the flower? So, in one moment, it has to become aware of itself, and in the next moment, it can watch the flower. According to Buddha, there are no two moments. There's only one moment available to the mind because in one moment if it becomes self-aware - in the next moment, the mind is new according to Buddha. There's no continuity in the mind. So, in the next moment, the mind again uses up one more moment to become self-aware.

This becomes a continuity where the mind can't observe anything other than itself because it is using up that moment to become self-aware. It's a beautiful argument that says, without the self, without the third entity that is independent of the mind and independent of the object that you're watching, experience is impossible. Because experience is not just about you experiencing something, it is also about you knowing that you're experiencing something. There is no meaning to experience without memory. Now, how can memory happen if the mind is momentary?

Buddha was right. The mind is momentary. The object is also momentary. But where the Hindu philosophers completely misunderstood him was, he did not talk about the nature of the self. He did not talk about the nature of the ultimate reality. He left it blank, preventing the creation of a philosophy on the nature of reality or truth, after having observed Hindu philosophy's evolution into just that. They had forgotten to inquire into the nature of truth. They had forgotten to go deep into meditation. They had simply become philosophers. They wanted to talk about the self, and they had assumed that "I am the self. I am the Brahman." Buddha saw that in his students and his disciples. He could see that was what was holding them back. Because intellectually, since they had assumed that they were the transcendental self, they didn't have the motivation to search for it.

Heart of the Matter

There are two primary centers from which a human being operates - the mind center and the heart center. Both are centers in the inner dimension of life; you will not find these centers on the outside. When I'm talking about the mind center, I'm not referring to the brain, and when I'm talking about the heart center, I'm not referring to the physical, beating heart. There is something deeper here to understand. The word "heart," the way we use it in the English language, is quite literally the center of things. When we say "Get to the heart of the matter,'" we're literally saying "Get to the source." The heart is the source center from which emanates all the beautiful, wonderful qualities of life - the seat of love, beauty, bliss - and the seat of the self. It is there inside you somewhere. You have to find it. You have to connect with it.

The mind is another center. In a way, the mind is a moving center; it's not fixed. The mind is mostly momentum and change - that is why it is the seat of chaos, confusion, and fear. The mind is not the seat of intelligence; the heart is the seat of intelligence. The mind only filters the intelligence of the heart, depending on the situation. The heart center is pure intelligence and pure awareness. Depending on how you're using that intelligence and what you're using it for, the mind filters it. That is why the mind can use the same intelligence for good as well as for bad. It can use intelligence to help you or hurt you, to create something or destroy something. Because it does not possess intelligence, it has no choice in how to use it. It is merely allowing the intelligence of the heart center to be used in a certain way.

MIND IS NOT THE BRAIN

Mind is inside us, operating at a certain level in a certain dimension. It is not the brain. It is not the brain because the brain is simply the center of the physical body where we recognize thoughts from the physical dimension. It is only an inverse process: if there is something wrong with the brain, it affects your thinking. If part of your brain is damaged, part of your memory is affected. But that does not in any way imply that all your thoughts are in the brain. Even if the door is damaged, the way information moves through it changes. For whatever reason, if the door is blocked, you cannot pass through it. So damage to the brain is quite literally damage to that part of the door that is allowing access to the thoughts. Thoughts, emotions, and desires are all happening in a certain internal dimension. The brain is, in a way, the filter for those thoughts because, as physical beings, we only have access to the brain from the outside. We don't have access to somebody's inner thoughts. Whatever happens in the brain, we simply assume that is where all the thoughts are hidden and that is where the human being is. That is why if you bump your head, it affects the way you think. But even logically, that does not explain where thoughts are actually happening. It only says the brain is a necessary organ and it has to be healthy. It has to be in a functioning mode to be able to access memories and to be able to interact with the mind.

Mind is a deep, vast concept, and the heart is even deeper and more vast. We are centered in the body, and when you turn inward, you are entering pure space. You're entering a dimension where there's nothing physical. The moment you sit and close your eyes and try to connect with your self, you will notice it is hard to pick a point to focus on because everything is changing inside. If you try to focus on one thing - let's say on a particular thought, you can only focus on it as long as that thought is available to you. When the thought moves you away, shifts you away from there, you drift with the thought, so you cannot keep your focus on a thought. Similarly, if you try to find an empty center within you, it is hard to recognize what emptiness is because true emptiness feels very different - that emptiness can be accessed only after a little bit of meditation. It is not readily available because the mind is so powerful. The mind is so readily visible that automatically your focus goes to some part of the mind that you recognize as emptiness, but that is not true emptiness. True emptiness is the emptiness of everything - the emptiness of feeling, of thoughts, and the emptiness of physical body sensation.

If you pay attention, although you cannot pinpoint exactly whether you are in the mind center or the heart center, you can recognize it by how it makes you feel. You can recognize the landscape by what it is doing to you. It is like there are two roads - one sign says "forest," and the other says "city." You pick one. Let's say you pick the one that says "forest." You start walking on that path. As you start walking, you start hearing the sounds of human civilization. You start hearing vehicles and people. You hear the sounds of the city. That will tell you that the sign is wrong - you're moving closer and closer to the city. Although you have not yet reached the city, there are enough signs to tell you that this path does not lead to the forest. There's no need to go there. Turn back. Come back to the starting point. The starting point is always the body. That is where you move from. So you come back to the body and say, "No, I want to go in a different direction. This sign says "city," but if that one is the city, this has to be something else. Because the mind is madness, it labels everything and it changes labels. Nobody is governing the mind, and it does not care. In one blink, if you lose awareness, it'll go and change the signs. It's always fooling around.

Let's say you take the other road that says "city." You start walking, and you start seeing more and more trees. The pathway is getting narrower. You start hearing the birds. You see an animal jumping in front of you. Although you've not yet reached the forest, it's giving you the signs that yes, I'm getting closer to the forest. Maybe the signboard was wrong. This is the path I want to take because I want to go to the forest. You keep walking.

Recognizing the mind and heart centers is all about recognizing the distinct feelings they each generate in you. You can't readily recognize it, but you can always recognize it by how differently it makes you feel, how it affects the way you act, and the way you look at the world. Now, with this understanding, we can look at a human being from the outside and come to a reasonable understanding as to whether he's operating from the mind center or the heart center. For example, politics and religion purely operate from the mind center. It has nothing to do with the heart. Why? Politics, by the definition of the word, is manipulation. You have to be political, so you have to rearrange things. You have to present things differently. Even if you don't use the word "political" in the literal sense as a political party or something, the very idea of politics is manipulation. You have to do politics. That's what it means.

Then there's religion. Religion is based on superstition. It's about playing with ideas, not just rearranging them, but covering them up. Religion tries to hide the truth by calling it something else because the truth is unknown. You don't know what heaven or hell is, what good or bad is, what pain or happiness is. For someone religious, these are just guesses because they haven't explored deep inside to understand these concepts. So, they hide their ignorance with different labels.

Covering up and manipulating are things the mind does, not the heart. The heart is about pure emotion and expression - it can't hide or manipulate. When you're in your heart, you're open and ready to connect. You see everything as part of you. But when you're in your mind, you're scared. You try to control and own things. How a person acts shows whether they're led by their heart or their mind. And it's not just individuals. You can see in entire cultures, which is stronger - the open heart or the controlling mind.

You're born with both the centers inside you. Both are necessary - the heart center helps you to connect with existence, and the mind center helps you to deal with the challenges of life. You need to know when to navigate to the mind center and when to come back to the heart center. When you forget the way back to the heart center, you go to the mind center and make that your home. You completely forget that there is a heart center.

Just as the mind is the masculine center, the heart is the feminine center. The qualities of the heart are closer to the feminine qualities: love, acceptance, and connection. The mind is a masculine center: aggression, force, control. Both are necessary at times, but you need to know how to navigate. You need to be in your heart center and once in a while move to the mind center to deal with the circumstances outside.

You don't need to navigate to the heart center unless you have already moved away from it. The heart is your natural center. Love and bliss are your true nature. You don't have to search for it, but if you do have to search for it, that means you have moved away from the heart center. One look at your life: How is it arranged? What are you thinking about most of the time? Are you thinking most of the time? Are you greedy? Are you jealous? Do you have thoughts of hurting someone to find satisfaction within you? Are you always in a state of agitation? You don't see a harmonious connection between you and nature. You look at nature as wilderness, something to be afraid of. These are all signs that you're stuck up in the head. You're more of a man. Coming back to the heart is to become the female.

Unless a man is willing to get in touch with his feminine qualities, he cannot move to the heart center. As you start moving away from the mind and closer to the heart, the landscape changes. The quality changes. The way you think and the way you see changes. If you're afraid of losing your masculine nature, you will not continue on the path. You will stop in the middle and turn back. That is why many have started walking toward meditation, and they've stopped in the middle and ran back to their masculine selves because they could see they were becoming softer. Their body movements were changing. The very practice of meditation, the act of sitting quietly and doing nothing, just watching your thoughts, watching your emotions, is feminine. Man is used to doing. The mind is used to doing something. It wants to manipulate, control, conceal, and do a lot of things.

Politics and Religion

Mind, by its very nature, is either political or religious, so it's not a surprise that the world has become so political and religious. If you don't control the mind, that is where it wants to be. The very act of choosing to sit quietly and accept life - to be in a state of surrender - you have to get in touch with your feminine qualities. Unless you're willing to drop your masculine self, you cannot move toward the center. In a way, that is what Buddha did when he left home. All the possessions he had were masculine because he was a man - because he was a prince. All the luxuries he was given were, in a way, to celebrate his mind, not his heart. It was his heart that was empty. That is what was missing. That is why he moved away to go in search of something. For the people who were steeped in the mind, this was a big surprise. How is it that a man can leave all these things and go away? But for him, it was perfectly natural because he wanted to meet the female inside him. It was that female who showed him life in a different light. "Look, there is suffering. Look, there is old age." It was the heart speaking to him, not the mind. Up until then in the palace, it was all the mind.

Buddha went out and started seeing life unfolding. It was unstructured life - it was not manipulated. When he was in the palace, his life was manipulated by one big mind, that of his father. His father had arranged his life in such a way that the heart was hidden. He had played the political game, but when he stepped out of politics, he could see the signs of the heart. The heart is not always joyful; even in pain and suffering the heart is authentic. As long as the mind is not manipulating that suffering, it is teaching you something - it is revealing something. That is what the Buddha saw. He saw the signs of his beating heart, and he was smart enough, intelligent enough to recognize that although he's seeing all these things outside, it is reminding him of something he needs to find inside him. There is something he's missing, and then his journey toward the heart begins. It was not about going away from his palace and moving into the forest, that's all from the outside. But on the inside, he had packed his bags and said goodbye to the mind. He said, "I'm done with you. I'm done with your luxuries. Nothing is real. It's all manipulation because eventually, I will suffer, I will experience disease, I will die, and so will my loved ones. So, I have seen your facade. I'm done with you. I'm never coming back to you." So he goes to the heart. And it was natural.

Buddha found a place where he could connect with the heart more easily. It is not that he could not have become enlightened in his palace, but there was too much of the mind, too much structure. It wasn't helpful, so he went to a more neutral space. Going to the forest, he did not go directly to the heart, but at least he went to a place from where he could begin the journey. He had the courage to say, "I am missing something. I want to connect with my heart." It takes great courage to acknowledge that there is a feminine side inside you. It takes great courage to connect with that center and accept it, and courage is not a quality of physical strength.

Man is disillusioned in believing that his courage comes from force. He's been obsessed with control and force because he thinks that's what courage is. He thinks there is only one courage, and that is of the warrior, the one who fights, the one who conquers, the one who wins over things. That's the whole nonsense of kingdoms trying to expand and assert their influence in the world. But true courage comes from the heart. True courage comes from acceptance. True courage comes from openness. True courage comes from surrender.

It was the custom of the men of Qazwin to have various images tattooed upon their bodies. A certain coward went to the artist to have such a device tattooed on his back and desired that it might be the figure of a lion. But when he felt the pricks of the needles he roared with pain, and said to the artist, "What part of the lion are you now painting?" The artist replied, "I am doing the tail." The patient cried, "Never mind the tail, go on with another part." The artist accordingly began on another, but the patient again cried out and told him to try somewhere else. Wherever the artist applied his needles, the patient raised similar objections, until at last the artist dashed all his needles and pigments on the ground, and refused to proceed any further.

Such is the nature of Man. He talks about courage, wanting to have a tattoo of a lion on his back to show that he's courageous, but he cannot take the pinpricks. He cannot deal with reality. The pinpricks of reality are silence. He cannot deal with silence. Man trembles at the thought of silence. The pinpricks are stillness, silence, bliss, and joy - qualities that are alien to him. He would rather put on a mask that shows him as being courageous. That is why a king needs a throne and a crown. He needs all those people standing around to cheer him because he's trembling inside. He's a small boy. He's a child. He doesn't even know who he is, so he needs all that. That is his identity.

The World of Ideas

The mind needs all the support it can get because it is not real. It lives in the world of ideas, in the world of words. Instead of calling him a pope, if you call him a dog, immediately he'll fall from that pedestal. It's just a word; it means nothing. If you were to address him differently and not give him the respect he expects, nothing matters because it's all a show, it's all a game. Religion is a show, a game organized by the mind, meticulously planned and structured for a certain purpose. It has nothing to do with existence, nothing to do with truth. A slight change in that arrangement makes his heart tremble. That's why reasoning with a religious person is challenging. It's hard to have a conversation or criticize them because the moment you question their beliefs, they tremble and may become violent.

Some of the greatest atrocities in the world have been committed in the name of religion, in the name of ideology. It is said that it is not greed that gives rise to the worst of crimes; it is holding onto a certain ideology. If you look at the biggest battles in the world, they haven't been battles of greed; they've been battles for an ideology, a belief. Six million Jews were massacred for what? What was this man getting out of it? Nothing. It wasn't greed. It was an ideology, a belief that he was superior to them. Where was he? Was he operating from the heart? Did Hitler even have a heart? No. He had completely shut it; he didn't want to go anywhere near the heart. That's why he never visited the chambers where people were being killed. He issued orders from far away because he didn't want to confront reality. He knew that if he started witnessing these things, perhaps the heart center would awaken and tell him, "You idiot. These are people. They have bodies like you, minds like you, families like you. They are children, babies, mothers, and fathers." But he never allowed himself that. He stayed in his bunker, sealed himself off, and gave orders. That's how he was able to unleash so much ferocity - he was stuck in the mind and wanted to remain there, disconnected from his heart center.

What is evil by definition? Why does evil exist in the world? These are questions Man has asked. Man has cursed God, wondering why there is so much pain and suffering. It's because Man has moved away from his true center. That's why there is pain and suffering. It's not of existence's making; it's his folly. He started playing with certain ideas, engaging with them so deeply that he completely forgot the fundamentals of life. He started playing with certain Christian ideas, like the cross, crucifixion, and all the rituals surrounding them, and in doing so, completely forgot that another human being, who doesn't believe in these things, is still a human being with a beating heart, a mind, and an aliveness.

Just based on his ideas, he rejected him, saying he was going to hell. He made an arbitrary separation between himself and them, and this separation is purely imagined. Where is a Christian? Where is a Hindu? Where is a Mohammedan? If you take away all your clothes and stand naked, how do you identify a Christian? How do we identify a Hindu? All our divisions are fashions; it's just a fashion statement. "I am fashionably Christian. I'm fashionably Hindu." Deep down, we're all the same. Moving from the mind center to the heart center is a great journey. It's a journey away from all the nonsense we've been dealing with - chaos, confusion, manipulation, and hatred. It's a journey toward love, silence, and stillness, and only an individual can undertake this journey. Community as a whole, and society as a whole, cannot take this journey because collectivity also belongs to the mind. Only the heart is individual. Everything collectively belongs to the mind. So you cannot start from the collective. You cannot be part of a community or group and say, "I'm going to turn this whole group into a loving community." People have tried and failed. Many well-intentioned people wanted to transform their society and change the way their communities functioned, but they operated from the mind center, desiring to change others. A group of people - a community - also comes from the mind.

JOURNEY TO THE HEART

The desire to change yourself, to connect with yourself, to look within - these desires come from the heart. And only you, as an individual, can make that journey. Yes, it's a long journey; sometimes it's painful, and sometimes it's confusing. But there's no other journey you'd rather take because the world is a testimony of what happens when you move away from the heart.

Everything evil, everything ugly that you see in the world exists because we have moved away from our true center. Just begin your journey. Sit, close your eyes, and try to recognize the feelings of love. Try to recognize the signs of the heart. This is a unique meditation where you're not looking for any physical point to focus on, but you're scanning the landscape of yourself. You're scanning your internal landscape to recognize the telltale signs of the mind and the heart. When you recognize the mind, try to avoid it - not by running away or suppressing the mind, but by understanding it. "Oh, this is the mind. This is what is happening here. Let me be closer to the heart." With a little bit of practice, you will understand that the heart is very close to you. The mind is far away. To be in the mind, you have to move toward the mind, but the heart is naturally there.

After a while, you will understand that the more relaxed you are, the more rooted you are in the present moment, and the easier it is to connect with the heart because it is natural. The more agitated, disturbed, or ambitious you are, the more you're in the mind center. So, in a way, both the heart center and the mind center are right there within your dimension, but the mind is slightly off-center. Every time you are in the mind center, you can feel that something is off. You're not rooted; you don't have the support of existence or the present moment. You need all kinds of artificial support. That's why a person dwelling in the heart doesn't need anything.

Jesus walked into Jerusalem with twelve people, but he could have walked all alone. He did not need multitudes of people cheering him. He did not need the support of an army or any physical assistance. A man, hardly clothed, with bare feet, walked to challenge a deeply entrenched religious belief system of two thousand years. And where did this individual get that courage? His courage came from the heart. He operated from the heart. He could see that the whole of Jerusalem had become a big mind. Humanity had lost its connection with the heart, which led him to overturn the tables of the money changers in the temple. His aggression came from the heart, stemming from love. However, the mind saw what it wanted to see: a trembling, fearful mind that had carefully arranged everything. For such a mind, one man was enough to create havoc, to challenge and potentially destroy that old illusion. Why was he crucified? Because the mind could not accept his truth. The priests began to tremble in fear, sensing that this man was speaking the truth. Otherwise, why crucify him? Simply regard him as a madman, cast him out of the city, and forget it. But they couldn't, because every time that man spoke, every time the madman spoke, he reminded them of the madness within themselves. It didn't matter that they had an entire support structure built around them; their madness was evident. They were clinging to an idea, a belief system.

Here is a man speaking the truth. One simple statement, he says, "Come back, become like a child," and then you tremble, realizing, "Oh, I've forgotten my childlike nature." The child isn't far away; it's right there, wanting to play, sing, dance, and embrace the whole world. But the man within you has constructed a completely different structure, living a fabricated life, a false life. It was inevitable they had no other option but to crucify him, to silence him. However, they didn't realize that truth cannot be silenced by killing it; truth cannot be killed. It has resonated over the last two thousand years. That's why time and again, there have been attempts to manipulate it.

How was Christianity born? Why does it persist? Because his truth still exists; it has to be obscured, and given a different meaning. Jesus was a man, and he wasn't speaking of a heaven somewhere outside or a kingdom up in the sky. He spoke of something inside you, and he embarked on a quest to find it for himself. He retreated into those caves, sat among those holy men, and learned how to go deep within.

All the different sects and divisions of Christianity are different ways of covering up the truth because people cannot accept these truths about Jesus. The moment you accept them, all your religious nonsense drops. You will stop worshiping him on the cross, and you will sit next to him, and you will ask him to teach you something. You will go back to his verses again. You will throw the Bible out because that is a manipulated text. It has nothing to do with the man, nothing to do with his truth, nothing to do with his heart. Read the Bible. It stinks of the mind. There's mind everywhere. Every page you turn, there's mind. There's no heart. But read Jesus' verses. If you can find his true verses, you will see there's a beating heart there. There's a mystic, there's a meditator speaking there. You cannot find him in your church because he was thrown out long before.

If you want to find him, you have to find him inside you. Not as a person, not as a personality, not as the one who sacrificed himself for you, but as the one who spoke for you, as the one who wanted to introduce you to yourself, as the one who just stood as a signpost that said, "Here." That is what Jesus is. You can replace the word "Jesus" with "here." All his teachings, every verse, every word he spoke, was reminding you of the here - "Come here. It is right here. Where are you going?" because religions had already put Man's search somewhere outside, Jesus was reminding them, "No. It is not out there." Christianity did not invent the idea of heaven and hell. It was already there. He could see that. He said, "Here, Come here." And that is what Buddha was talking about - "Come here. Where are you going?"

Every man who's worth listening to has only spoken about the here, he's not spoken about something outside of you. Then where are you searching? How long will you search on the outside? How many lifetimes more? It is time to turn inward. That is where everything is. That is where your true center is. All you have to do is just keep looking for it. Keep navigating the landscape. Yes, you will stumble in the darkness. Yes, you will make a few mistakes. Yes, you will cling to the mind for a while, but eventually, you will find the center. Because it is the center. And something is drawing you toward that center. Know that as much as you're looking for the center, the center is also looking for you.

Just like the apple on the tree, when it gets disconnected, it has to fall because it belongs to the earth. The tree has taken the apple away from the earth. The nourishment of the apple, the juice of the apple, the taste of the apple, it all belongs to the earth. It is only in a different form. The earth longs for it. And when the time is right, it takes it back. It assimilates it. You are the same. You can go as far away from the heart as you want. You can live in your mind as long as you want. But eventually, you have to come back to the heart. Eventually, you have to merge with the heart. That is your true hope. That is your true space. Keep looking. Keep searching. One day, accidentally, you will just fall into the center. And that'll be your greatest flowering. That moment you fall into the center, when you know who you truly are, that is when you will know everything there is to know about the mind and all its manipulations. And that is when you will know where to be.

Dancing with Shadows

INNER VOICE

How do you start from the most chaotic place in the universe - the voice in your head - and go to the quietest part, the most peaceful, serene part of you? The journey from chaos to silence. Let me start with a beautiful passage from the Gita. Arjuna asks Krishna, "What is the definition of a steady person, a person who's steady-minded?" Krishna says, "A person is said to be of steady mind when he is content in the atman by means of the atman and when he has renounced all desires which are produced by the mind. A person is said to be a sage of steady intelligence whose mind is not agitated in misfortune, whose desire for material pleasures is gone, and whose passion, fear, and anger have disappeared. A person is of steady insight who is renounced on all sides, who does not rejoice or bemoan upon attaining anything whether pleasant or unpleasant, and who completely withdraws the senses from the sense objects like a tortoise withdraws its limbs into its shell."

This is a beautiful passage where Krishna is, in a way, describing one's journey from the mind to the self. He's talking about how the mind is the seat of pain, fear, anger, desires, and a person who is caught up in the activities of the mind, who is fully identified with the mind, who sees himself as nothing more than the mind, can never be steady. Steadiness comes when you withdraw yourself from the outer world of senses to the self, just like a tortoise withdraws itself to the shell. That is where it finds comfort, and rest. That is its home. Every time it sticks its neck out, it is anxious. It is disturbed. It is in fear. It is in danger. That is how our situation is when we are entangled in the mind. When we are fully identified with the mind, we have stuck our necks out of our shells, fully. Naturally, there's always fear - the fear of losing something, the fear of judgment, the fear of rejection, and above all, the fear of death.

Only the one who is rooted in the self, at the center of their being, can be steady. Trying to find steadiness in the mind is like trying to stay still in the middle of a raging stream. The effort is futile. Your own life is a testimony to that. Every time you try to find some sense of peace, some sense of relaxation, some sense of certainty, and you look to the mind to provide that, what has the mind done? It has only added to the uncertainty, chaos, and confusion because, in its efforts to provide you with what you're looking for, it has pushed you into more desires. From one view of the society and the world we live in, we can see what the mind has done to us. It has replaced contentment with a search without realizing that contentment and a search can never dwell in the same house. Search, by its definition, means something is missing. Contentment, by the very definition of the word, means there is nothing to search for.

Contentment and search are opposites, and the mind knows only searching. By its very nature, it cannot find contentment. How can you experience contentment when you are fully identified with something whose very nature is to search? How can you find peace and relaxation, and enjoy the present moment when you're not content? Contentment is the foundation on which all these emotions stand. You cannot be peaceful if you're not content. You cannot enjoy the present moment when you are in the process of searching. So, Krishna says it's the steady one who withdraws themselves from the world of senses.

Irresponsible Mind

That's where the mind is. The mind is playing with the senses, utilizing them to add to the confusion, to add to the chaos, whatever might be the intention of the mind. Its intentions might be good. It is your mind, and it might be trying to help, but what if your mind is blind? What if it wants to help you cross the road and it does not know that it is blind? That is the situation. Every time you want to cross the road, the mind comes in first, "I'll help you." But it doesn't know that it cannot see. That is why it always takes you right to the middle of the road and leaves you there. Now you have to figure it out for yourself: What do I do from here? At your darkest hour, when you need the greatest support, the greatest help, your mind deserts you. It panics. It does not take responsibility. It does not say, "I'm sorry, I pushed you into all those desires. For the last ten, fifteen, twenty years, I've been blindly dragging you from one sense pleasure to another. I am the one who's responsible for the way you look, the way you feel about yourself, for all your agitation and chaos. I'm sorry." But the mind doesn't accept it. It just disappears. It is scared, it does not want to take responsibility, and it's gone. And there you are, alone, contemplating all the things that you should not have done, all the things you could have done. Your whole life seems meaningless, not because you did not achieve something great - it's because you missed all the simple joys of life.

When you look back at your life, the biggest disappointment wouldn't be lack of accomplishment, but not being able to say with certainty, "I lived. I was there." When you turn back and look at your life there will be so many things, but there'll be one thing missing: You. That's the saddest feeling, to look at your life and think, I wish I had lived more. I wish I had been there in my experiences. I wish I had replaced some of my blind chasing and running with stability - with an experience of myself. I should have given more importance to myself, my mind and body, my thoughts and emotions. And above all, I should have paid attention to my inner voice. Because that inner voice - which I mistook for my own voice - was nothing more than the voice of my mind. That's where I faltered. I could not make a simple distinction between my voice and the voice of my mind because I did not learn the art of listening. My voice was subtler. My voice was quieter. On the contrary, my mind was louder, and I was listening to the loud mind - not the silent voice that was behind it."

That would be the biggest regret. Something took you on a different path away from life, away from all that you are. Everything you are searching for, you could have experienced in this very moment. You don't have to go anywhere, but you are entangled in the mind, and it doesn't know anything other than searching. Even if you were to introduce the mind to what you're searching for, the mind can at most go around it, circle it, but can never touch it. If you were to introduce your mind to happiness, it would come close to it. It would try to understand what that happiness is, but it can never experience it. So, it will always live in the illusion that you need to do something more to be happy. This is very important to understand. By its very nature, your mind cannot taste the truth. And truth is where you should be. Truth is who you are. Truth is where all the best qualities of life are: peace, certainty, contentment, joy, and bliss. It's all in that truth. But the mind cannot see, cannot touch, and cannot be with the truth.

It's not that you don't know that happiness is only in the present moment. You know it. It's not an entirely new concept. It's not that you cannot understand that life is in the present moment. Understanding is not the problem. The conditioning has taken you so deep into the mind that just that simple understanding, that intellectual understanding, isn't enough. That understanding has to deepen and become a memory. It has to seep into your mind, into your body, into every pore of your being until it becomes very clear to your being that the present is where you should be. Intellectually, it's not a difficult concept to grasp.

How can you be happy tomorrow? You are here. This is the only reality you can experience. Even when tomorrow comes, when you experience that tomorrow, you will only experience it as now because you cannot experience anything other than the now. And yet, your mind keeps on putting you into the future. It keeps on pushing you into the future or the past. It's not because you don't understand it; it's because the conditioning of the mind is very strong. Withdrawing from the senses is not just a matter of will. It is not just a matter of decision. It is a matter of technique. You need to know how to do it. That is the tricky part. You need to understand the process of withdrawal. It has steps. You cannot suddenly withdraw to your inside. If that were the case, it would have been easy to say, "Oh, I'm too addicted to my mind. Let me go back in." Even to recognize what the mind is, what the self is, when the mind is active is an accomplishment.

Now, how do I know who to listen to? That itself is a method. So, let's understand how to listen to the inner voice, what to listen to, when to listen, and how to slowly move inward. The entire objective of watching your inner voice is to start from the loudest part of you - your mind - to go to the quietest part of you.

There was an interesting psychological study conducted by researchers at the University of Illinois to understand the cognitive processes: how the mind processes information and how it responds to sounds, as well as the actual process of hearing. They wanted to comprehend what actually occurs when we listen to something. So, they decided to experiment with a group of individuals. The study group was given headphones and made to listen to sounds and words. They manipulated the sound in such a way that one ear was listening to the sounds much more loudly when compared to the other.

There was another twist they added to the experiment, which the subjects were not told about: They inserted a few words that sounded phonetically similar to a few other words, essentially grouping them together. Listening to one made it easier to listen to the other phonetically similar-sounding words. However, the subjects were not informed about this. They were simply told to listen to these words and recollect them later.

While conducting the study, the researchers asked the subjects to repeat the words they had heard. The researchers expected that, because the human mind naturally identifies patterns, the subjects would hear these phonetic words, these similar words, more frequently. However, the research turned out to be entirely illuminating. The subjects were hearing more words being repeated in the louder ear, rather than recollecting phonetically similar words. This outcome was a big surprise and is known as the cocktail party phenomenon. In a crowded environment like a cocktail party, the mind tends to tune out sounds at a similar volume level and pays attention to any sharp or distinct sounds.

The conclusion drawn from the experiment was that the mind is more acute toward the volume of sound than the actual content. It doesn't pay attention to the content itself but focuses more on the way that content is being presented.

Survival Instinct

This is very significant to understand. The mind is listening to the loudest part of the mind. What does that mean? It means it is blind to the content. The mind is not as smart as we thought. We believe the mind to be so smart and sophisticated, capable of listening to all different kinds of sounds, picking out what is most important and relevant to you, and presenting it. However, through the study, we discovered that the mind is much more primitive and simple. It picks up any loud and sharp sound without considering the content.

When you try to understand why this happens, there is a clear explanation: the human mind has conditioned itself for survival. In the wild, sophisticated ideas, subtle concepts, deeper meanings

- these are nothing compared to a sudden loud noise. A sudden loud noise signifies danger, so the mind naturally tunes itself toward listening to loud noises. For the mind, a loud noise, a bitter taste, or a sharp prick is infinitely more important than music or profound philosophical understandings of the self.

Survival is what the mind is all about. It does not comprehend that it is no longer living in the jungle. It doesn't grasp that it's now in a completely different environment - a world of words, ideas, and concepts. Its primary instinct remains fixed on overcoming the fear of death, to keep you alive. Hence, it gravitates toward anything loud. This, in a way, explains why meditation is hard and why something as simple as connecting with your inner silence becomes challenging. The mind is constantly in survival mode, where silence is the least important thing because it poses the least danger to your being, and thus, the mind doesn't pay attention to it at all. The same principle applies to stillness. The mind pays more attention to movement than to stillness. Why? Because when you're still, the danger is minimal. When you're asleep and your body is still, there's no perceived danger. However, when you're in motion, the mind's entire focus shifts to the body because movement implies potential danger.

All our senses are tuned toward sharp sensations, but in meditation, that is exactly what we are trying to avoid. We're attempting to withdraw the mind from all the sharpness, the alertness, the constant disturbance, toward the calmer part of us. When you listen to the mind and how it interprets those words, it links everything to survival. Even an idea or a concept that has nothing to do with survival becomes linked to it, creating fear because the mind is a survival mechanism. It doesn't recognize that we've created a civilization that has moved away from most dangers. It's not about constantly worrying about being eaten anymore, but the mind still operates as if that's the imminent threat. This is where it becomes most disturbing. A slight change and the mind acts as if neglecting it means certain death, filling your thoughts with scary images. This is also reflected in your dreams. How can you withdraw from this? That is the bigger challenge.

The mind, by its very nature, is not designed to turn inward. It will not turn inward because its biggest fear is failing in its responsibility to protect you. The mind is like the security guard you've placed at the gate; it's not meant to enter the house. It resists coming inside because it knows that if it sleeps within, there's no one guarding the entry. So every time you try to coax it inside, saying, "Come in, it's okay, there's comfort and relaxation," it hesitates, glances inside, and rushes back to the gate. This is what happens in meditation. When you attempt to relax, to be quiet, the moment it touches that zone of silence and stillness, it panics and retreats to the entrance, resisting being there.

This is where a method, a technique, and practice are necessary. You can't merely instruct the mind; you have to slowly guide it inward because initially, you can't leave the mind out. You're identified with the mind. When you attempt to go inward, a part of the mind also has to enter because your identity is deeply intertwined with it. When you go in, you're still conversing with yourself. The only time you can leave the mind outside and go inward is when you've stopped speaking - when there's no mental voice. As long as there's a voice conversing within, you have to persuade it to turn inward.

MIND, MEET SILENCE

The easiest and simplest way to get your mind to turn inward is to introduce the mind to silence. Don't attempt to drag it; allow the mind to be there. First, identify what the mind is. It's not a physical entity sitting there. It's not images or movement. The mind is simply your inner voice. What you tell yourself constitutes your mind because images alone don't matter. It's when the mind begins qualifying those images, talking about them, that it exerts its influence on you. Otherwise, you could sit and observe your mind like a movie without any physical form. Why are you unable to do it? Why can't you simply sit and watch your mind like a movie? It's because your mind isn't just images; it's someone sitting next to you, constantly whispering into your ear. Every time you attempt to observe your mind, it says, "What are you doing? You've been sitting for five hours!" When in reality, you might have only sat there for five minutes. The mind is armed with all sorts of tricks and it knows you thoroughly. Its objective is to pull you away from that moment because you're sitting there, still, doing nothing but observing, and it doesn't like it. That voice is your mind.

What happens when you start paying attention to that voice? What happens if you make it your method, your technique to watch that voice? This is what happens: Initially, when you start watching that voice, your mind, which is you, only listens to the loudest, the sharpest of sounds. It does not take into account any subtlety - it listens to the loudest of voices. You start watching it. Every time there's a conversation, you watch it.

Now, here is a beautiful fact about the mind: When there is a conversation happening in the mind and you don't watch it, when you don't pay attention to it, the mind keeps on increasing the volume until you pay attention to it. You are lost in your daily activities, so your mind keeps on amplifying it. First, it'll introduce the idea: "Let's see if he takes the bait." It says, "You need to get this thing done now," but you don't act on it. You're busy doing something else. Then it goes for a walk and comes back: "You need to do this now." Watch it. The volume is higher. You ignore it. It comes back again, comes back again. It keeps doing this until that voice is so loud that you cannot do anything - you cannot listen to anything else. It does not care what you want. It wants you to act on that.

That is how the mind functions. But what happens when you start watching - the same process reverses. When you pay attention, a conversation comes just like a wave, and this time you are alert. You're not lost. The mind does not have to strain to get your attention. You are ready even before the thought comes. In fact, you're watching it from around the corner. You're watching it come. And when it comes, because you're fully alert, there's no need for increasing the volume. It just presents the conversation. You watch it, and then it goes away. Because you watched it, something in the mind registers that this conversation has already been acknowledged. It labels it as watched. So, anything it labels as watched - when the mind comes back again - it reduces the volume a little bit because that thought has already been watched. It does not have to strain to get your attention. Next time when the thought comes back, the volume is lower. When the mind has already watched a thought, why does it keep coming back? Because the mind is blind.

The mind is not as sophisticated as we think. It is a simple mechanical process. As long as that idea has any momentum, it'll come back. That is the nature of the mind. That is why we keep thinking about the same thing a million times - even when we are done with it - because the mind is not sophisticated. The mind is a dumb repetition machine. All that smartness and intelligence comes from somewhere else. That is what you're trying to understand. Where does this intelligence come from? If it is not in the mind, where is it?

So, the next time it comes back, the volume is lower. And now, you're ready. You're watching it. Again. The mind labels it as watched twice. It comes back again. The third time when it comes, the volume is even lower.

If you pay attention to the mind, you will see ideas never completely disappear. Their volume reduces so much that you start listening to something else, but the same conversation is going on. Let's say there is a nagging worry, that you've been thinking about. If you have watched it enough, it starts going back to the background, but it doesn't disappear. It is still there, but now there is something else that is more important. Quite literally, your mind is now attuned to listening to something even louder; a new thought has come. The same process repeats. It comes back. Are you watching or not? Remember, if you don't watch it, it'll come back with a higher volume. You cannot get rid of a thought without watching it. Let me repeat that. It is impossible to get rid of a thought without watching it. A thought that is not watched is your biggest nemesis. A thought that is not watched is your mental noise. A thought that is not watched is your ultimate source of suffering. A thought that is watched slowly goes into the background.

The practice, the method, is to sit and watch every thought. Again, not images, not movement, not shapes, just the voice. Watch every conversation. Watch everything you're telling yourself. Of course, when you first begin, your mind will start with the loudest of sounds, and the loudest of sounds are the outside sounds, not the inside sounds. Initially, you won't even be able to listen to your inner voice. You won't even know where this inner voice is, because you are listening to sounds that are happening outside: Somebody is talking, a vehicle is moving, or you're listening to an insect buzzing or the sound of thunder. Your senses are totally attuned. Remember, your mind is a survival mechanism. It is still in that survival mode, totally outside. It does not know that you are walking on a different path. It does not know that you are a Buddha striving to realize that Buddha nature. It still thinks you are another animal in existence. The mind is that primitive. It sees you as just a piece of life that has to be protected. That's all.

WATCHING THE NOISE

Somewhere deep down, you are more. That is what is pushing you toward meditation. That is what is pushing you toward awakening. Initially, you will start from the outside. Don't get frustrated because you're not able to listen to your inner voice: "Oh, my technique is to watch the inner voice. I'm not even able to hear my inner voice." Don't worry about it. Start from the outside. Listen to the loudest of sounds. As long as you're paying attention, those sounds slowly start moving to the background because now you've paid attention.

Notice how easy it is to handle this mind now. It's the same mind, but because it's not screaming, it's easier. And then slowly, the volume of the outer conversation matches the volume of the inner conversation. Then, for the first time, the mind cannot make the distinction between an outer voice and an inner voice. Your meditation has gone so deep that now it is beginning to talk about what's happening inside. The outside voice is still there, but it's far away. That is how you move inward - not by fighting with the mind. Not by trying to drag it inside, but simply by watching it. Take away its energy. Take away its volume. If you try to change the volume of the conversation, the mind won't let you do it. You have to simply watch it. That's it.

Then slowly, it starts presenting you with the conversation that's happening inside. And then again, you're paying attention. You're watching everything the mind is saying about the inside. It still has to exhaust a lot of conversations that are inside. In fact, it doesn't take too long for it to exhaust the outer conversations, because outer conversations are fixed to what you're experiencing here. But your inner has much more depth to it. It has all your memories, all your experiences. So it takes longer.

Once you turn inward, you will be in that zone of listening to the mind much longer. And then slowly, a day will come, when for a moment the voice has become so soft, so quiet, that without the awareness of the mind, there is silence introduced. The same mind that was carrying noise, that knew nothing else but to carry the noise, for the first time, picks up silence and brings it to you. It's the first glimpse of silence. It will shock you with what's happening here. There was a moment of absolute silence. When you touch that silence, it is so pure, so pristine that there's no mistaking it. You will know it is there, and your own mind has brought you to silence. Again, don't jump right on it. Understand the trick of the mind.

If you jump on that silence and say, "I want this silence again," when asking for it, you have forgotten to watch and you have let two or three thoughts pass by without watching them. When they come back, they come back with a higher volume. That is how a desire takes you away from the present moment. Even when you're inside, when a desire arises - it could be the desire to experience silence, or it could be the desire to experience enlightenment. A desire is a desire, no matter the content. The moment you start desiring that experience, in that desiring process, you miss a few thoughts, and they come back with more and more volume. Because you missed a few thoughts, you start worrying about it. "I'm not able to stay in the present moment." And every time you do that, you're missing a few more thoughts. Before you realize it, you've missed the whole train. Now, this train has come back with twice the volume and the cycle has started again. Slowly, you're spiraling back to the top. Instead of going deeper, you're moving higher and higher, up to a point where you have to get up from your meditation because now you're unable to go deeper. It's just too much noise.

You see the process, the beauty of the process - just watch. And then slowly, it'll keep bringing silence again and again and again. And then, one moment will come when each compartment of that train, - which is your mind - will be carrying silence. There will be nothing in it, nothing to say, nothing to disturb you. Just pure silence circling.

You moved from the chaos of the mind, a mind that knew nothing but noise, the loudest of loud noise.

Now it has become a vehicle for silence. Your own mind - you have tamed the beast. You have tricked it - artfully, craftily, with patience, with practice, with a little bit of effort, and a little bit of playfulness.

Embellishing Silence

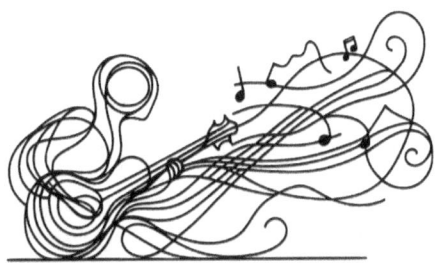

Each one of our senses is complete by itself, although we use them together, moving from one sense perception to another. Each one independently can give us a complete perception of life. Seeing by itself can give us a total sense of life. What do I mean by the total sense of life? How can it be total when you're unable to hear, smell, taste, or touch? What I mean by a total understanding is if you are deaf, or for whatever reason if you are unable to feel life, if you are unable to smell or taste, if you only could see, then your entire understanding of life would happen through your visual senses. There would be nothing lacking there. It appears to be lacking only to the one who uses multiple senses.

THE WORLD OF SENSES

For the one who has attuned himself to just seeing because he does not have the other senses, for whatever reason - maybe he was born with only one or two senses - there is nothing diminished in his quality of life. This might come as a surprise. You might be thinking a blind or deaf man should be depressed, but that's not at all the case. More often than not, they have a sense of innocence. They seem to know how to enjoy life just using whatever senses that are available to them. Why is this? Each sense is its own language. Senses are not connected; they are basically a language to make us understand what life is. Seeing is its own language; listening is its own language. Similarly, smelling and tasting are their own languages. And we can notice this in animals. Some animals use certain senses predominantly. Some animals don't see at all, but they still go about living their lives perfectly. Some animals don't hear. Some animals don't see color, but nothing is diminished in the quality of life because that is their language. The universe has chosen to reveal itself to them through a certain medium.

As human beings, we predominantly look at life through the visual senses. Although we have the faculties of smell, hearing, and taste, we don't use them as much to navigate, explore, and understand life. A simple difference would be how much you use your smell as opposed to your dog. Your dog lives in the world of smell. Yes, it can see and hear, but it uses the sense of smell like the way we use our eyes and hands - to see things, to touch things, to get a sense of what's happening around us. We smell only when it is really necessary. Otherwise, it's a sense that is there somewhere in the background. We also don't use touch as a navigation tool for life, but some animals are predominantly touch-based. If they're not touching and feeling their environment, they can't move around.

Each sense is a door through which we can enter being, provided we understand the language of that sense and have attuned ourselves to it. Just like seeing can open the doors to your inner silence, you can start with watching. It could be watching your breath, watching a flame, watching a beautiful flower, looking into the mirror - all visual meditation techniques. Then you can enter your being through other senses. For now, let us keep our dominant visual sense aside. Let us forget that we have eyes. Let us forget that we can see. Imagine you are born blind. How would your perception of life be different? If you were given a choice between listening, smelling, tasting, and touching - you could only pick one out of these, and that's the only way you're going to understand life, - which one would you pick? It's more likely that you would pick the hearing sense because the range of experiences in the hearing sense is broader than touch, smell, or taste, but it's not as broad as the visual sense.

You wouldn't select one sense above the other because inherently these senses are not superior to one another, it's how we have interacted with the senses. For human beings, the visual sense is the most dominant, followed by hearing, then touch, then smell, and finally taste. We use these senses in the same order. Our first go-to sense is seeing, and then we listen. It is a good order. I don't know how the human society would look if we were to reverse this order. If we wanted to taste before seeing, if we wanted to smell before touching if we wanted to touch before hearing, and if we wanted to hear before seeing.

The entire construct of life that we experience makes sense to us because that is how we move. We first open our eyes, getting a visual sense of what's happening around us, and then we try to listen. If something is interesting, if it piques our curiosity enough to investigate, we move closer, we touch it, just like you would first look at a flower. You might observe it from far away - its colors, movement, texture, lights, and shadows capturing your attention - then you move closer. Perhaps you don't hear the flower, but as you get closer, you begin to hear everything happening there. While standing far away and watching the flower, it's purely visual. As you get closer, perhaps you can hear the rustling of leaves. Getting even closer, you might even hear the plant moving in the wind. Then comes touch - you would want to feel the flower. Following that, you would want to smell it. You can stop at that. Tasting it is optional. That is the progression of the senses.

Between Notes

So if you were to pick one sense out of the remaining four - leaving the visual sense out - you would pick hearing. And if you are born blind, hearing would be a complete sense. There would be nothing missing there. If you look at human society, listening has been an integral part of connecting with ourselves. Despite the dominance of the visual senses, we have always enjoyed listening. The biggest testimony to that is the sheer variety of music we have created. Listening is not just about hearing. There is a big difference between hearing something, listening to something, and feeling it. When hearing is the only thing you're doing, that hearing can become all your other senses put together. You can see, feel, smell, and taste through hearing. Your hearing becomes your entire body.

You can explore life just as you would with your entire body using your hearing alone. You can start from the outermost layer of recognizing the sounds, and then you can recognize the rhythm and the tune. Each faculty you add to it is like writing another sentence that tells you something about what's happening around you. Rhythm and melody teach you something. The intensity of the sound teaches you something. There's a difference between a shriek and a laugh - both come from the same source, but they touch you, and make you feel in totally different ways. Why? Because the intensity registers differently in the mind - small variations in sound.

Look at nature. Nature, in a way, is music personified using colors. Nature is visual music. How can we say this? Look at how a plant grows. Observe the rhythm of its movement. Notice how the branches are arranged. There is music in how the petals of a flower are arranged. There's music in the way the ocean waves, in the rustling of leaves, in the movement of the clouds. Because we are so visually tuned, we don't perceive all these things as music. If you were to forget that you can see, if someone were to describe to you what nature is, what's happening around you just through listening, you would realize that life is very rhythmic - it has a tune to it. For example, seasons - they have a rhythm, an order, a flow. Now, what is the difference between music and noise? Noise has no order; it's pure chaos. You cannot grasp noise because there's no beginning, no middle, no end in the noise. There's nothing to hold on to - it's just a random arrangement of sounds with no intelligent intersection of silence. It's just noise. That's why noise, after a while, is irritating, even deafening. So, what does this mean? It means it's not the sound we are interested in; it's actually the silence interspersed between two sounds that our being is trying to connect to.

When we listen to music, although we tend to think, "I am listening to music," if we pay closer attention, we will see that we're trying to listen to the silence. Music is only embellishing the silence. It's an ornamentation of silence. Music is just the language for silence because you cannot directly perceive silence; you perceive it through music. Between two notes, you wait for the next pause. That is what your spirit longs for. And if there is no silence, if the music were to be continuous, one sound after another, with no rhythmic interspersion of silence, that would be noise. Look at nature. Nature is musical. Nature is music because it knows when to pause, when to move, when to change the tune, and when to change the intensity of the tune - there's harmony in nature. Consider the word "harmony." It's the word associated with music, the same word used for nature, and the same word for when we are in tune with life. When we are in harmony with life, we are healthy, happy, peaceful, and connected. When we are not in tune with nature, that's when we experience discomfort and disease. We are out of tune.

No Words

Look at the word "universe." What does it mean? It means "one tune." The entire universe, everything that we experience, is one tune played in different ways. We are all vibrations on a single musical instrument. We have our independent, individual identities, but we cannot vibrate independently of the instrument. And what is that instrument? When we are connected to the body, the body is our instrument. When we are thinking, the mind is our instrument. When we are interacting with the world, the world is our instrument. Every moment, we can either be in tune with our minds, with our bodies, with our selves, or we can be in chaotic noise. Music, especially instrumental music without any lyrics, allows this connection because the moment you start verbalizing, you are engaging your mind. It is possible to verbalize without engaging your mind, but it is hard.

Instrumental music is how we have been celebrating some of the most important occasions of life. If you look at human history, the farther you go back in time, music becomes more and more instrumental, more and more primordial. It starts moving closer and closer toward the primordial sounds of life and nature. If you go to the simplest of cultures, the most primitive of cultures - cultures that have not been polluted by too much thinking or too many ideologies

- you will see their musical instruments depict the sounds and voices of nature, such as the calls of birds and animals, mirroring the way nature speaks to them, then we started adding words and lyrics.

Music as entertainment is purely a modern phenomenon. If you go back in time, you will see that at one point, music was restricted to royal palaces - it was performed exclusively in front of kings. The king used to have individuals or a band who dedicated themselves to learning these musical instruments, and the music was played only in his presence - it was not available to the general population of his kingdom. That's why you didn't see musical theaters or places of music in any of these kingdoms. However, if you were to go to the palace, to the place where the king lived, there was always a dedicated music hall.

Now, where does this come from? If you go back a little further in time, you will see that music was played only in a religious setup, in front of the deity - what people used to worship - what they called "God" or divinity. First, music was an offering of thanks, expressing gratitude to the divinity, then, as a meditation to connect with your inner divinity. The farther you go back in time, you will see that music was more religious, more spiritual, and more meditative. The music we see now is simply a deviation from the meditative center. That's why instrumental music can be used as a form of meditation all by itself, without any other method, without any other technique.

Music for Sattva

If you can learn how to see and feel through music, if you can connect with the vibration of music, if you can see music as a complete language, then it can lead you to enlightenment. It can do so more joyfully, with more celebration, and with less noise and chaos of the mind. Initially, when you begin listening to music, you can use it as a cleanser of thoughts. The difficulty of entering meditation when you're just starting is the noise of the mind, the constant conversation, and the mind's attempts to explain and understand meditation. After a while, that itself becomes the biggest source of disturbance because meditation takes time to sink in for you to experience it - but your mind is impatient. It begins to overdo, adding too much. Consequently, after a while, you may feel like giving it up because you're unable to keep pace with the mind. Your mind desires quick experiences, and if you're unable to achieve that, there's a good chance you'll give up. You can avoid this by using music because when you're listening to instrumental music, if your focus, awareness, and attention are entirely on the music, then you're not listening to the voice in your head. You're not listening to the desires of the mind; instead, you're listening to something more simple, more primordial: rhythm, tune, music, harmony.

You can start with listening first. You can choose meditative instrumental music. Yes, music by itself is meditative, but there is such a thing as music that is not conducive to meditation; it's created for a different purpose. Music can serve various purposes - to relax you, to stimulate your senses, to evoke anger, to bring sadness; it's a language of its own. So, it can encompass everything, touch every emotion, and reach every chord within you. Hence, you need to select music that naturally calms you down. Going back to yogic terminologies, you need music that induces a state of sattva, not rajas or tamas. What is Rajas? Rajas is over-excitement and over-stimulation, so you don't want music that overstimulates your senses; you cannot achieve a meditative state. Simultaneously, you don't want music that induces tamas, which is sleepiness. You don't want it to be so slow, boring, or monotonous that you're unable to maintain focus. Seek a balance - sattva music - music that stimulates your senses adequately but also keeps you relaxed.

Meditative instrumental music - be it the sounds of a violin, flute, piano, guitar, djembe, or tabla - that is created without the desire to impress you, is important. Music can either be used to touch your soul or impress your mind. As a meditator with some level of accomplishment, you can discern the difference between these two kinds of music: music that merely captivates your mind and music that soothes your soul, music that goes deep. Choose instrumental music that naturally draws you in, and that naturally evokes a meditative sensation. Start listening to it, focusing entirely on the sound, then the rhythm of the sound, the tune, and the silence in between. Forget your mind, your ego, and your body. Let that music completely submerge your ego. Become the music.

For a moment, pretend that you are blind. Don't visualize the musical instruments while you're listening. Don't visualize the person playing the music, and don't imagine yourself sitting and listening to the music. Set aside all entertainment and dive into the meditative exploration of music. This is important because we have been listening to music since the beginning.

Some of the oldest musical instruments can be traced back to forty thousand years ago. There was a bone flute found that has been dated to that time. Music has always been an important and integral part of human communities, but why hasn't it transformed the human race? It hasn't taken people to that meditative level because we have not used it as a science of self-transformation. We have not viewed it as a meditative science. We've enjoyed music, and that enjoyment has become more of an entertainment than an exploration.

When using instrumental music as a meditative technique, you should try to avoid the pitfall of entertainment. When you entertain yourself with music, your mind is also entertained, and you don't go deeply into the self. You can enjoy the music, experience it, and go deep into it, but the word "entertainment" stays on the surface. Entertainment aims to create a moment of excitement. Instead of seeking excitement, aim for depth. Slowly transition from the sounds to the silence, because that is your destination. That is what you're truly seeking. The music is speaking to your inner silence, which is why you enjoy it.

Think about it - your body has no inherent reason to enjoy music. The body is physical; it needs food, sleep, and rest. Why should the body need music? Music is the proof - the definitive proof - that you are not just a body; you are something more. You are something subtle: silence, stillness, wakefulness, consciousness. It's natural for you to enjoy music because there are no barriers in your universe; the walls exist only in your mind. Internally, it's vastness; there's no one hindering your movement, rhythm, or tune. That's why music thrives when it resonates within. When it can penetrate inside you, it resonates even more. Consider the word "resonate" - it implies happening in a certain dimension. Resonation requires an internal chamber. What exists within us to bounce off? There are no walls, no restrictions—just pure inner space. And yet, where does this resonance occur for music to happen? It resonates with your consciousness.

WHERE IS MUSIC HAPPENING?

Music touches the screen of your consciousness, stimulating you. Scientists have studied music and concluded that it stimulates certain parts of your brain - creative centers, emotional centers, and intelligence. However, their focus has been on studying the impact of music on the brain, not on your spirit or self. Science has yet to investigate the nature of consciousness; it remains fixated on particles and materials. Eventually, science might discover the need to explore subtler elements; that perhaps the universe is composed of consciousness, aliveness, music, rhythm, and tune, and maybe it has nothing to do with particles.

We've been stuck with physical things because of our visual sense - because we see things. That is where we went into investigation, and we didn't ask a simple question: If we were born blind, how would we investigate the nature of the universe? How different our science would be. How different our theories and concepts would be. So, as far as science is concerned, music is just stimulating - and yes, it has a positive impact on the mind and the body. But if you were to ask a meditative person, if you were to ask a Buddha, he would say you are music. That is why you enjoy music. If there were no music inside you, how could you enjoy music? Music has nothing to do with hearing. Your whole body, your whole mind, and every cell in your being can connect with music.

Beethoven composed one of his best pieces of music called "The Ninth Symphony" when he was completely deaf. He started developing hearing problems in his twenties, and by the time he was in his mid-forties, he completely lost his sense of hearing. That is when he composed his best music. He composed "The Ninth Symphony" when he was in his fifties and he had lost his hearing. It is impossible for us to even understand this. How can you create music without hearing? You can. Beethoven started developing different ways of listening to music when he started losing his sense of hearing. He loved music so much that he started figuring out different ways of connecting with music. He used to put his head on the piano and listen to the music through the vibrations because his hearing was gone - he listened just through the vibrations. There are examples of people learning music just by putting their ear to the door of the auditorium, just picking up the vibrations.

Music is not just hearing. Music vibrates the very fabric of space. It vibrates the fabric of consciousness. That is why it goes so deep. We have not allowed music to help us go deep in transformation because we've been stuck in the visual senses too much. The moment we listen to something, the moment we hear something, we want to go and see it. That is where we shut the listening sensors. If you were to throw away seeing for a while and just be with listening, you can see how deep it can take you, how far it can go. That vibration is what you're trying to connect to - not just the sounds, but how those sounds are dissolving the walls, the rigid walls that you have created for yourself. What does music do? It penetrates all your artificially created ideas of yourself. It shatters your idea of a physical body. It shatters your idea of a limited being because when you're listening to music, if you pay attention, you can see that the listening is not happening in one place. It's not just happening in your ear. Even if you were to completely close your ears, you can feel music.

Music is happening in a certain dimension, and as you start going deeper and deeper and become attuned to listening, you can get to a point where you become the very space in which music is resonating. That's when you realize the one who's listening to the music is not sitting here. He's everywhere. The consciousness, which is allowing the music to happen, is not restricted to time or space. It is not restricted to the body. It is not restricted to the mind. Something is happening here. The language of music begins to unravel its mystery. Initially, you are only reading the tune. You're only reading the sounds and a little bit of silence. And then it starts speaking to you. It'll start composing poetry. It will start deciphering the nature of your soul. Music becomes a teacher. Then when you feel like knowing more about yourself, knowing more about meditation, you will go straight to music because you've learned how to listen to it. Because music is a language on its own, just like seeing, smelling, and tasting, music is its own language, and it's complete in itself. It represents the totality of life. Nothing is lacking in music.

Each one of our senses is complete by itself. They don't use the other senses as a crutch. We use them because of how we experience life. But in existence, each sense perception is designed to take you all the way from the inside to the outside. And you can use music to move from the outside to the inside.

Dancing with Shadows

LAUGHTER IS SUNSHINE

Only human beings can laugh. Think about that for a moment. Some animals display signs of laughter, some behavioral traits that can be recognized as laughter, but they do not laugh. At least not in the way you do, bringing an emotional connection to the laughter, using their whole body, laughing for the sake of laughing, laughing because they can see the funny side of things. Animals can never do that. There's something interesting about that. It takes a certain level of intelligence, a certain level of awareness, to see the funny side of things. And it takes the ultimate courage to see the whole of life as a joke. There is nothing serious about life, except that we have made it into a serious affair - the natural process of life and the way humans interact with that process.

The Ultimate Joke

What is it that we do with life? What is it that we do throughout the day? At the end of the day, what is it that we recognize as life? You cannot help but see the whole thing as a big joke because we're going nowhere; there is no tomorrow. We are accomplishing nothing because everything goes back to the same process of life. All our greatest civilizations that have come before us testify to the fact that everything lasts only for a while. The Egyptian civilization, the ancient Indian civilization - there is not a civilization that didn't believe that it was the ultimate, that it was the zenith, that there cannot be anything beyond it. The Romans felt the same way. When they built the Coliseum, they thought there was no way anybody could build anything bigger or grander than that, and yet we have. Everything gets recycled. Life assimilates it. Nothing lasts forever. And while we were creating those things, we created them with utmost seriousness. I cannot imagine those building the pyramids laughing and enjoying themselves while building them, or, for that matter, while building the Colosseum or any ancient civilization.

There was enormous effort and a lot of seriousness involved, but if you look back at it, you can see it was all a joke. They could have spent their time enjoying life, laughing a little more, just having that perspective that life is here and now, and whatever we are creating, we are creating for our joy. There's nothing serious here. There was a time when Man wasn't this serious - nowhere near as serious as he is now. Look at the way Man moves about now. He wakes up serious. He has a lot of things on his mind. He wants to get a lot of things done during the day. And while he's getting those things done, he has to be concerned about making sure that he's getting those things done in the right way. We use the word "concern" in a positive way, while the word is purely negative. If you're concerned about something, that doesn't mean that you are caring for it - you are cautious about it. It simply means you're not laughing. It simply means you're not enjoying the moment. You're concerned, and there's always something to worry about.

Let's say you stop worrying about your health - all your worrying disappears. You can transition from worrying about your health to fretting over your finances, the well-being of dolphins, the threat of nuclear weapons, or the potential collapse of the economy. You can keep on endlessly worrying about things because worry is about the future, and the future is unknown. If it is unknown, you can imagine whatever you want. You can imagine all the things that might never happen. But Man wasn't like this. There was a time when he woke up with very few thoughts or desires in his mind. Maybe there were a few activities, but he was always ready to laugh.

Look at any indigenous culture. Laughter is there. Laughter is there as a community therapy. They gather around and laugh, but not as a laughter meditation. We need laughter meditation. Modern man needs laughter meditation. They didn't need it - laughter came naturally with the way they were living. They could see the funny side of their activities because they were not chasing after grand, big ridiculous dreams; they were closer to life, hunting, gathering, cooking, eating, and playing with children. Humor was natural, but something changed along the way. Of all the various things that have made Man serious, the single biggest culprit is religion. All religions have been serious. Seriousness has been their business because they figured out very early that nothing sells like fear. It is the easiest thing to sell.

By nature, there is something in Man that can easily trigger fear because there's a part of him that is unknown. He's exploring life. He's trying to understand himself. He does not have all the answers. He wakes up in a strange world where there is lightning, thunder, ocean waves, and eclipses, and he does not know why these things happen. Without contemplating all that, he can go about his life, fearing when he has to fear and laughing when he has to laugh.

You don't need a reason to laugh. The content is everywhere; you just need to look at it from a slightly different perspective. Now, if you are unable to, then again, it's fine. Laughter by itself can create laughter. Just the sound of laughter, just the way your body moves during laughter, can create laughter. Laughing meditation is about laughing because you're laughing. You don't need a context or a reason, although you can add reasons to it. You can sit in a group and tell funny stories or jokes and laugh, but laughter doesn't need any of that. Wake up in the morning and first thing, just start laughing. Before going to bed, the last thing, laugh. Initially, it will simply be a mechanical process. Just take a few deep breaths and forcefully get all the air out of your lungs. Do it two or three times, and then start making the sounds of laughter. And then automatically, that sound of laughter will trigger laughter in you. Because you're trying to laugh, there's nothing there to laugh at, and that itself is so funny. Just listening to you laughing, you will start laughing. Have a nice, deep, belly laugh.

We laugh, but only once in a while. Our laughter doesn't go deep because we are so cautious when we are around people, and we are so protective of our self-image. We don't laugh with a sense of self-abandonment. We are always holding on to ourselves. We don't want to let go. In laughter meditation, you can go all the way. Have a nice, deep belly laugh, let your entire body vibrate, laugh for no reason, and laugh until your jaw hurts. Laugh until you start crying. There's no need to stop in the middle because there is no purpose for laughing. It's just to laugh for the sake of laughing - there's no external reason. If there's an external reason, then after you've laughed enough about that, you need a new reason. But if you're laughing for the sake of laughing, you don't need any reason.

Scientists say laughing is healthy - it stimulates your nervous system, muscles, and blood circulation. It increases positive hormones, known as endorphins or happy hormones. It helps you relax and also deeply impacts your mind. Laughter is cathartic; it helps you release pent-up, accumulated, and suppressed emotions. The human body and mind are reservoirs of suppressed emotions. When we don't want to express something, we push it deep inside our minds and bodies, hoping to never find it again - but it's always there. In moments of disturbance or pain, it surfaces. Laughter is an emotional catharsis. When you laugh for no reason, something releases inside. The knots of fear, anxiety, and uncertainty begin to untie themselves because the mind and body recognize that, for a moment, there's an opportunity to forget their fears and pain. It starts seeing laughter as therapy. When you repeatedly come back to it - let's say once in the morning and once in the evening, you can remember throughout the day that there's a release waiting. Just knowing that there is a release helps you not hold onto negative emotions for too long. The mere thought that, no matter how serious or worried you are, at the end of the day, you will laugh, helps you stay detached.

Think about it: People who go into cyclical loops of anxiety, stress, and depression have forgotten how to laugh. They don't have a release mechanism. There's only intake - there's no outlet for emotions. Imagine you're accumulating all these thoughts, and those thoughts are multiplying. They're having babies; they're producing on their own. One thought gives rise to two, two gives rise to four, and there's no way to throw it out. More often than not, it's a negative thought that multiplies ferociously. A positive thought has patience; one thought might give rise to two once in a while. But a negative thought is different. It is eager to multiply. It is eager to spread its negativity. So, before you know it, you're filled with all kinds of unnecessary thought processes. Laughter is a release. Use it as a valve to throw out all that you don't need.

You can do this meditation alone for about thirty minutes in the morning and thirty minutes in the evening, or you can do it as a group therapy. If you're finding it hard to laugh and if you can somehow create a small group - it could be anywhere. Even once a week, gather a bunch of people. Instead of going to the church on a Sunday, gather around and laugh. That'll take you closer to your true nature. It has the possibility of introducing you to your divine nature - not by believing in ideas of heaven and hell.

A belief is a belief. Whether you believe or not, you're not going to get there. There are no real places called "heaven" and "hell." If you are still believing in heaven and hell, then you need laughter meditation. It is highly recommended that you wake up in the morning, revisit your beliefs - all your serious beliefs - and have a good laugh because it's all a joke. Religion is the biggest joke in the world. It has never taken anybody to heaven and never thrown anybody into hell. It has never given anything to anybody except for just a feeling that somebody is there to take care of you. Except for postponing your search, except for forgetting your search, religions have done nothing.

The mind of Man is deeply religious. Just because you're not going to church, just because you're not going to the temple, just because you call yourself an atheist or call yourself agnostic, non-religious, or whatever, doesn't mean that you're not religious. Religion has seeped deep into the human mind. Now, how do you unknowingly know that you are still governed by the laws of religion? Your seriousness. If you are serious about life, somewhere religion has done its work. You might call it by a different name. "No, I'm just working toward my future, securing my future," or whatever it might be. Dig a little deeper. You will see the fundamental idea of seriousness can be traced back to religion. Before religions, Man wasn't like this. There was no reason to build cathedrals, no reason to build the pyramids, no reason to keep on imagining the future. It's religion that took Man away from the present moment and put him in the future, and he's still in the future, although he might deny it - "I am no longer religious, I have gone beyond religion, I am my own man, I have my own understanding."

Postponing Happiness

That seriousness is there as an undercurrent, and it shows in all his activities. It shows in how he treats himself, in how he treats others - everything is a serious affair. He's living in a hostile world, so he has to compete. Where do all these things come from? Where does ambition come from? There is a difference between creating for the joy of creating and being ambitious. Ambition is purely a religious phenomenon; it is not a secular phenomenon. It is a big misunderstanding to think ambition comes because individuals want to create. No. Creativity never leads to greed. Creativity is pure joy. There are no goals and no deadlines - you're doing it because your creative energies are pushing you to create.

Look at how Man moves now. He moves with ambition, a desire to conquer, and a desire to win over things. All this can be traced back to religion because it is religion that first started preaching about subjugation. Man didn't know anything about subjugation, about suppression, about postponing his happiness. Religion introduced the idea in Man of postponing your happiness - "This life is not the most important thing; it is the next life. What you do here is only in service of God. You don't have to laugh now, sing now, or dance now. You work. You work to build our cathedrals, you work to build our temples, you work to build our stupidity. You are in service of God." God never wanted you to do any of this. Has God ever asked you to serve? Do you know where that word "serve" comes from? It comes from religion. It comes from the ambitious mind of Man. Otherwise, why would you ask someone to serve? You would ask them to laugh, to sing, to enjoy life. If you are really concerned, if you really love another human being, the last thing you would ask them to do is to serve. Who are you serving? While serving, you are in servitude, in bondage, and what joy can there be in bondage? Religions have kept Man in bondage.

Although the traditional ideas of religion have waned a bit, and people have made a conscious choice to move away from dogmatic beliefs, the underlying current that is pushing humanity is still very much religious. We are deeply conditioned. That is why we need laughter. That is why we need a release. That is why we need a mechanism to completely reject all that has been added to us. In laughter, this happens naturally, because when you're laughing, you are disturbing all the religions. Imagine you're sitting in the church, and in the middle of all the ceremonies, you just start laughing. Do you think people will gather around you to laugh with you? No. They'll throw you out. Your laughter is a disturbance because they are pretending to be serious. Because they're only pretending, your laughter reminds them that everything they're doing is a joke and they are unable to laugh - they've become too serious. Otherwise, what is the necessity not to join in the laughter? Why not just enjoy that laughter?

It's a serious affair. They plan and think about it, and they stand in the queue for hours, very serious throughout that journey to the temple. Nobody is laughing, nobody is enjoying. Why? Because the very idea of religion is opposed to the natural flow of human life. Religion is artificial; it is man-made and imposed from the outside. Everything beautiful in life emerges from inside as a natural outflowing. You cannot impose anything onto life. When you impose it, it burdens life, shackles it, takes away the laughter, takes away the joy. Religion is purely a creation of Man. Yes, there is religiousness, spirituality, something we don't see, don't understand, a higher truth to life. There is that search, but that search is not serious, not somewhere outside you, not beyond this life - it's all right here. Your search is in your breath, in your body, in your mind. None of these things belong to religion; they belong to existence. Yes, there is a yearning to connect with something higher. Even some of the greatest scientists believed in religiousness. Although they might not follow any religion, they acknowledged the quality of religiousness.

For example, when Einstein was asked, "Are you a religious man?" he answered, "There is something invisible, an invisible order, an invisible force beyond everything we know that moves life. I am religious in the sense that I believe in that. Only in that sense, I am religious. Not in the sense that religions have been talking about - believing in heaven, believing in hell, believing in a savior - no." That is religiousness. So, you don't have to be an atheist to step away from religion. You can be religious and still step away from religion. You can still hold on to the mystery of religion, the mystery of life, and get to the truth and reject religious dogmatism.

What we have been given in the name of religion are just ideas and concepts that push our search beyond this realm of life. So it is natural that Man has become serious. The moment he's born, he's condemned. How can he laugh? How can he laugh when you tell him his life is a sin? He's been thrown out of the Garden of Eden. He has to earn his right to get back to the garden. Right from the beginning, you are telling him that there is something wrong with him. The basic processes of life, the basic desires of life that arise in him - if you're condemning him, then you're suppressing. This has happened for centuries. And remember, although you are here and your body is here, your memories are all about the experiences that have happened in this life. There is something inside you that has a memory of everything that has ever happened. It has not forgotten its past suppressions. Memory is not just about what you're experiencing now. Your body has a memory of the past, the past that you haven't even seen, haven't even experienced, but it has the memory.

That is the deep conditioning. It is not as simple as, "Okay, I've picked up these desires" or "I've never been religious. I never went to the church. I never believed in all that. I am free from religion." No, it is not as simple as that. You are a part of the same collective unconsciousness of Man; you belong to the same stream that has been moving in a certain direction, a stream that has been unnaturally moved in a different direction. Its flow has been affected. Dams have been constructed. Religion is the biggest dam that stops the flow, that obstructs the flow, and you are a part of it.

You need to recognize if you are unable to breathe freely, if you are unable to laugh freely, if you're unable to enjoy each and every moment of life fully, that is a clear sign that you are a part of the same stream of humanity that is being diverted in a different direction. The conditioning is there. That is why we need methods. That is why it is not simply a matter of saying, "I want to become joyful now. I want to reject my religion. I will change my name from a Christian name to some other name." It's not about rejecting any of that. It's about recognizing how deeply these dogmatic ideas have seeped into us because there is a collective unconsciousness whether we like it or not.

WE ARE ALL CONNECTED

Somewhere, deep down, we are all connected. Suffering somewhere in the world resonates in your inner being. Suppression somewhere in the world speaks to your being. Injustice somewhere in the world takes something away from you because we are all one. Deep down, we are all connected. We are all moving images only appearing to be separate. When we're not thinking about the image, when we just close our eyes and connect with the aliveness within us, my aliveness is not different from your aliveness. That is why when we laugh, we all laugh the same way - we don't laugh differently. There may be minor changes and minor differences, but laughter is laughter. When two people are laughing, you can always tell that they are laughing. You will never be confused: "Is that laughter or something else? Well, I laugh like that, but does that mean that he's laughing like that?" There's no confusion because deep down we are all one. Our emotions are one. Our pain, our fears, our laughter, our joys, they're all connected.

The way we have been treated, the way we have been fooled - literally fooled because we did not know how to read or write - we were afraid. These qualities were enough for perfect subjugation. "I don't know what truth is. I don't know how to read." Now here is a man who knows how to read. Right there, you put him on a different pedestal. Right there, you treat him as an authority figure just because he knows how to read and write. And then he says, "These messages are coming from God." I don't know how to verify these messages. I am just a simple person. And why would I want to take on God? Now, he makes you believe that if you go against him, you're going against God. If you don't believe in him, you're going against God. And what kind of God has he presented to you? A God who punishes. A God who tortures you. A God who throws you into hellfire. Naturally, you say, "Alright, enough, I believe. Leave me alone now so that I can go back to my kids, I can live my life." It's almost like you have no other choice but to believe because if you don't believe, he'll keep on coming at you. He'll keep on talking about how sinful your life is. And the moment he's able to gather a group of people - then he has the support of a group of people. That is why it is so hard to break away from your religion - there's so much support for it.

He's already gathered his flock. He's already mesmerized them.

If you try to be an individual, if you try to break away, you have to break away from all that. And people are naturally social creatures. We love to be loved and we love to love. We don't like isolation, so we accept - "For the sake of my soul, for the sake of my spirit, for the sake of my children, let me be a part of this." Somewhere deep down, most of us know that there's nothing there, but we still go through the motions because we don't like the feeling of being disconnected.

Just laugh. Wake up in the morning and just laugh. Laughter is your connection. Laughter is your community. Laughter is your refuge. You have found something more valuable. A billion people can gather together and they can all believe in the same ideologies. But if they're all serious, one man, amidst all that, who is laughing, is more important. He's more valuable than all those billion people put together. You don't need the support of a billion people if you know how to laugh. because when you're laughing, you are an individual. You're connecting with your authentic self. And when you compare the crowd to individuality, there's not even a match. The crowd is just an idea. They don't even know why they are huddled together. They don't even know why they are believing in those things. They don't even know why they are singing the songs or reading those sermons. They are just repeating it like parrots. It just feels good. There's no logic. There's no reasoning. There's no inner transformation. But when you laugh, when you treat it as a practice, a method to unwind yourself, to discard all that unwanted nonsense that has been added to you, you are truly taking birth again. Everything is getting renewed from the inside.

It's a simple meditation. You don't have to add too many things to it. Sometimes you can speak about your problems and laugh. Sometimes you can read from your bible and find whatever reason to laugh. But in laughter meditation, you don't need another reason. Just start making the sounds. If you want, verbalize the sounds, shout like animals, create some funny voices, make funny faces - it doesn't matter. Whatever tickles you, whatever generates a good belly laugh, use it. And one day, while you're in that deep ecstasy of laughing, when you've forgotten all about laughter, when you've forgotten all about worries - your worries and fears - something will show up. You will see something. You will experience something - the disappearing of the one who's laughing. That's when you realize there has never been anybody laughing. There has never been anybody crying, suffering, moving, or thinking - it's all a happening. I am a happening. I am not a thing. If you're just a happening, what is there to worry about? Then you can happen in the most joyous way. If you're just a happening, there is nothing to change. There's nowhere to go. Nothing to accomplish. Joyfulness and laughter are a natural consequence.

MIRROR, MIRROR

Let's talk about a profound, mysterious, and scary meditation technique: Watching the mirror. What can be scarier than looking at your own face for extended periods of time? If you think you know yourself, if you think you know what you look like, if you believe you know how you think and are in touch with your emotions, try the mirror meditation. It will, for the first time, reveal things that will scare you. It will show things you could have never imagined about yourself. There's a reason for this. Most of the time, we simply skim the surface of life. We form opinions about ourselves based on the judgments of others. Most of what you know about yourself comes from the people around you - the voice of your mother, father, friends, family members, the community where you live, and, to a certain extent, your religion and the language you speak.

AM I REAL?

Who are you beneath all this? When your name is taken away, when the voices in your head are silenced, who are you? There's a firm assumption on which your entire perception of reality rests: that assumption is that you are real. You've never questioned this assumption, never asked this simple yet profoundly significant question: Am I real? You've not been introduced to this question because it's a very dangerous question. It can lead you in a very different direction from the one society wants you to take. Nobody will introduce this question into your being because it's an authentic question. Why assume that you are real if you can investigate and find out for yourself? What if there were a way to actually figure out if you are real or not?

Now, what do I mean by "if you are real?" Everything you know about yourself comes from your perception of yourself, and most of it is connected to your self-image, which is reinforced every day. You wake up in the morning, and there isn't a single day that goes by without you looking into the mirror. The moment you look into the mirror, your entire life is linked to that self-image. You don't have to keep looking in the mirror; you only have to glance to know "I am there," and then you go about your life.

Now, imagine if there were no mirrors in the world. Imagine if there were no way to see your reflection. Imagine if you looked into still water, but there was no reflection. You looked into a mirror, there was no reflection. You looked into, let's say, any shiny object, but there's no reflection. How different would your reality be? More importantly, how much of a difference would that make to your suffering, your pain, your fears, and your frustration? Have you ever thought about how it might well be possible that the single biggest reason why human beings suffer more than animals is because we look into the mirror and they don't?

It's profound when you think about it because every day they wake up to the same reality, pretty much the same circumstances - except for minor differences that we all experience as individuals and as animals. Life is one for all of us. And yet, they don't suffer nearly as much as we do. Could it be because they don't reinforce that self-image every day by looking into the mirror?

We have not been investigating in this direction. We have simply assumed that the person I'm looking at in the mirror is me. Who else can it be? What if that assumption is not true? What if there is more to your self-image? What if there are more things hidden there? Not only more things but what if there are multiple you's?

When you sit and watch the mirror - not as a glimpse, not as a judgment - but as a practice, a method, a technique, you are going deeper into the inquiry of understanding the nature of reality. More importantly, the nature of form. What is form? Is it real? You don't even have to go too far mystically to try and understand this. Just look at the progression of our scientific understanding of the nature of reality. If you go back in time, the farther you go back, the more outward is our nature of investigation into reality.

Look at the pyramids. As much as we think about the pyramids as a religious symbol constructed on the basic presumption of an afterlife, they were created for the pharaoh to experience all that he had experienced in this life to continue after death. A pyramid was constructed that gave him all the comforts, and all his needs for the next life. This is a religious interpretation of what the pyramids are.

Pyramids are also astronomical instruments. They were primitive astronomical structures created to track the movement of the stars. So were the stones at Stonehenge. Although they appear as symbols created by humanity to leave a mark during their construction, they were built based on a certain astronomical understanding of the universe. It was Man's way of trying to connect with the universe.

If you go back even further, Hindus had a clear understanding of the sun being at the center of the solar system and the nine planets revolving around it. Galileo proposed this, and he was absolutely rejected because it was believed that the Earth was at the center of the universe, but Christianity would not accept the theory that the Earth is just another planet revolving around the sun. Thousands of years before Galileo, the majority of Indian temples had a separate section where you walk into a chamber and find the sun god right in the middle, with many of the other planets represented as figurines of different gods. This is known as the Navagraha. You circle this as part of your prayer, as part of your ritual, circling it a few times, and then you go about your life.

Although now it is performed mostly as a ritual, when it was constructed, it was built based on a scientific understanding of the nature of reality. When you are creating a model of the universe, it has to be scientific. The approach is scientific. Think about it: without telescopes, without all the modern equipment we have now, they were able to track the movement of celestial bodies. And out of the millions of stars, they were able to identify the difference between a star and a planet just using their naked eyes, just by the power of observation. So, Man has always been on a quest to know what reality is.

If you look at the progression over the last few hundred years, we have been moving closer and closer to ourselves in terms of investigation. The ultimate pinnacle of that is particle collision, the accelerators that are created to understand the nature of fundamental particles. What is the fundamental nature of reality?

We started with the sky. We began with understanding the sun, the moon, the ocean waves, and eclipses; we wanted to comprehend the seasons. The entire humanity is filled with knowledge of the outer world. Now, here we are for the first time doing something so obscure, so difficult to even explain to people. But if you were to talk to any of those scientists who discovered the Higgs boson, what they called the "god particle" - it doesn't matter what they called it - they were looking for a field, an energy field, that appeared to be giving mass to matter. Up until now, we had assumed that matter is real, that it is solid. So, if you're able to take a chair and start breaking it down into smaller and smaller pieces, eventually, you will get to the smallest of particles.

Now, that smallest of particles is what makes up the whole universe. That's what makes up a chair, that's what makes up you, that's what makes up me. That is the assumption with which we started our inquiry. We began dissecting the chair, the trees, and the human body, going deeper and deeper. We found molecules, then atoms, and then we discovered that even an atom can be divided into multiple parts. We found electrons, and neutrons, thinking that was the ultimate particle. And then we realized we could further divide it.

Experiments were conducted: Under certain conditions when two particles collide at certain speeds with a certain energy, they break up into even smaller particles. So, we continued investigating, only to conclude that there is no particle at the minutest of levels, at what we call the quantum level. When we are searching for that ultimate particle, it disappears. Scientists completely confirmed that what we were searching for wasn't there. That's when the inquiry began into whether there is something else that is making all this happen.

Matter isn't real. Elementary particles don't have mass. What a discovery that is! You call it a particle, but it does not have any mass, which means it cannot be solid or physical. Even if you bring millions or billions of them together to make a chair, that chair will not have any physical properties because it lacks mass. It only appears to be real.

When scientists began investigating this omnipresent field, they named it the "Higgs field" after Higgs, its discoverer. Regardless of the name, they were aware of the existence of such a field. When an elementary particle interacts with this field, it acquires mass. So essentially, mass is nothing but the interaction of a particle with this field. They were searching for what they called a Higgs boson. Discovering that particle would prove the existence of the Higgs field.

In 2012, we found the Higgs particle. We discovered the Higgs boson, confirming that the Higgs field is real. That completely changed our understanding of reality. It marked the end of the search for tangible things. Until then, our quest had focused solely on physical entities: earth, sun, moon, stars. We had never investigated the nature of a field, an energy field.

Now, for the first time, we are on the brink of understanding something beyond what our senses can perceive. Up until now, all scientific inquiries have revolved around "What I can see and understand. If I don't see it, it's not part of my scientific investigation. I have to see it. It has to move. It has to do something." But for the first time, we are investigating an invisible entity that cannot be seen, touched, smelled, or tasted. It's simply referred to as a field.

What have the mystics been talking about? What have the meditators been discussing? What have awakened people been alluding to? They have spoken about that invisible field more than anything else. In the spiritual and mystical community, we refer to it as consciousness, aliveness, or awareness. Because when an individual personally experiences this field, it's not merely a field - it embodies your true nature. You can't label it as just a Higgs field because it's "my field." When you experience it, it's your consciousness, your aliveness.

Jesus went so far as to call it, "That is me. You have to pass through me." It's akin to a scientist saying that every particle has to pass through the Higgs field to become real. Jesus was expressing, "You have to pass through me to realize the truth," because he identified with that consciousness, that aliveness. Look at the beauty of life - two words can differentiate experiences so distinctly.

How am I connecting Jesus and the Higgs boson? Why not? If you examine the properties of that field, its interactions, and what they are discovering, a day will come, sooner or later, when we must conclude there is a correlation between what the mystics have been speaking about and what we have been discovering. In a way, what a meditator has been trying to subjectively discover inside themselves has taken thousands and thousands of years to reach a point where we can understand it objectively.

Ultimately, the basic conclusion is that matter is an illusion. It's purely a matter of perception. Matter is mostly empty space. Then, what about your body? If your body is mostly empty space, what is holding it together if not for your habit of looking into the mirror? When you look into the mirror, you are reinforcing your self-image. Throughout the day, you can go about your life knowing that you've looked into the mirror and you know who you are. All those assumptions would be questioned when you sit and watch the mirror.

The Technique

This is how it unfolds: You sit in your comfortable meditation posture and keep a mirror in front of you where you can see your entire body. If you're sitting on the floor, ensure that your whole upper body is visible in the mirror, not just your face - that would be too unsettling. Besides, you cannot examine your face from that close a distance. Let it be your entire body. Dim the light; don't keep it too bright because you need to keep your eyes open and look into the mirror. If it's too bright, it might strain your eyes.

Mirror meditation is beautiful to perform in the evening. If you have to choose two meditation techniques, one for the morning and one for the evening, in the morning, you can do a breathing meditation or watch the flower meditation - any meditation that helps you relax. But in the evening, you can try this adventurous meditation. Mirror meditation is perfect for evenings, especially as the natural light dims and the sun sets. The evening sets the mood, serving as a reminder to let go of your self-image.

Imagine if you are in a perfect natural setup. You're not living in an artificially constructed home with mirrors and lights and all that. Imagine if you are living in nature, You are going about your life throughout the day. You're hunting, gathering, eating, doing all kinds of different things. And then the evening sets. What is the evening symbolizing? It is telling you to return. Come back home. If you have gone hunting, the evening reminds you to come back home. If you have gone gathering, if you have gone doing something - come back home. Because slowly the light is disappearing, And eventually, when the light goes out completely, you cannot even see yourself. And if you cannot see yourself, you cannot see anything else around you. You are in complete darkness. Your body is gone. Now what activities will you perform using the body?

The evening is a natural reminder that our self-image is just made up. Even within the same day, we have to let go of it at some point in time. It is so hard for us to see all this because we don't inquire deeply. We want to hold on to a certain idea of life and we don't want to question all this. We have never questioned why should there be a day and why should there be a night. Why should my body look like this? All our questioning has been about what do I do with this body? What is the purpose of my life? What can I achieve with this body? We have never questioned the basic reality of the body.

So, in the evening, as the sun is setting - if you are in an artificial setting, dim the light - create the atmosphere, sit, and watch the mirror. Something strange happens as you continue with the practice. You will notice there will come moments when the image in the mirror flickers. Initially, it will be fixed, solid, mirroring exactly what you're doing. If you're sitting still, the image is sitting still. If you're blinking your eyes, the image is blinking. It's merely a reflection of your actions.

However, there will come a moment when it will do something you didn't intend or expect, and it will startle you. How is this possible? Up until then, your entire assumption has been that you are real and physical. So, a mirror is simply an inert reflective material, with no influence on how it projects the image. Whatever is in front of it, it just reflects. But one thing you did not take into consideration is consciousness and awareness. Awareness has a choice whether to register or not to register the reflection in the mirror.

Up until now, you had assumed that as long as your eyes are open and you're looking at your image, the image has to be there. But when you go deeper, you will realize there is somebody else observing this. There is a consciousness, an aliveness that is behind the body, behind the mind, witnessing this entire process. A moment will come when it will grow lethargic, bored of observing the mirror. You've been watching the same thing repeatedly, day in and day out, for at least an hour a day. Twenty days have passed - thirty days have passed. In one instance, you relax, no longer interested in the mirror. At that moment, it flickers. For the first time, you'll know without a doubt that your image disappeared, albeit for just a fraction of a second. In fact, it was for a minuscule duration. But you sense something is occurring here. That's your first cue to inquire deeper. And so, you continue.

That experience resurfaces again after a few more days of meditation. It happens again. Now you are certain it wasn't an accident. Something is indeed occurring, and you persist. This occurrence repeats with more frequency. Almost every day when you sit in front of the mirror, there comes a moment when your image simply disappears for a fraction of a second. Now you are certain that something different from what you expected is taking place.

Continue to meditate. Let it not scare you. Your assumptions are being tested. If you don't give up, if you don't get scared, if you can hold onto the practice, a day will come when that one moment will extend to two moments. That moment when the image disappears extends to two or three moments. If it can extend to just one second, something has changed inside you. For that one second, if what you're seeing has vanished, it registers in your consciousness as an authentic experience that you can never shake off, because you did not make that image disappear and your eyes were open. You did not ask for the image to vanish. Everything is gone, all dark, in a flash. How? That is the first sign that your body is not real, it's pure empty space. There is nobody sitting in front of the mirror, yet there's this strong assumption that you're there. It's because you have conditioned yourself to perceive yourself in a certain way, but that conditioning can be broken when you go deeper.

Because you've not gone deeper into seeing, you've only stayed on the surface, never allowing existence to reveal that the image is an illusion. However, of course, you can still feel the solidity of the body. You can still smell, taste, and hear sounds. All these aspects contribute to your perception of reality.

When the image disappears, it startles you. But it doesn't startle you as much as awakening or enlightenment would because there are still many other familiar sensations - the warmth of your body, the sensation of your breath - still present. However, what mirror meditation has revealed to you is that your senses can be deceived, and there is no trick involved. Watching the mirror isn't a magic trick; nobody tricked you into forgetting the image. It happened naturally.

That should make you ponder: "If I didn't do anything additional, and if it is still happening, maybe that is the true nature of reality, and I'm getting closer and closer to it. Maybe throughout the day, I have been doing something to keep the image alive. And when I don't do anything, when I simply sit quietly, when I relax, naturally, I am being erased. Why should the image disappear? I didn't want it to disappear, and nobody instructed me to do something. I wasn't doing anything - I was just sitting quietly. Why did it naturally happen?"

That is a significant thing to understand. So, that means when you're not artificially adding to this self-image, your natural state is formless, which is what happens when you go to sleep. There is nothing to be scared about. Every day for a few hours, you completely forget your body. You exist as a nobody. And yet, you're not scared because when you wake up in the morning, the mirror is always there, and you can go and look at it, saying, "Oh, I'm here." But it should scare you. Sleep should scare you because you're losing the consciousness of the body. However, because you've gotten into such a beautiful habit of it and you are certain that you're going to wake up in the morning, you have no trouble falling asleep.

Imagine if I were to tell you, "Go to sleep, but there's no guarantee that you're going to wake up." You would be afraid of going to sleep. That's similar to what happens when you look in the mirror. When the image disappears for the first time, there is that fear: "What if this is permanent? What if I can never come back to this image?" But after a while, you will understand that you can always return to your image, although it's a projected image because it's more of a memory, more of a remembrance. When you want to see your image, it's always there. But when you don't want to see it, you can withdraw your awareness from the visual sense, and you don't have to see it.

Apart from the mirror and the image and everything disappearing, before that happens, the image also changes. Sometimes you will look beautiful; sometimes, you will look ugly. Sometimes you will appear as a nice, gentle, good person; sometimes, you will seem like a criminal, because all those facets are inside you, you're not just positive. There are a lot of negative emotions, a lot of things hidden inside you, and all that gets projected. When you're sitting still, just looking into the mirror, you're providing a screen for your emotions to play on - where the hidden emotions can emerge. That's when you realize there's nothing more beautiful than the human face, and there's nothing uglier than the human face. The same face, when filled with anger, jealousy, worry, and fear, appears ugly. And that same face, when relaxed, smiling, loving - what can be more beautiful than the human face? And you can see all that right there. Your face reflects. Play with the emotions. Sometimes your self-image changes in terms of age; sometimes you look younger, and sometimes older, although you're not consciously doing any of this, you're just sitting and looking into the mirror. But all these things are happening. Why? Because of your consciousness, your awareness.

Consciousness and Awareness

Up until now, you've only used it momentarily - to look into the mirror, to observe your activities. Now, for the first time, you're asking your awareness to focus continuously for an extended period, but the nature of your consciousness is such that it doesn't concern itself with the image. It attempts to withdraw itself. So, while you're trying to maintain focus on the mirror, your awareness is attempting to go deeper inside because you're relaxed. Each time it shifts from the external to the internal, it traverses through various layers - your childhood, your self-image, your emotions - and that's what gets projected. There's a scientific reason why your image keeps changing, why your emotions keep fluctuating. Even though you remain fixed, even though your mind is fixed, something traverses from the external to the internal.

As it navigates through the landscape of your mind, body, senses, and emotions, occasionally, it manifests because of your heightened awareness. In that moment of awareness, you're not truly observing the mirror or the projected self-image; you're observing the internal. For the first time, you're using the mirror not to perceive the outside, but to investigate the inside.

Up until now, you've used the mirror only to see the form. But for the first time, you've used it more like a microscope. A microscope, not just a mirror. And look at the beauty of it. You cannot create a microscope without a mirror. You cannot create a telescope without a mirror. The mirror is how we investigate the nature of reality. Here, for the first time, you're using a mirror to look inside. Not inside your body, not the cells, not the bones, not the muscles - you're looking inside the dimension of the form that is your body. You're looking into your thoughts and your emotions. See how far you can go. Once the withdrawal happens completely, more often than not, the image goes blank. Your eyes are open, but you're not at all interested in looking in the mirror. Then just gently close your eyes and turn inward. From that point onward, you don't need the mirror. Your mirror meditation has ended. If you are fully dedicated to the practice, if you're practicing mirror meditation at least for an hour every day, within a matter of a few months, you will turn inward, and then you don't need to look into the mirror. Yes. You can go and look at it just to relive that experience because now you know how to go inward and forget the image. It's fun to see your image disappearing. It is magical.

Once in a while, you can look in the mirror. When you're standing in front of the mirror, just go into deep meditation. Connect inside and see how everything disappears. And then, after a while, you can do this even without a mirror. Just stand anywhere, keep your eyes open, but turn inward. Notice how everything disappears. For the first time, you've got the key to go inward. Reality is not as fixed as it seems. It is just like what the mystics have been saying. Form is just an illusion. Your aliveness doesn't come from the body. Your aliveness is what is supporting the body.

Let me end this with a small example. Imagine if you were given a toy as a child, and you were told to play with that toy throughout the day. That toy is your most important possession, and you have no conception of other toys and other things. This is the only toy you have. You start playing with it. You carry it wherever you go. You take care of it. You bathe it. You clothe it. If the toy gets damaged, you repair it. You make sure that it's in good condition. You give it a nice place to rest because that's your world; that toy is your world.

Imagine, with a snap of a finger, in a single moment, I made your body invisible. Now there is only the toy. There's nothing else there. The toy is moving. Sometimes it is sitting, sometimes it's sleeping. It is reflecting on itself. It is taking care of itself. There's an invisible hand that is nurturing that toy, but you cannot see that hand because we've made the body invisible. That is the relationship between us and our bodies. Our bodies are the toys that we started playing with. Our consciousness and our aliveness are that invisible hand that is nurturing us. Everything we are doing, we're doing it through consciousness. Our bodies are just toys, but we have played with them for such a long time it has become our absolute reality.

Now, although we are the consciousness, we think we are the toy. Although you are the aliveness that is nurturing the body, you mistake yourself to be the body because of conditioning. You've played with this toy - everything you've done, you've done with this toy, and the one who's doing it has always remained invisible. So there was no way for you to know the actual doer, the actual awareness, the actual consciousness.

When you sit and watch the mirror for the first time, you are trying to connect with the one who's playing with the toy. Of course, he has to be something above and beyond the toy. He cannot be the mind. He cannot be the body. He has to be transcendental. And what else have we been searching for? That ultimate transcendental reality, which a mystic calls self, consciousness, aliveness, and a scientist calls a Higgs field. It's the same reality, the same field. When we move through that field, we become real. So we are not real. It's that field. It's that consciousness.

If you can start with this much understanding, and then let the experience take you, sooner or later, this intellectual understanding will become your experiential understanding. That is what you need to be striving for. Theoretically, you can read. You can read the philosophical scriptures. You can read ancient mystical scriptures. You can study what's happening in these colliders. But none of that matters unless you sit and go through a practice. That is why meditation is indispensable.

You could spend twenty billion dollars creating that machine. But even with all that money and all those resources, you cannot add one ounce to the experience of an individual. Only an experience can transform an individual. If an individual is to see himself as something more than the body, he has to experience it.

Even if the entire scientific community in one voice came and concluded that yes, matter is not real, we are all imaginary, and consciousness is real, it does not make a difference to your quality of life because it is not part of your experience. It is something you simply heard and registered in your mind. That's about it. When you're angry, when you're frustrated, when you're in pain, these things don't come. Your knowledge is of no use, but that meditative knowledge that is distilled inside you will stay with you. That is why meditation is indispensable.

Understanding is fine. It's the first step. Experience is the ultimate. Become a seeker of experience. Then whatever it is that you are searching for, you will know it. And ultimately, you will become.

MOTHER NATURE

There exists a deep connection between Man and nature. This connection is not imagined; it is not a concept or just an idea. Man comes from nature and is an extension of it. What better way to renew and revisit that connection than to turn it into a meditation? You can engage in the natural process of observing nature, something that comes naturally to us. We enjoy being in nature, observing its changes, listening to it, and feeling its presence. Nature is our home. So when you're meditating in nature, you're closest to your being, closest to your home. Of course, if you're sitting and meditating in nature, just ensure you carry bug spray and such. Nature is not always kind; she doesn't conform to our imposed sets of morality. She doesn't distinguish between a hungry mosquito and a teacher. If the mosquito is hungry, it can take the blood of anybody; there's no distinction.

Perhaps this lack of differentiation is why we are so enchanted by nature and also terrified of her.

In one corner, a hummingbird visits the flowers - its gentleness, its softness - without harming the flower, and the flower not harming the hummingbird. They exchange something precious for each other's lives. The hummingbird gains nourishment, and energy, while the flower utilizes the hummingbird to spread pollen, multiply, and expand.

In another corner, there could be a gazelle being torn apart by a tiger or a lion. The sheer beauty and cruelty of this are beyond human conception. Consider that there's a reason why nature is so enchanting, so raw and pristine. It's because nature isn't consciously created; nobody shapes or designs it for a specific purpose. It lacks artificial motives and purposes; it can be both beautiful and cruel, kind and harsh, nurturing and life-taking. This duality makes nature fascinating and ensures it remains so. It stems from a deep, unconstructed space. Part of nature comes from within us because if there were no individuals to observe nature in a certain way, or to make sense of things, nature wouldn't appear as enchanting.

Change

There is a deeper unconsciousness within us that connects with the unconsciousness of nature. Simultaneously, nature reminds us of all the qualities of life, everything we miss - its momentary existence, teaching us to perceive life as an overflowing stream that stops for no one, indifferent to our plans. It is ever-changing, offering only one momentary experience at a time, no more than that. It doesn't concern itself with tomorrow or yesterday; it merely seeks to exist in this moment. That's it. This serves as a reminder of what we lack in life: the transient and constantly evolving nature of life itself. Understanding change as an unalterable fundamental quality of life can make it more comforting. That's why we say change is the only thing that cannot be changed; it's an eternal law of life.

Imagine if you were to go far away, let's say, on some space exploration. You move away from the Earth. The universe is a very desolate place with no air, no heat, no light, eternal darkness, eternally cold, and brutal. Compared to that, Earth is a paradise. We are living in a paradise, and we are not seeing it. Outer space is desolate. There's nothing there. We've been searching for signs of life, for anything that remotely resembles a possibility of life, but we are only searching. At this point, Earth is the only reality. It is so easy to miss all this. It is so easy to lose that perspective on where we are - how much nature is a part of our being, and how much of a healer nature is.

In one sense, I'm optimistic about all the space exploration because imagine when the human population becomes too much for the Earth to handle. It allows us to step away and live on other planets, leaving Earth to be herself, for the mountains, for the forest to reclaim the land, for nature to be in her purity, in her pristine state. And then, Earth would become the spa of the whole universe. You could be anywhere. If you think about relaxation, if you think about rest, there's only one place that'll come to mind: Earth, because there's no other place like Earth. There's no other place like home. We can keep on searching, and we'll continue to search.

Eventually, we'll come to realize that we are living in a paradise. To use the phrase, "We are living in the Garden of Eden." We were never vanquished; that is only an idea. We have always been here, and we will always be here. This is our garden. This is our home. When you sit in nature, try to establish that connection. Try to reduce the influence of your ego.

The Technique

Sit, just sit comfortably, and start listening - listening to the sounds of nature. Listen to the birds, listen to the rustling of leaves, listen to the wind blowing, listen to the conversations between you and nature. There is always a conversation going on there. You're not able to hear it because your mind is so noisy. Your mind is trying to interfere with every experience. Gently quieten the mind and try to see if you can establish a direct connection between your body and existence outside. See if you can forget your physical form for a while. When you're sitting and meditating in nature, the most beautiful experience is experiencing nature in her totality, not trying to separate individual experiences and individual senses. If something is interesting to listen to, listen. If there's something beautiful to watch, watch. If there's something nice to smell, smell it. If there's something nice to feel, feel it. Abandon yourself in nature. Lose yourself. Just see if you can become transparent for nature to flow through you. Even for a moment, simply imagine that you're transparent.

Imagine there's nothing solid, nothing physical here. If there's nothing solid to hold on to, then everything you're experiencing is nature. The reason I've been referring to nature as "she" is because nature is "she." The qualities of nature are feminine - in her acceptance, her love, her genuineness, and her ability to heal. Nature is feminine. The reason why you have to reestablish the connection with nature is that you have been conditioned to nurture your masculine nature and not your feminine nature. You have become very rigid in your emotions, in your thoughts, in the way you connect to yourself. That is why one Hindu sage says that when Westerners come to my programs, the first thing he has to teach them is how to cry. The Anglo-Saxon male definition gives no room for crying, gives no room for expressing your emotions. It is not a surprise that the Western man finds it difficult to connect with a woman. You cannot connect with a woman unless you are in touch with the woman within yourself because a woman is a different phenomenon of life, just like nature. She moves differently. She breathes differently. She thinks differently. She walks differently.

The feminine side of you is the nature within you. When you are not stuck in your ego, when you're not stuck in your thoughts, when you are relaxed, when you're not chasing after wild dreams and desires, your natural state is to connect with the feminine inside you - all the subtle, soft qualities of life. When you're sitting in meditation, try to re-establish that connection with the soft nature within you. Try to see if the feminine inside you can connect with the feminine energy of nature. Look at a flower. If you were to give a gender to a flower, would you call it masculine or feminine? There is nothing masculine about a flower. Man has gone so far away from nature. He has disconnected himself from nature; he's become too rigid, too firm. When you're sitting in meditation, it is an opportunity for you to unwind, to reset your masculine clock, to reset your masculine emotions. Step down from the pedestal. As of now, you're sitting somewhere high up on a throne, which is the ego. Nature is down here, and that's where there's a disconnection. Step down, descend, use your breath, use your body to descend from your head, and then dissipate your energies to the outside.

Nature gives you plenty of reasons to watch her. Every moment is new; there is nothing monotonous. Every moment, there is a new sound, a new sensation, a new movement. The shadows are changing, the colors are changing, and if you're sitting longer in meditation, the light is changing, the sun is changing, and the moon is changing. When you're sitting inside four walls, when you are cut off from nature, it is easy to feel boredom, to feel like meditation is just a monotonous activity and that there's nothing new happening. You cannot feel that when you're in nature. In fact, you just have to deal with the disturbance of nature. If you have a fixed idea that your meditation is going to be relaxing and peaceful and there won't be any disturbance, then you might be in for a disappointment because nature is nature; she does not listen to your expectations. So instead of looking at relaxation, look at connection.

Even if the sun is a little too harsh, if there are too many bugs bugging you, embrace them. Okay, embrace their disturbance and sink deeper into meditation. You can meditate in nature anytime you're there, not just when you're sitting and consciously meditating. You can be in a mindful state when you're simply taking a walk - just feeling your footsteps, listening to the rustling of leaves, the whole sensation of being in nature, and the awareness of life all around you in its variety. If you are feeling alone, if you are feeling disconnected from yourself, there's no better place to start than in nature. But you cannot walk into nature and carry your mind, your thoughts, and your ego and expect to connect with nature. Nature requires silence, it requires stillness. Nature does not interfere with a noisy mind. If your mind is noisy, you will not be able to let existence in. That is why it has to be a meditation, it has to be a practice.

Half Awake, Half Asleep

I'm also of the opinion that the earliest meditations started as a way of connecting with nature. There was a deep desire in Man to understand nature, to be with her, so maybe he simply sat, listening to the waves, listening to the trees. He just enjoyed that process. He was not trying to meditate. Nobody was teaching him meditation, just the silence of being in nature. The connection with nature would have pushed him to simply sit. Instead of moving around, he would have just relaxed and observed nature. Perhaps the first awakened man was awakened entirely by nature. There was no other teacher. Now, some teachers will introduce you to the idea of meditation, who will introduce you to the realms of the inner being, the self, and the breath. But there must have been a time when Man should have gone into meditation naturally.

If you think about meditation, it's a state where you are half awake and half asleep. It's almost like somebody has to sing you a lullaby while you are awake so that you can start relaxing. Your mind will not sing you a lullaby because your mind is always in action. It wants to push you to action. If you think about it, how did Man connect with that half-sleep state? If you just sit, close your eyes, and listen to nature, you get the answer right there. Just the sounds of nature, the rhythmic movement of the sounds, the way nature sings and speaks, it is almost like a lullaby. If you're just sitting and listening to nature, you get to deeper states of relaxation. There is nothing harsh there. There is melody, there is music there. In a way, nature meditation is a combination of multiple meditation techniques. It's like watching a candle flame, listening to music, watching your breath, and connecting with your emotions, all at the same time because nature herself is alternating between all your senses. Sometimes she's stimulating your hearing, sometimes your feeling senses, and sometimes she's captivating your eyes. But she does not take you too far away - the enchantment is right here. So it gives you something to watch without drifting in the mind. Something to hold on to. Nature herself becomes the anchor for your meditation.

Watching Pain

How do you watch pain and eventually go beyond it to ultimately connect to that center of silence and stillness where there is no pain?

A few things are important to understand about pain. Pain is not an objective reality; existence has no conception of pain because pain is an experience. Without the one who is experiencing the pain, the pain has no meaning, because it is not a fixed, objective reality. It is a byproduct of the one experiencing pain. Through your conscious understanding and your conscious observation of pain, you can reduce your pain, increase your pain, or completely transcend it. The control rests with you. How do we know this? Since all of us have experienced pain, we can generalize it as a common experience. There is ample evidence of physical, emotional, psychological, spiritual, and all kinds of pain. There might be some difficulty finding pleasure, but you will have no trouble finding pain in the world —it's everywhere. Babies don't come out laughing; they come out screaming in pain. What is that pain? Why should pain exist at all? At the same time, there is no denying that we experience pain in our own unique way. There are varying degrees of pain tolerance and varying levels of experiencing pain. Some experience more physical pain, some more psychological, and some more existential - that feeling of disconnect, loneliness, or boredom. However, each individual experiences pain differently. Why is this? Is there something inside the individual? Is there something an individual does to pain that changes the way they perceive it?

Why Pain?

Why is there pain in the first place? There are different explanations for it. One is the psychological explanation - the pain of being thrown out of the womb. For nine months, the baby is there in the womb, comfortable, blissful, without fear or worry, not having to figure out what to eat, where to rest, or how to find warmth. Everything is taken care of by the mother. The baby isn't even breathing in the womb; the mother is breathing for it. The oxygen flowing through the mother is transferred to the baby. So, there's hardly anything the baby has to do except be there blissfully for nine months. The body has no conception of pain; maybe there's a little discomfort when it turns and tosses once in a while, but it's not experiencing pain.

However, birth is a violent act for the baby, not just a human baby, but for any baby coming out of the womb. Suddenly, they're thrown into a strange world where everything is new, and they have to breathe for the first time because their whole body is in the amniotic fluid, including their lungs. Now, for the first time, they need to clear all that out, clear the liquid out, take the air in, and experience life anew. The body has to acclimatize to a new environment. It takes months, sometimes even years, for the body to adjust to the environment, but there are certain things it never gets adjusted to. No matter what it does, there will be a few things that the body cannot accept.

Each body is different. This is where our understanding of allergies, our understanding of tolerance to certain diseases, and immunity all come into the picture. So right from the beginning, the body is fighting. It is not delivered into a nice, blissful environment where it is perfectly adjusted. Now, all it has to do is figure out how to walk, how to talk and learn how to live. It's not that simple for the baby because every moment is a struggle. Everywhere we see babies going through the same process, experiencing the same suffering so much that we have become numb to the processes. Otherwise, if you think about it, these are not simple processes: learning how to walk is not a simple process. It takes a lot of effort and a lot of falling. It takes a lot of time as well, and there is pain involved. Then, there is learning how to talk.

Self-identification in children is not as great, so the child forgets most of this pain because self-consciousness develops after a few years. That, in my opinion, is a survival mechanism because if the baby were to develop self-consciousness a little too soon, either in the womb or right when it comes out, the pain of those first few years of trying to adjust to a new environment would psychologically damage the child forever. And that is where, for the first two to three years, self-awareness is very little. At the end of three, four, or five years, that's when the child starts acquiring self-awareness, and by then, it has forgotten most of that pain.

The body remembers the pain. It has its own memory. Your mind might not remember the experiences in the womb or the experiences of your first few years, but your body remembers them. Throughout your life, in one way or another, it keeps reminding you of that pain. And throughout your life, you're trying to go beyond that pain. Psychologists say that this emotional trauma of coming out of the womb is the single biggest pain that humans try to overcome. In everything they do, they're actually seeking the comfort of the womb without even realizing it. It manifests in different ways of going beyond pain. That's why people are always seeking pleasure. That's why they're addicted to sleep, drugs, alcohol, and all sorts of things that numb the body's pain - anything to divert attention away from the body.

Look at the world of entertainment that Man has created for himself. Movies are a classic example. What are you experiencing while you're sitting and watching a movie except for lights on a blank screen? And yet, you choose to engage with that experience. You choose to live in that experience, to laugh and to cry, although you know it's all made up, and it's not even a great trick. It's a flimsy trick. One of your fellow humans created it with a little bit of effort. You probably even watched the making of the movie and then you've gone back and watched it and still cried. Why? Because there is a deep desire to escape the pain of the body. There's a deep desire to go away from the present moment. This desire to be able to watch pain and to transcend it needs to be understood.

The pain is there, but because it is an experience, your self-consciousness is what attaches pain to you. Otherwise, the pain is restricted to the body. For a child in the womb and immediately after birth, the pain is purely a physical experience. It is not psychological; it is not emotional because there's no self-awareness. It is only later that this pain becomes psychological and emotional. Now, your pain is no longer restricted to your body. It is completely intermixed with your cognitive processes.

There was an interesting study conducted that introduced the theory known as "The Gate Control Theory of Pain," which became a significant study in terms of understanding the nature of pain and its impact on us. The theory concluded that there is a gate in our spinal cord that regulates the movement of pain up and down from the body to the brain. This gate controls how much pain should be sent to the brain and how much of it should be experienced.

This study is interesting because, until then, it had been thought that physical pain is purely a body stimulus: If I hurt your body, if I take a pin and prick your body, there's no way for you to regulate how much pain you should experience. There is an external stimulus passing through your body, reaching your brain, and your brain reacts to that pain. It responds to it. Other than that, there's nothing you can do about it. The pain is beyond your control.

Watching Pain

Let's say you experience a pinprick. Up until then, we had assumed that it was purely a stimulus. Your body records that pain and sends the signal to the brain, and the brain reacts to that pain. There's nothing much you can do about it. You have no control over how much pain you can experience - it's purely a physical stimulus. But what this experiment suggested was that the way you interact with pain, the way you associate yourself with that pain through your thoughts and emotions, changes its intensity.

The study was conducted with individuals who were given a pain stimulus. One group was also given something pleasant to think about - something to divert their attention away from pain. Another group was simply given the pain stimulus. The study showed that those who entertained positive thoughts and engaged in pleasant activities of the mind experienced significantly less pain compared to those who only experienced the pain. The study concluded that your mind regulates your pain; it is not just your body. Your mind controls how much pain you should experience.

This has a direct correlation to watching the pain during meditation because when you're observing the pain, you're engaging your mind in the process. You are consciously observing the pain. Through the practice of observing, the mind regulates pain, allowing you to change the way you experience it.

Watching Pain

Something interesting happens when you start watching pain. Firstly, none of us have a conception of what it is to watch pain because we more often than not try to avoid it. We attempt to distract ourselves or run away from pain. If you examine medicines and the way we treat pain in the medical profession, there's great emphasis on killing it. It doesn't matter whether you're addressing the actual problem or not; there's a strong desire to eliminate the pain. Suppressants, stimulants, painkillers - all these offer immediate, quick pain relief. They don't address the underlying problem causing the pain, but they work. Why? Because pain is an experience. There's nothing tangible there. It's an experience created by the mind. These shortcut methods can numb the pain of the body, but the problem is that there's no opportunity for you to understand pain.

You will always be addicted to something external to you. It's not that if you're unable to sleep and take sleeping pills, you cannot sleep well. Yes, you will sleep well. But what is it doing in the process? It is addicting you to those pills, slowly diminishing the possibility of natural sleep. There might even come a time when it would be impossible for you to sleep without the pills due to the addiction. The same applies to painkillers. There's a purpose behind the pain you're feeling; it's crucial to comprehend it.

However, if you look for a quick fix and attempt to bury the pain, the mind and body react in their own way. The mind amplifies the pain, as it needs to signal to you that something is wrong. It's the mind's method of capturing your attention, the body's means of communication.

Basically, physical pain is the language of the body. That's how the body communicates. It's how the body says, "I'm tired. I am experiencing this pain. You've stressed this part of your body too much. Give it some rest - Oh, I've cut my finger." Without pain, you wouldn't be able to take care. In fact, we can observe this in patients who have lost the ability to experience pain. Normally, you might think, "What a blessing that is, to not experience any pain no matter what happens." But if you actually look at these patients, it has completely ruined their lives because they cannot even change their position in bed - there's no indication from the body that it's time to shift their weight. Even the simplest of things become problematic. They start developing all kinds of issues everywhere they sit - they don't move their hands, legs, or body - leading to sores, ulcers, and various problems due to their inability to experience pain. So, pain is a necessary bodily mechanism. That is the language of the body.

When you try to suppress your pain using any artificial means, because the necessity of the pain remains, your mind starts to exaggerate even simple sensations. That's why those addicted to taking painkillers often talk more about pain than normal people. They experience pain in even simple bodily changes that most normal people don't even care about. They hold onto it, discuss it, and try to deal with it, but using those suppressants actually increases the pain more. So, there's no way to artificially suppress pain and understand it. And without understanding, there's no way to transcend pain.

In meditation, in yoga, pain is viewed from a completely different dimension. It is seen as a momentary attention that your mind and body are craving. Pain is not looked at as physical or permanent. Of course, there are a few pains where there is severe damage to the body or severe damage to the mind. Those extreme pains, of course, need intervention. You have to take care of them; you can't simply watch if you have cut your finger. You have to first take care of it, and then you can probably watch the pain that you're experiencing inside. Barring those, most of the pains are experienced while just sitting quietly.

Imagine you're sitting and meditating. You experience pain. Your back aches, your spine hurts, your leg itches, you feel the urge to shift or scratch - you experience an array of sensations, but that pain can be observed and understood. Something magical happens when you begin to observe pain; you'll notice it moves in waves, up and down. Pain isn't a fixed reality; it's a phenomenon. It moves much like the mind does - in waves. If the mind seeks your attention, you can observe how it starts gently, perhaps talking about something, and then it intensifies if it doesn't receive attention. Just like a wave, it begins slowly, gathers momentum, builds up, and then recedes. Initially slow, it gradually intensifies until it becomes unbearable, prompting action - a scratch, a change in position, or some form of response. This is how most people perceive pain - as something that cannot be transcended. If you're in pain, the common belief is that you must distract yourself, or else the pain will completely consume you.

In meditation, the process of pain should be observed entirely - when it builds up, as it reaches a certain intensity - without attempting to distract yourself. Instead, observe it more closely, more intensely. Then, magically, you will notice that the scales tip, and the pain begins to subside. Without taking any action, just by observing, you understand how pain functions. Give it a try. When you're meditating and a strong urge to scratch or itch arises, refrain from doing so. Just sit and observe. Despite any external events, like a war, famine, or pandemic, nothing outside will matter until you scratch that itch. Your entire focus, your entire being, will fixate on that itch. That's the nature of the mind, the nature of the body.

Once the mind decides to get your attention, it does everything to achieve that. That's why a small pimple on your nose can draw more of your attention than a world war. You feel compelled to address it. Anything happening to the body, anything occurring on the body, is very real because whatever is happening on the outside is inconsequential compared to what's happening in the body. In fact, all the pain we experience externally pales in comparison to the pain we experience through the body. It's because we experience pain through the body that we can empathize with others' pain. Otherwise, we'd have no way to connect with external pain. Most of existence is blissful; it's the body that experiences pain.

Einstein goes to work, experiencing severe groin pain, evident in his face. His assistant asks him, "Is everything alright?" Einstein responds, "Everything is alright. I am not." That's how it goes. Everything seems fine. Existence is fine. Birds fly, flowers bloom, people carry on with their lives - some in suffering, some in laughter - they have found their way in life, and everything continues. But there is pain within you because you have a body. And the body is not just a body; it's also an absolute pain receptacle. There isn't a part of the body unfamiliar with pain. Why? Because the body is born out of pain. It lives in pain.

Watching Pain

Until you discard the body, some level of pain will persist. The only reason you don't constantly think about it is that you've learned to identify varying degrees of pain. Only when the intensity reaches a certain level do you label it as pain. Right now, you could be in your most comfortable posture, with no health issues or exertion. Your body might be completely relaxed. Yet, if you were to close your eyes and start meditating, you'd notice the existing pain. You're not creating any pain; you're simply closing your eyes and observing - try it. There's so much pain in various parts of the body.

Now, why aren't you acknowledging it? Because you don't designate that discomfort as pain. For you, pain requires a certain level of intensity before it grabs your attention. That's when you address it. It's another kind of survival mechanism. If your body constantly reminded you of every small itch, movement, or discomfort, you'd be too disrupted to function. However, pain is a constant reality. You don't need to rely on your mind to comprehend this constant reality of pain. If you truly want to understand the extent of pain as a constant reality, go sit in one corner, close your eyes, and focus your awareness on the body. You'll notice the entire body throbbing in pain.

Experiencing Bliss

You have not experienced something completely devoid of pain. Consciously, you don't know what not being in pain is, but you do know what it is to be in bliss. There are moments when you have experienced bliss. For example, in sex, in orgasm, you experience that single moment when you are not feeling the pain of the body at all. In fact, that is what you call an orgasm. That is what you experience in that moment of awakening, in that moment of enlightenment - you experience a tremendous surge of bliss. It is bliss that is indescribable. But if you think about it, there is no such thing as "bliss" in existence. Existence is existence. Consciousness is consciousness. Consciousness means it has no qualities. And yet, you experience it as tremendous bliss. Why? Because you've been living in pain all your life. Your body has been in constant pain. That is why the experience of stepping out of the body feels so blissful, so spectacular.

There isn't a single individual who has experienced enlightenment and has not come back from it to speak about the sheer magnanimity of the experience, the sheer bliss of it. Now, where is this bliss coming from? It's coming because for the first time, you are experiencing something other than your body, and everything in existence is blissful except your body. Your body is the seat of pain. That is why we have organized our society the way we have - without the ability to consciously watch the body. Without learning how to watch pain, we will always be addicted to external things.

You don't have to accept pain as an eternal reality of your life. People have been saying this - they've been telling you that pain is a part of life, everybody experiences it, and you are nothing special. Your pain is no different from our pain. "Go through it." We tell the same thing to children. As adults, we accept it for ourselves, and that's why we are tolerant of pain outside. When we see suffering outside, somewhere we have become numb to it. Unless it reaches a certain level of intensity, we don't bother about it. People could be torturing each other at home. The husband could be torturing his wife, or a wife could be torturing her husband. Emotionally, they could be going through a lot of turmoil. Kids could be suffering as a consequence of that, but we have become numb to all this. Why? Because life is suffering. This is how it has been since time immemorial. It is a part of life, so experience it. No. There is a way to go beyond pain.

Transcending Pain

Because pain is an experience and your mind is involved in it, your body is involved in it, you can watch pain to a point where you can completely transcend it. There are enough examples of individuals who have meditatively watched the body and have transcended the pain completely. That is what awakening is. That is what enlightenment is. If you believe that awakening is real, you should also believe that going beyond pain is real. You don't have to blindly believe in it, experiment with it for yourself. Start with a scratch, start with an itch, start with some discomfort in your body. Don't give in to the pain. Don't surrender to the pain. Don't accept the pain. Just watch it without any judgment, without any desire to change it, just simply observe it. Notice how the pain reaches its absolute peak, almost to a point where it's literally like somebody is pushing you hard to act on it. But if you're able to hold on, the pain subsides.

Pain is an intensity. It cannot stay at the same level. It is the very nature of the mind, the very nature of the body, that nothing can stay in your consciousness forever. It has to come, and it has to go. Because you've been distracting yourself, you've not been watching the complete process of pain creation, reaching its intensity, and subsiding - you've always stopped the process in the middle - you have not watched the other side. In meditation, you watch it. You watch it go all the way, and then let it subside. If you're able to do this a few times, then the next time when a similar pain arises, you know not to do anything. It reaches a sudden intensity and then drops.

After doing this for a while, there is something intelligent within us that recognizes that this pain that the body is trying to create to draw your attention is useless because it has tried so many times and has failed. This time, it completely reduces the intensity of the pain. It comes already expecting that you're not going to react. That is how every single tingling sensation of the body, every small sensation that you were reacting to before, now you are easily able to overcome it. You're hardly even registering that pain because you have changed the conditioning of the body. You've changed the conditioning of the pain body. Now your body is conditioned to tolerate most of these minor discomforts.

This doesn't mean that you have gone beyond pain completely. That can never happen, even after enlightenment. When you come back to body consciousness, if somebody pinches you, you will know. The body will always know the pain; it's just that the intensity is different. Notice your own pain. When you are experiencing any physical pain, you immediately bring your mind to it - "Oh, maybe I won't be able to get rid of this pain. Maybe this is going to be a chronic pain." You know you've experienced pain like that a hundred times. It has come and gone. But somewhere, when you're experiencing the pain, your mind makes you believe that you will not be able to get rid of it this time. With meditative watching, with mindful watching, you would be able to keep the mind away from the physical pain of the body. So when the body is going through the pain, you will not exaggerate it. You will not amplify that pain using your mind. You will just keep your mind aside. You're just watching the pain, and the body learns to accept that pain. After a while, something even more beautiful happens. Because you're watching the pain so intensely, every time there is pain, your attention shifts from the watched to the watcher. Your energy is slowly being drawn away from what you're watching, which is pain, to the one who's watching. The one who's watching is in no pain. How can he be in pain? He's the one who's watching the pain.

There has to be something inside you that cannot experience pain for it to register pain. If there is something inside you that can never be out of pain, then there's no way for it to record pain. If you want to create a painting, you need to start on a blank canvas. You don't start on another painting. Why? Because you would not be able to see this new painting. Now why is it that you can see pain? How is it that you can experience pain? Because there is a blank canvas inside you that pain cannot touch. It only shows you the pain. It never becomes a part of the pain. That is where your attention will eventually

Watching Pain

shift. Your energies will shift to that blank screen, which is consciousness, which is aliveness. And once you're rooted, once your centering shifts from the pain body to the painless self, you have found the keys to transcending pain.

Now it's completely in your control. How much pain do you want to experience? How much do you want to bring your mind into that process, and how much do you want to step away from it? When the pain is intense, you will know how to take care of it. If you want to escape that pain completely, you know the pathway. Instead of running to pills, drugs, alcohol, and all that, you will go inward. The one who has learned how to go inward to escape pain has found the ultimate solution for transcending pain without depending on anything external because it's your own insight. Nobody's stopping you from going there. You don't have to pay any toll. It's your own being. Just go straight. You don't need to be addicted to drugs. You don't need to numb your pain. You don't need to run to the doctor for every small silly thing, and you don't have to suffer when you see suffering outside because somewhere you know the way. Out of compassion, you will share it, you will teach it to people: "This is the way to go beyond pain," or you will blissfully experience that non-pain self of yourself without interacting much with the pain outside. Either way, you are out of pain. And it all starts with the simple process of watching pain consciously and not accepting that pain is an eternal reality of your life. You can transcend pain just by watching it.

JUST FOR FUN

It doesn't matter what it is that you are trying to move toward. If it is in the future, it cannot be your true nature. You're chasing a figment of your imagination. Sometimes it's necessary to contemplate the future, but you cannot live there. Sometimes it's necessary to reflect on the past, but you cannot build your home there. You have to come back to the present moment. And when you come back to the present moment and act without bringing in the past or the future, playfulness is a natural consequence. In fact, all creatures of existence are meant to be playful. We come into this world as expressions of playfulness, and that is also why the journey of life is brief. We cannot stay here forever. If it were not a play, if there were some grand spectacular purpose, and if you were meant to be burdened by that purpose, then life would not be this transient. Experiences would not be this fluid.

LIFE IS A PLAY

Look at life. Every moment is changing. No two moments are the same - there's nothing fixed. It's almost like we are all playing the parts that we are assigned. Shakespeare, in his Macbeth, gives these beautiful verses. He says, "Out, out brief candle, life's but a walking shadow, a poor player, that struts and frets his hour upon the stage and then is heard no more." He's referring to life as a poor player who frets his hour upon the stage. He's given a brief duration to play, and he has the stage only for that duration. But he moves reluctantly. In a way, he's referring to that lost playfulness in us, how we have forgotten to be like children. In other words, he says, "All the world's a stage, and all the men and women merely players." What is the role that we have assumed? The purpose is easy to dwell on, and it is also interesting to contemplate - what is my purpose? What do I do with my life? In a way, it comes naturally to us, but it is this very questioning of the purpose that takes us away from playfulness because a play cannot have any purpose. The play itself is its purpose. What is the purpose of life? Life itself is its purpose. There is nowhere to go. There's nothing to accomplish because, by the very nature, life is designed to only be a playful experience. You come empty-handed; you leave empty-handed. You cannot possess anything. You cannot hold on to anything. You cannot carry anything from this life to your next life, so how you live each moment is what determines your quality of life. If that is all that matters, if how you live moment to moment is all that matters, then playfulness seems to be the most natural, the simplest, and the easiest way to live.

Meditation is no different from this. Meditation is another pursuit. As far as the mind is concerned, as far as the body is concerned, it's another desire. This is important to understand. Although the ultimate objective of meditation is to transcend the limitation of the mind and the body, when you're beginning the journey, the mind looks at it just like any other activity - you need to relax. Think about it. Even relaxation commands without understanding that you cannot be forced to relax, but that is the nature of the mind. "Oh, you're too agitated. Now you need to calm down. Now you need to stop thinking. Why are you continuing to think?" The mind does not understand that it is contributing to the same noise. But there is no other way. When a desire is introduced into the mind, there is no difference between a worldly desire and an otherworldly desire. A desire is a desire for the mind. There is a way in which the mind has conditioned itself to chase something - by being restless, agitated, disturbed, and by not being content with the present moment. That is how it has learned to push you into the future to keep chasing your dreams and desires. It does not understand that meditation is something totally different. Yes, you are pursuing a desire in meditation. You want to experience deeper levels of relaxation. You want to become enlightened, but it does not understand that the objective of meditation is to transcend the mind itself.

Getting to the Center

The language the mind uses, the strategies, the techniques the mind uses to push you into meditation are useless because it is trying to do the same thing that it does in the world. That is where trying out a few totally nonsensical techniques comes into the picture. In fact, these are what I would call techniques without any technique. Try and jump into the present moment without any help, without any crutches. Try and see if you can connect with the void. You can start with a simple assumption that there is something I am looking to experience. There is a center I want to touch, and I know it is not my mind. I know it is not my body. So if it is not my mind, if it is not my body, then I don't know where that center is. I don't know what that center is. Just assume that you don't know and imagine the center. Purely imagine it, construct it in your mind.

What can you do with a center? It's simply a center. Even if you tell the mind to imagine it, there is nowhere to take you away because it's only a center. A center is pointless, dimensionless. It is simply an imagined sensation, you could say. It's an imagined feeling. It's an imagined experience that you want to connect with. Let us, for a moment, call it void, nothingness. You don't know what nothingness is. You don't know what nothingness feels like, but just assume that your ultimate objective is to become nothing - to touch a zone where your mind is not allowed, where your body is not allowed. All experiences have to stay away from that center. If you're able to imagine this center, when you decide to touch that center, forget everything your mind and body are trying to do.

Let's say you pick a technique of watching the center of a circle. Just imagine a circle, or you can even draw a circle. Now, put it in front of you and just imagine the center and keep your awareness on that center. Don't put a dot. Bring in your imagination to construct the center and keep your awareness there, so you're not looking at the circle. You're not looking at that sheet of paper or whatever on which you've drawn the circle; you're trying to simply focus on that emptiness that is in the middle of the circle. When you know there is a circle, that means there has to be a center. So just try and be at the center.

Every time your mind tries to enter your meditation, keep it outside the circle. Every time your body sensations begin to disturb your meditation, put them outside the circle. Yes, it is nonsensical because how can you artificially push the mind out of the center when you are using your mind to imagine the center? You're using your eyes to look at the circle and your body is very much there. All the sensations are very much there. But just play with the idea. Don't ask too many questions.

This is a nonsensical meditation. Don't ask, "How is it possible to simply watch nothingness? What do I do? How do I keep my mind out?" There's no method here. How do I keep my mind out? How do I keep my body out? How do I relax? No questions. Just enter the void. It's a direct method. There's no technique. You can do this instantaneously, and you can do this in the middle of your other meditations as well.

Let's say you're doing the watching-the-breath meditation. You're trying to keep your focus on the breath. And naturally, that effort involved to keep your awareness on the breath is stressing you out. It's disturbing you. Immediately jump into the void. Just imagine a circle and imagine yourself being in the center of the circle. Just experience the nothingness.

Of course, you can hear your mind. You can listen to the conversations in your head, you can feel the sensations in your body, but try and ignore them. Just be in the void. For a moment, think like there is nothing there. Whatever I'm experiencing as my mind, whatever I'm experiencing as my body is outside this circle. Let me try and put it outside the circle. Now, how do I put it outside the circle? By not dwelling on it. By going to the center. It's very simple. When you are listening to your thoughts, you can either make that your center or you can go so deep within yourself that you can create your own center where all those conversations of the mind become periphery. Just imagine the circle, imagine the void, and jump into it.

Bright Light Meditation

You can also visualize bright light. For a moment, just plunge into the world of your imagination and turn everything that you can see into bright light. Just imagine pure white bright light engulfing everything. Your mind, your body, everything you're listening to, everything you're feeling - just turn it into light. And then you can also shift to light and darkness. Play with light and darkness. Sometimes keep your eyes open and suddenly shut them and go into darkness and try to expand the darkness inside. Don't leave any gray areas. Just imagine everything is dark. You're sitting in a dark room. Your mind is dark. Your body is dark. Everything is dark. Imagine the whole universe to be just black. Anyway, when you turn off the lights, when there's no sun shining, darkness is an existential reality. Everywhere you see it's darkness. As daVinci says, "Start every canvas with a wash of black. For everything in nature is black. Colors and lights are added to the experience, but the fundamental canvas, The background, is always dark." Just imagine it. Imagine the light. Imagine the darkness. You can call it the "Eyes-open and eyes-closed" meditation. I'm keeping my eyes open and keeping my eyes closed.

Just play with the idea, then play with all your senses with the condition that you should not move. You should be in a meditation posture and not lose your awareness of what you're doing. Keeping your watchfulness intact, play with the sensations. If there is a sensation of pain, see if you can intensify that pain. Use your mind and see if you can exaggerate that pain. See how far you can stretch that pain. You'll be amazed that you won't be able to stretch the pain too far. By the time it reaches a certain level, it immediately subsides. And then when it's beginning to subside, try and see if you can imagine the pain disappearing more and more.

Just for Fun

Sometimes imagine that there is no body. It is a nonsensical meditation, so you are not using your senses. Your senses have tricked you into believing in a certain reality that, "This is your mind. This is your body. This is what meditation is. This is how you need to approach it." Break all the boundaries, keeping just these two rules in mind: stillness and awareness. As long as you're still, as long as you're aware, you can play around with your meditation. Bring in the natural playfulness.

Shakespeare says there's a child hidden within all of us. It is about discovering that child. It is about connecting with that child. And what better place to do it than in your meditation? Because the mind is involved, is always clouded by the ego, and is in this constant state of agitation to achieve things, to accomplish things, it tries to do the same thing in meditation. But you as an individual should approach meditation differently. Not only with playful meditation. Your meditation itself should become playful. That is when you will not be burdened by moments of disturbance when you are unable to sink deeper into your being. When there are disturbing thoughts, you won't take them too seriously. When your meditation session ends, you will forget all about it. Then you're again coming back to it fresh.

REMOVE THE MIND FROM MEDITATION

Without playfulness, meditation will seem like an arduous effort. It will feel like "I'm putting in so much effort and what am I getting out of it?" This attitude of "I am putting in the effort, I need to get something out of it" is all in the mind. Take the mind out of your meditation. Enjoy the process. Once you learn how to enjoy meditation, then you will not be worried about how quickly you're going to become enlightened or how far you need to travel. You will approach it differently. You will start playing with the whole idea of enlightenment. And you will use the mind. You will use the body. Now, that whole arena, that whole space of meditation becomes your playground. Now there is enthusiasm. There is a spring in your step to go and sit in meditation because it's no longer a burden. You've thrown away the desire to become enlightened. You've thrown away the desire to become peaceful. Look at the stupidity of it. If desires are what is stopping you from being peaceful and relaxed, how can you make being peaceful and relaxed into a desire? That is exactly what the mind does. It turns everything into a purpose.

The mind is mechanical. It does not know how to sing. It does not know how to dance. It only knows how to repeat what you have already put there. It only listens to songs - it does not create the song.

Playfulness comes from the heart. Playfulness comes from a totally different dimension. The mind is a regurgitating machine. Whatever you add to it, it mechanically repeats it. Relaxation - it repeats it. Peace - it repeats it. If you tell it to dance, it'll repeat the word "dance" a hundred times, "dance, dance..." It does not understand anything other than boring, monotonous repetition. When you step away from the mind, playfulness is a natural consequence because existence is playful, and you are an expression of playfulness.

Think about it: if human beings were created using the mind, imagine if two people said, "Okay, now we need to create a baby. Let's check out a plan. Let me do this and you do that. At the end of this process, we'll create a baby." Is that how creation happens? Can you plan? No. It happens as playfulness. Think about it. Sex is one of the greatest acts of playfulness. Sex is nothing but playfulness. If you take away playfulness from sex, it is one of the silliest, most awkward things two people can ever do. There's no logic to it. There's no purpose to it. It is sheer playfulness. And what comes out of that playfulness? Life. When playfulness is such an integral part of life, why not make it an integral part of meditation? That is probably why existence is not burdened. Existence creates without having the desire to create. It is spontaneous. It is natural. In Zen, it is called "wu wei," or "effortless action." There is action in nature, but there is no effort. It is only the human mind that clings to effort. Again, what is effort if not for the recording and the comparison of activities?

Effort is not the effort that you're putting in at the moment; there is no such thing. Effort is always a recollection. Pay attention to all those moments when you are burdened by the thought "I'm putting in so much effort." Notice you are always talking about effort after you've put in the effort or before you're putting in the effort, and not when the effort is happening. When it is actually happening, there is no effort. It is simply an activity. When something is happening, you can't bring in your mind, but the moment you stop that activity, the mind floods in. Before you get into an activity, the mind is there reminding you, "Now you need to relax. Now you need to go deep." It tries to artificially manufacture effort because there's no mind in existence. Nobody is instructing the tree to flower and fruit. There's no deadline. There's joy in creation.

If you want to take away all the enjoyment of creating, just set a deadline. Imagine this: Just plant a sapling and say, "You are free. I'm going to provide water for you and I'm going to give you manure. You are free to move in whatever direction you want. You can draw as much sunlight as you want. But the only condition is, at the end of two years from this date, I want fruits." Imagine if it has to live every moment thinking about producing fruits. Its whole life is ruined at that very moment. You have taken away its momentary joy. You have taken away its peace. You have taken away its relaxation. You have taken away its playfulness.

That is what has happened to the human race. Man is meant to sing and play, laugh and dance, live and die. But what have we done instead? We have burdened him right from childhood. We have burdened his mind; we have burdened his body. We have added so much to him. By the time he becomes an adult, he has lost his playfulness. Wherever he goes, he's carrying this additional weight. Now, what happens if you weigh ten times more? How can you play? Your body doesn't move. Everything hurts. That is what has happened to us. Our egos have stiffened us. Why are we searching for peace? Why are we searching for relaxation? Why are we searching for that connection with nature? We have been living in a delusional framework - delusional conditioning where we have postponed everything into the future. We have postponed our happiness, our joy, our peace, and relaxation. That is why we are longing for it.

The whole of humanity is burdened by nothing real, just these ideas. We don't understand that when a simple idea is introduced into the mind - when the mind takes hold of that idea, and if it does not know the consequences of that idea, what that idea is doing to it - it is lost. One such idea is that your life is a sin. That's enough. You've destroyed playfulness right there. Another idea is that you have to be somebody in this world. Gone. How can you be somebody in the present moment? You can be somebody only in your imagination. In the present moment, you are a nobody. In the present moment, you are just a small part of the vast tapestry of life. It is only in your imagination that you can sit on a throne and feel like "I am somebody now." But in reality, you are just a part of everything. In reality, you cannot be somebody. You cannot even be something.

Fear of Losing Ourselves

In reality, you are a flowing, ever-changing phenomenon of life, and you have to jump into that stream. You cannot be afraid of jumping into the stream and cling to the banks. That is what we are doing. We can see the natural flow of life. We can recognize it. But we are afraid to jump into it. We are scared of losing ourselves. And the same thing happens in meditation. We want to go deeper. We want to experience something transcendental, but there is fear of losing ourselves. If you watch closely, that fear is not your fear, but the fear of your mind, the fear of your ego, because your ego does not know playfulness. Ego looks at playfulness and laughs: "What are you doing? You're wasting your time singing. You're wasting your time laughing. You're wasting your time playing with lights and shadows. You're wasting your time drawing an imaginary circle and trying to be in the void. What are you talking about? You're going to become the void. You have to be somebody." It tries to take you away from playfulness.

Try a few nonsensical meditations. Bring in your imagination and just play with the whole idea. Sometimes just move around with some definite purpose. Say, "I want to go from here to there and walk." But before you get there, stop in the middle. Don't go there. Your mind will be confused. "Why did you stop? You are supposed to go there." It's nonsensical. I am trying to tell you that you are the one having the conversation with your mind. I'm trying to tell you that there is no necessity to accomplish everything that happens in the mind. Tell your mind, "Everything you desire, you've been trying to push me to accomplish it. Now I'm going to desire a few things and I will make sure that I will not accomplish those desires." Then, imagine ice cream. Create a desire inside to eat an ice cream. See that ice cream being in the refrigerator. Walk toward it, but stop in the middle and turn around. See what happens? Do it a few times. Slowly, you'll be drawing control away from the mind.

You're doing nothing special. You're just being nonsensical. Your mind has become too sensible. It has become too smart. It has arranged itself so cleverly. It is not allowing you to break its mold. Ultimately, the objective of meditation is to break the rigid brick wall of the mind. And the way to break this wall is to be a little nonsensical, be a little playful. Start with this. And slowly, you can turn every moment of your life into playfulness. And when your whole life becomes playfulness, then where is worry? Where is fear? The moment you are playful, you are also acknowledging the transient nature of life. Because when you're playful, you cannot be thinking about the future. When you're not thinking about the future, life is only one moment. That's it. You're not even thinking in terms of "I have a short life, I need to play." That again is the mind. "You only have this many years. Are you playing well? Are you playing enough?" Don't let the mind come into playfulness.

True playfulness begins and ends in the moment. This purpose, this moment, is complete by itself. Your purpose is just to be here. There is no tomorrow. There is no yesterday. There is no trying to accomplish things. There are no goals. Just be in the moment and see how much you can create out of that joy. It is a total misunderstanding that just because you don't have desires, just because you don't have goals, you will be useless. You won't create anything. You will just rot in the present moment - not at all.

Look at nature. Look at existence. She does not have any goals. She does not have any purpose. But can you create the way she creates? Look at the abundance. Look at the joy with which she creates. We are the center of creativity. We are expressions of creativity. What is burdening creativity is this one-dimensional goal-oriented approach. You take that out, and every moment you will find something new. That playfulness itself will become your creative joy. Then you can turn every moment of your life into meditative playfulness, and before you realize it, you have progressed. Now to bring back the language of the mind, you have progressed. You have reached the depths of silence. You have even accomplished enlightenment. The language of the mind is used to describe that, but that is not how you get there. You get there by playing - by sinking deeper into the moment.

Dancing with Shadows

Breaking the Rules

Primordial meditation breaks pretty much every conventional rule of meditation, while, of course, staying true to the purpose of meditation. The ultimate objective of meditation is to break the method. The mind loves method and structure. It loves familiarity. In meditation, while these things are useful, they can also be an obstacle. Too much reliance on structure or familiarity is what leads to stagnated zones of comfort in meditation where you touch a certain zone and you explore it a bit. Then the mind starts enjoying that exploration. It starts qualifying it, it starts thinking about it, and then it starts putting rules and restrictions around it. And before you know it, it has built a wall that you have to scale to go deeper.

The obstacle in meditation is always the mind, and not just at the beginning. The mind is there throughout your journey. Throughout your journey, you have to deal with a mind that is constantly trying to build a wall, put you inside it, and say, "You have arrived. This is what you were searching for." The ultimate objective of the mind is to end this weird search that's going on so that it can go on uninterrupted on its outward search. Your inward search and the outward search of the mind are contradictory. You cannot be going inward while believing in all that the mind wants you to believe. You cannot be chasing your worldly dreams and desires blindly when you want to go deeper and understand yourself, when you want to transcend the limitations of your mind and body. Your desire to transcend those limitations, your quest to transcend those limitations, clashes with the mind.

There is a meditation through which you can keep the mind always in check by being more chaotic, more moving, more disturbing than the mind. It is a meditation that counters the mind using its own devices. What is the mind if not for movement, change, excitement, a surge of energy, images, experiences, feelings - everything that activates your senses is what the mind is. The mind has control over you through the senses. When you're sitting quietly in meditation, trying to go deeper, your mind is using your sense perceptions to push you out. That is why going into meditation is harder compared to going out of it. It takes a long time before your meditation deepens so much that going inward becomes easier compared to getting out of it. The sheer bliss of it, the sheer joy of it, the sheer magnanimity of it is so intoxicating that your mind and all its enticement, all its scheming to bring you out, is useless because what you have found is infinitely more precious than what the mind can offer.

The mind is using all that is available. It shows you things. It's making you listen to things. It's reminding you of all the wonderful experiences you can have. It's trying to push you out of meditation, but what you're experiencing is so fulfilling, so complete, that you listen to the mind, you acknowledge it, but you act only when you want to. Now this happens only when you have gone deep enough into meditation. Initially, it's a struggle against the mind. Every time you try to go in, the mind will use the senses to pull you out, and that is why meditation is challenging. Although it is one of the simplest things you can do, it is also very tricky. It takes intelligence, awareness, and a deep understanding of the nature of the mind to break through this.

Path of Knowledge

One of the popular methods of meditation has been the path of knowledge: You understand what's happening so that you can deal with the mind. But still, understanding also belongs to the mind. You can intellectually understand something. It is not that hard. You can clearly see that the mind is noise and you are moving toward silence. That is what you want to experience. The mind is movement. You're moving toward stillness. You can clearly see and understand that the mind is the obstacle, and yet you cannot break away from the mind just as easily as you got to understand it, because understanding the mind and having control over the mind are two completely different things. The first layering of understanding also happens through the mind - it's intellectual understanding. That intellectual understanding has to seep in and go into the body. The body has to acquire that understanding for it to counter the mind.

Take any skill you develop. Initially, you are introduced to that skill intellectually. Let's say you want to learn driving. First, you learn the basics of driving purely intellectually, using your thoughts, using your mind. But why is it that just with this much intellectual understanding, you cannot start driving? If you just start driving, assuming that now you understand how to drive, you will meet with an accident. Why? Because your mind still has not assimilated that knowledge and passed it on to the body where it can stop interfering. When does your driving become smooth? When your mind is not interfering. When the knowledge has seeped into the body and the body has the memory of what driving is. As long as you have to think to drive, you are still learning. It's not that you don't know what driving is. Intellectually, you know what a brake is, you know what a clutch is, you know what steering is. You know all the traffic rules. Despite all the knowledge, you are still unable to drive smoothly; that's because your mind is still there. As long as the controls are with the mind, you cannot do anything smoothly. All the things that you do smoothly now were once owned by the mind, and that was your learning period.

Your ability to speak, your ability to walk, your ability to dance - if you know how to dance - initially, they were all in the realm of the mind. That is why learning is hard, and it happens only when the mind lets go of the knowledge and the knowledge starts seeping into your body. The mind is not at all required. That is when smooth movement begins with anything you're learning. That is when the deepening of experience happens. In meditation, on the path of knowledge, you have to spend a lot of time in the company of your mind before the understanding seeps into your body. Now, this is the most challenging part of meditation because you are only trying to meditate, just like initially, when you are sitting behind the wheel and you're driving, you're only learning how to drive. That is why the experience is not pleasurable. Far from enjoying driving, you are scared to death because the entire control is with the mind. Your body has not yet acquired the necessary skills.

Primordial meditation is a way of bypassing the mind altogether. It is a way of countering the mind using its own tools - movement, change, action, effort - the things that the mind understands. There is a beautiful saying by Immanuel Kant. He says, "From such crooked wood as that which Man is made of, nothing straight can be fashioned." Man is a crooked piece of wood, and what makes him crooked is the crooked mind. It never does anything straight. The truth is right there. Bliss is right there. You're not even an inch away from it, but your mind is so crooked, so twisted, so devious that it cannot go straight to it. It goes around it. It hops about it, it skips it, it jumps it. Once in a while, it goes a little close, tries to get a sense of it, freaks out, and runs away.

The mind is crooked because its ways are crooked. It has shaped itself to see the very things that are not there. The mind cannot see what is, it cannot experience truth, and it cannot experience reality. The mind, by its very nature, is a device created by the senses to aid in perception. So, it is an extension of the senses. How can the mind see anything other than what the senses can see? In a way, the mind is the slave of the senses. If you stop giving signals to your mind using your senses, if you stop seeing, hearing, smelling, tasting, and touching, what happens to your world of dreams? What happens to your world of desires? Imagine for some reason that immediately you lost all your sense perceptions. You cannot see, hear, smell, touch, or taste. At the end of six months, what would be the nature of your dreaming? What would be the nature of your desiring? Would it be more intense? Will you have more dreams? Will you have more desires? Or will you have fewer dreams and desires? Would your disturbance be more or would it be less? It would, of course, be less because no new disturbance is being added. The mind only has the existing disturbance to deal with and it keeps on going back to it. It tries to bring up the thought processes that are already there because nothing new is being added. There's no new chaos being added. You're not seeing someone being murdered for the disturbance to be added. You're not seeing a new earthquake. You're not seeing a new president. Its all old problems. After a while, the mind gets used to it and then the disturbance settles down.

When you stop adding to the mind through your senses, you don't have to remove the contents of the mind to reduce the disturbance. Naturally, after circling for a while - I mean, it's the same thoughts - it gets bored. The mind needs new things, new excitement. And once the mind gets bored, that is when the real stuff begins. That is when your actual journey starts. When the mind is bored, something else begins to awaken. Your body begins to awaken. Your awareness of the body begins to awaken. You will start experiencing things with a heightened sense of awareness. Because now, your mind is bored, it does not want to interfere too much. It is speaking somewhere in the background. But you've heard it enough to listen to it but not act on it. That's when deepening happens. But you have to go through this entire process. You have to sit, close your eyes, you have to understand the mind, and fight with it, for days, weeks, and months, then you gain control of the body.

Disturbing the Body

In primordial meditation, you use the body - you use the movements of the body. You use the energy of the body to counter the disturbance of the mind. In fact, you disturb the body so much that your awareness shifts from the disturbance of the mind to the disturbance of the body. By your very nature, your inside is designed to watch only that which is most disturbing - that which draws your immediate attention. That is why, irrespective of all the dreams and desires of your mind, if you suddenly cut your finger, it does not matter. Your whole universe, the mental universe, stops and you need to take care of that bleeding finger. Why? Because it's immediate. It is intense. There is pain. You have to take care of it. So what happened to your disturbing mind then? What happened to that mind that you could not stop? A single pinprick can stop the entire movement of the mind. If you think about it, it could be racing somewhere. It could be thinking about work. It could be thinking about achievements. It could be thinking about building something in the future. It can have the grandest of plans, but one small pinprick and something inside you says, "Leave all this nonsense and take care of that," because somewhere, something inside you, even without your knowledge, is aware of who you are and what is truth and what is lies. And that part of you knows that your mind is a lie.

Your body is the truth. So, anything happening in the body gets immediate attention. Look at it this way: Every time your body calls for attention, how does it do it? It does it through signals. It does it through the pain signals it gives. That is the only language the body has. So, as long as you are experiencing the body differently - anything other than normal, the pain need not be too intense, just a little bit of change, something different happening here - your entire attention will be on the body because the body is spectacularly more important than the mind, and your inner self knows that.

MIND IS TIME

On the contrary, the mind is very flimsy. Most of the time, it is worried, it is anxious. It is trying to run away from something imaginary. Consider what stresses the mind the most. Is it something real or is it something imaginary? If you try to understand the nature of the mind, you will see that the mind is most anxious about numbers. Numbers are what stress the mind, not the actual experience of life. For example - How old you are? How much money do you have? How many friends do you have? Observe that all these things have something to do with numbers, something to do with quantity. "I want to make it big in life." What is big, if not for a number? "I want to be a part of something important." Now, what is that important? There is a process. *If* you go a little deeper and understand the nature of the mind, it is afraid of being lonely. It is afraid of not being in the company of others. And what are all these things? At the end of the day, they're all numbers. One is a number. Many is a number. Big is a number. The single biggest source, the single biggest instigator of stress, is our obsession with numbers.

The mind is an accumulator. It loves to remember things from the past, stacking them one on top of the other. The mind is obsessed with how much it can remember and add to, while your true being doesn't even care about it. Modern society is more obsessed with numbers than any previous culture. Consider indigenous cultures - they didn't focus on dates and specific days. What is today's date? Is it Monday, or Tuesday, or the 25th of March? Those details didn't matter to them. Modern society uses these dates to create stress. Imagine for a moment that there are no calendars and no numbers - half your stress would vanish. If you don't know what day it is, what would cause you stress? It all starts from there. "Oh, today is Monday. That means yesterday was Sunday and tomorrow will be Tuesday." The cycle continues. "I have one week to finish this." Time becomes a factor. Then fear creeps in - they're all connected, and the mind spirals. It forgets reality, it forgets the present moment, and it starts chasing.

Many indigenous cultures didn't even possess a word for the day. There was no specific term to designate "today." They recognized the changes in the day, knew morning from evening, and were attuned to seasonal changes. They were fully aware of everything happening around them but had no need to designate a specific word for "today" or even "yesterday." For instance, in native Indian storytelling, tales always commenced with phrases like "a long time ago" or "once upon a time." Stories never began with specifics like "two hundred and thirty-five years ago" or some particular date. Date or time was irrelevant; what mattered was the essence of the story. Just consider how much mental burden vanishes when you don't have to remember the sequence of past days.

Imagine for a moment being beyond that. If you remove that aspect, the entire stress and strain of the past and future disappear. There's no necessity to remember specific dates or contemplate some future event. The mind revels in remembering dates because, once again, it's a number. It loves to assign significant meaning to numbers, such as your age. Internally, you might feel like a child, but the moment you tell the mind, "I am so-and-so age," it forgets its natural capabilities and starts dictating, "For this number, for this age, this is how I should behave, these are the things I can or cannot do." A mere number has shifted you from the present moment into the domain of the mind.

The body doesn't encounter such problems. It holds memory, remembering everything that has happened to it, yet not in terms of numbers. That's why, compared to your mind, your body exudes tremendous peace. It moves when it desires, rests when it needs to, and when it needs your attention, it communicates through pain. Simple as that. It doesn't craft stories, fabricate tales, push you into the future, or pull you into the past. None of that. Returning from the mind to the body means returning to our true primordial self. There was a time when we were predominantly a body. The mind served minimal purposes then. We used it occasionally for contemplation, to reflect on recent events, some storytelling, a bit of reflection - that was it. The bulk of the time, the entire human mechanism revolved around the body.

If you don't observe your body in the wilderness, survival becomes unlikely. In the wild, once you begin daydreaming, it's over. Modern humans might struggle to survive in the forest because they'll walk and instead of staying attentive to their surroundings, they'll start daydreaming, potentially falling into a ditch. Alertness and awareness are essential survival tools in nature; they keep your body safe. Observe an animal in motion, like a hunting tiger. While it seems entirely focused on its prey - watching every move - it's also keenly aware of its body. It moves carefully and deliberately, conscious of each step and attentive to sound, tail movement, and ear adjustments. Watching a hunting tiger means witnessing total awareness in action. There's no room for the mind or thoughts. Imagine if the tiger began thinking, "What if I miss?" or "What if I'm not fast enough?" It would fail before even attempting because a momentary distraction could trigger an involuntary body action. That distraction could make it move too quickly or spook the prey, resulting in hunger. If the tiger daydreamed a couple of times, it would be out of the game of life.

Awareness and alertness come naturally to the human body, provided that we embody what we were meant to be. Presently, humanity needs to navigate back to its primordial nature to access its higher self. At present, people are too immersed in their minds, lost in their own worlds. To transition from the mind to one's authentic self through meditation, one must traverse their primordial nature, which is their genuine existential essence. This aspect cannot be bypassed. Consequently, the deeper one goes into meditation, the more profound their understanding becomes regarding life and their instincts, connecting deeply with basic movement and fundamental awareness. It's a journey that traverses the primordial self, allowing in primordial meditation a reconnection with the original primordial body one was intended to embody.

The Technique

The objective is to remove civilization from the body and the mind. It is to go back to the caves, where we came from. It is to return to that time before calendars and dates, before numbers and deadlines. Go back to the time when we didn't care about yesterday or tomorrow, to that moment when awareness was our primary nature. How do we do this? What is the method? First, ensure you have enough space to move around. Primordial meditation involves using your body, so you will move around a lot, and you cannot predict your movements. If you cannot predict your movements, the only thing you can predict is that you don't want to hit that wall, so make sure the wall is as far away from you as possible. That is the only thing you can predict. If you're practicing this in a group, make sure there's enough space between two individuals. Choose music that resonates with your primordial self - natural sounds, primal music, as carnal and bodily oriented as possible, such as drums, didgeridoo, any type of percussion music, or bass - anything that puts you in a state where you are not here, not in the twenty-first century. "There are no walls here. There are no people here. I am an eternal being trying to connect with my eternal self through eternity. So, I have to forget this time, I have to forget this form, this life, to connect with something that has always been there." Choose music that does not remind you of anything modern.

First, stand still, absolutely still, and bring your awareness to the body. Just watch your body and use your breathing to coordinate that observation. Take about ten to fifteen deep breaths to prepare your body for movement. As you breathe in and out, let go of the mind and focus on the breathing. Now, direct your entire focus and awareness to the breath. Gradually, let the music draw you into that primordial space where you move from the outside to the inside.

After about ten to fifteen breaths, release your body, let it go, and allow it to move freely in response to the music. Do not interfere with the body. Your primal instincts are still present. When you're about to fall or hurt yourself, those instincts will naturally come in to protect you. There's no need to worry. Letting go is the challenge, not protecting yourself. You tend to be overly protective. Even when attempting to move, you're very self-conscious and overly cautious. Drop that protective nature and allow the body to move. Jump, shake your body, connect with that primordial inner body that lacks the concept of where it is and what it is doing.

Let your body move on its own, and simply acknowledge the movement. Be aware of every movement, every sensation. It could be listening to your heartbeat or sensing your blood pumping inside. It could be feeling the sensations on your skin or the pain in your muscles - it doesn't matter. As long as you're not thinking and your awareness is fully on the body, you are in meditation. Let the body move. Use the body's movements as a way to cast out all that is unwanted - ideas, repressions, everything that has seeped into your body - just throw it out. See if you can purify the body by moving in an unstructured manner.

When your body starts to move without the command of your mind, without your conscious knowledge, it begins to cleanse itself. Let's say you move like an animal - a tiger, a bird, or a snake. In those moments, you are becoming something entirely different.

Your mind is so confused that it doesn't even know how to interfere with this process because your entire awareness is on the body. Imagine you're writhing on the floor like a snake. What will your mind do? It cannot sit and cheer you on because it doesn't understand what's happening. For ten to fifteen minutes, be with the body. Move with the body. Throughout this process, if you observe, your mind is arrested.

In regular meditation, while you're watching the breath, your mind is constantly talking, constantly disturbing you. Here, you stop that by keeping the awareness completely on the body. This is how the method works: By shifting your awareness from the noisy, chaotic mind to the body, and increasing the chaos in the body, you connect with your original body, which is devoid of the mind. Your body can exist by itself without any mind. Your mind only comes and goes once in a while. You are predominantly a body, but as of now, you have become more of the mind. So you're trying to pull back the control.

Start moving intensely for ten to fifteen minutes, however you wish, without any restrictions. Then, at the end of those fifteen minutes, either sit down or lie down flat and connect with your inner stillness. Continue to observe the body, but notice how suddenly you are thrown into a zone of stillness. Without any effort, relaxation is naturally occurring because you've stressed your body so much, you've strained it, you moved so intensely that you have exhausted yourself. You're sweating profusely, your neck is hurting, your legs are hurting, your whole body is writhing in pain. If you have moved without a care in the world, your body should hurt. If you have not controlled your movements, your body should hurt. In a way, this is also an exercise for the body. At the end of it, if you finish and just walk away, you're missing the most important part.

In meditation, you sit quietly and connect with your inner stillness. Notice how you begin to experience a sinking feeling as if you're going deeper and deeper. This time, because you're already so tired, your mind will not interfere with that sinking; it will let you go without interfering. Those few moments when you can go deeper and leave the mind behind - that's what you're looking for. You can do this in the morning or the evening, whenever you have that energy. You want to actively involve yourself in the meditation. Whenever you feel your mind is getting too noisy and disturbing your meditation, you can do this.

There's enough flexibility to move however you want, to do whatever you want in this meditation. The only condition is that your awareness has to be fully on the body. When you lie down or sit still, your awareness has to be on the inner stillness. You are using the body as a prop to dive deep into your being. Keep alternating: fifteen minutes of movement, ten minutes of stillness, and repeat. Do this at least two or three times until you're exhausted. The final step is to completely let go, lie down, and try to connect with your inner self. Now, just be there in that zone of silence for as long as you can.

You are intensely aware of the body throughout the practice. All the effort you were putting into dealing with the mind goes straight into deepening your meditation. The disturbance of the mind is taken care of naturally. Why? Because there was a time when the disturbance of the mind was not much; you only had to go back and connect with a primordial body that knew how to be a body. As of now, the body has forgotten to be the body because you have forgotten to be you. The mind has hijacked your senses completely. It has taken over your being entirely. So when you sit quietly and try to meditate, your mind attempts to disturb you. It becomes a battle - either you win or the mind wins. More often than not, for most people, the mind wins, and they give up on meditation.

Primordial meditation is a way of breaking through the structured functioning of the mind by introducing so much chaos that the mind goes blank. After a while, it has to shiver at the very thought of trying to interfere with your meditation. If it attempts to interfere, you will create chaos on your own. There's something beautiful about consciously created chaos: When chaos is consciously created, it no longer remains chaos; it becomes a transformative process. Unconscious chaos that happens in the mind is what is disturbing. When you naturally introduce chaos to the body and you're aware of it, that chaos becomes your transformation.

Primordial meditation revolves around connecting with your primordial body through chaos so that you can find clarity. Moving your body to connect with inner stillness - within that contrast, within the rhythmic movement between chaos and silence - you will connect with the true nature of your being, which is eternally silent and has been watching the entire process right from the beginning. The first step when you stand and watch your breath is the same watching as the last step when you lie down and attempt to connect with your inner self.

What you've done in this entire process is give yourself a better opportunity to watch the watcher because you've observed the watcher in two completely different states of being. One, when they're totally chaotic, behaving like an animal, and then when they're totally silent, as if they've touched a zone of absolute peace and relaxation. In both of these, you will notice the watcher is the same, the self is the same. Something isn't changing. Without striving to connect with that unchanging part of you, you will naturally be drawn into that zone. That's what your search is for - to accidentally fall into that space that is your own, away from the mind and away from the body, just you.

Dancing with Shadows

Read Yourself to Enlightenment

Let me introduce a new meditation technique. I'm surprised that this hasn't been a common meditation practice. It's what I call "reading meditation." How do you meditate while reading? How do you deepen the experience of reading by infusing it with a meditative nature and cultivating meditative qualities in your reading? How do you transform the simple information you're reading into profound knowledge?

Reading and meditation are indispensable. Whatever it is that we're searching for using meditation, that quest is presented to us via language. Without language, there's no way for us to comprehend what it is that we're searching for. Why? Because what we seek is very close to us. And anything so close to us isn't easily grasped intuitively because of our proximity to it. It's easier to perceive things that are far away. Language isn't necessary for this. Whether there's a word for the sun or not, whether there's a word for the moon or not, you can look at them and recognize them. You'll discern the difference between the sun and the moon. You don't need language or someone else to tell you what they are. Experientially, you know it.

But what about your breath? It's one of the closest things to you, always present. Yet, unless someone introduces you to the idea of the breath, you can live your entire life without ever observing your breath or knowing that such a thing exists.

LANGUAGE

Language is crucial to communicate the simplest and yet the most profound truths and still, there's no consensus among scientists, linguists, or archaeologists regarding the origin of language. There isn't a clear understanding of why human beings developed language. It's not just language itself, but the complexity and depth of human language that sets us apart from everything else. What distinguishes a human being from any other animal? It's our obsession with language. We don't merely use language; we inhabit it, immerse ourselves in it, we live and perish in it. Language, for us, is everything. There's no humanity without language. That's what sets us apart from everything else. But still, there's no clear consensus on why we began speaking.

There are different theories, and one suggests that early humans began imitating animal sounds. This theory, termed the "bow-wow" theory, involves listening to a dog barking and assigning a symbol to denote the dog based on that bark. Similarly, hearing a bird's sound and designating it by that specific sound. That's one theory - that we started imitating animals. Another theory proposes that we began vocalizing our inner emotions - the sounds of cries, pain, happiness, or joy. As we started expressing these sounds, eventually with a degree of sophistication, it evolved into language. Then there's another theory centered on social interaction. It suggests that because we desired group interaction and sharing within a community, we started developing language.

All these theories have one major flaw: none of them can explain the sheer variety and complexity of language. Language doesn't necessarily have to be complex to identify an animal, express emotions, or be useful in social interactions. A glance at the animal kingdom provides the answer. Some birds imitate other animals and birds, yet they don't use sophisticated language. They have no trouble identifying different creatures based on sound alone. In fact, they don't even need language; they can simply remember the sound and discern the animal from it. Creating another word is unnecessary; if a dog barks, they know it's a dog, whether or not there's a specific word for it.

Similarly, for inner emotions, why designate a word like "cry?" The moment you observe someone crying, you understand that emotion. Language is the least important tool for expressing emotions. Emotions are much more intuitively recognized by observation and listening. Regarding the social interaction theory, animals constantly interact with each other, forming groups - sometimes even complex ones - yet there's no sophistication in their language. They communicate using basic sign language, simple sounds, movements, and expressions of emotions to convey everything. Thus, none of these theories provide a clear understanding of the origin of language.

In my understanding, language originated because human beings sought to share something that cannot be easily shared. They aimed to converse about something that isn't easily spoken about. The immense complexity of human language arises from our attempt to reach something incredibly close, something inside us that is inseparable from us. We've been endeavoring to explain this in as many ways as possible, endlessly attempting to define that internal something. This is the only way to comprehend the complexity of human language, the poetry, and the sheer variety of it. It's more than just social communication or vocalization. If it were merely that, a few books would have sufficed in the entire span of human history for us to read, understand, and communicate. However, the vast body of work produced by humanity demonstrates that language serves a completely different purpose. It is about communicating the incommunicable and sharing the unsharable. It's a longing to articulate something that can only be experienced in silence. This inseparable connection between meditation and reading scriptures stems from this understanding.

As a seeker of truth, the first thing you are introduced to is understanding the scriptures. Yet, it's not merely about starting or ending with knowing what you're searching for. Reading is a continuous process in the journey of meditation because it involves different ways of using language that has trapped you in this realm. All the notions about who you are and the nature of reality are encoded in language. The way you use language shapes your perception of yourself and the world.

Reading holds significant importance in a spiritual journey because while reading, you're attempting to both relearn and unlearn what you've absorbed.

You're striving to reinterpret the decoded language of words to discover their true meaning. The more you read, the more you comprehend that what you're reading isn't as straightforward as it appears. There is a deeper layer here. When you encounter a beautiful piece of poetry, a mystical verse, or descriptions of love, transcendence, or consciousness, you realize that the scriptures discuss something not easily found externally. In fact, they address something that you can never discover externally - it's hidden somewhere. That's where your journey begins - that's where it continues.

Recorded Knowledge

If reading is such an integral part of life, of being human, and of meditation, why not transform it into a beautiful meditation? Language forms the foundation of everything, even your life. After you're gone, no one will care about your appearance, your hair length, your race, your wealth, or your fame. However, if you've spoken something, if your words are recorded somewhere - just one verse, one line - and if that holds meaning or significance for someone's life, then you will be remembered.

Consider human history. Do we know what Buddha or Jesus looked like? Do we have details about their physical features, how they walked, and their voices?

These details are entirely irrelevant, and yet, here we are, two thousand five hundred years since Buddha's time, speaking about him, remembering him. He's not our family member, and there's no direct physical connection, yet we remember him. Why? Because he expressed his thoughts and shared something profound and meaningful that resonates with us. His teachings offer a pathway for liberation, helping us break free from the shackles of life. That's why we remember him.

Before the 1800s, Egyptian civilization was largely silent. Despite the presence of the pyramids, temples, sophisticated architecture, and monumental structures they had constructed, we knew very little about Egyptian culture. In fact, hieroglyphics - the Egyptian language - were considered a dead language, leaving us unable to comprehend anything about their civilization. Then, in the 1800s, one of the most significant archaeological discoveries occurred: the unveiling of the Rosetta Stone. This discovery enabled the decipherment of hieroglyphics. For the first time, the stone contained inscriptions in three languages: Egyptian hieroglyphics, another language commonly spoken in Egypt during that era, and Greek. By comparing these inscriptions, scholars were able to decode and understand hieroglyphics, leading to a better comprehension of Egyptian civilization.

Just think about it. Without that one stone, that one tablet, one scripture, we would know nothing about the Egyptian civilization. It is that stone that helped us understand their language, their culture, their traditions, their customs, and then the whole Egyptian civilization came to light. It is a modern phenomenon. The pyramids have been there for centuries, but nobody knew anything about the people. It doesn't matter. We can create the greatest of monuments, but at the end of the day, human civilization and you as an individual can only be remembered in words, and it is only words that can lead us inward, and point us in a direction that is impossible to see without words.

The Technique

Acquiring knowledge is as important as sitting in meditation because when you're sitting in meditation, you have to know, at a certain level, at least at an intellectual level, what it is that you're trying to do. Your understanding has to deepen. If there are limiting belief systems that you're holding on to, you have to clarify them. That is the job of the scriptures - it has always been the work of a teacher. Sitting in meditation on your own is a modern phenomenon. If you go back in time before the internet, before the printing press, you learned meditation only by going to a teacher. So, he is your scripture. He is your teaching. He's supplementing you with the necessary knowledge, clarifying your doubts, and answering your questions. And then you're going and sitting in meditation, and all that knowledge, all that understanding is deepening your meditation. In the modern world and going forward, individuals will be able to practice meditation on their own because of the wealth of knowledge that is available in books.

When you're reading a book, you are reading the words of a teacher. It's almost as good as being in the presence of a teacher. Of course, being in the presence of an actual teacher is the ultimate because you can get something more than words, but just using words, you can understand what the teacher is trying to say, and then you can sit in meditation. Now, what if you're able to bring these two together? When you're reading, just observe your body posture. It is very close to your meditation posture. You can assume the same posture that you would assume in meditation when you're reading. You can sit cross-legged, rest your back, and sit in a comfortable posture, just like you would do in watching the flower or watching the candle meditation, but you are reading a book. You're watching the book - with a minor difference. The minor difference is that here your mind is engaged. Your body is still, and your breathing is relaxed, which means you are ready to go deep into meditation.

When you read - what you read is important. You can read pretty much anything and go into meditation. But if you're reading something that can illuminate your understanding of life, that can illuminate the understanding of the body, if you're reading something connected to meditation, then the meditative process is strengthened even more. So when you're reading, you can practically, in that very moment, try and apply that knowledge to your body. For example, you're reading a verse from the ancient scriptures that means, "I am Brahman, I am the creator." You're sitting in meditation. What is it that you're creating? At that very moment, you can go into the inquiry. Not deviating too much into the mind, you can just observe - "The scripture is saying that I am the creator. What does it mean? What am I creating right now?"

If you observe the entire process, you are only sitting and looking at some notations and symbols on a blank sheet of paper. Your mind is what is creating all the images and all the experiences. How can you not be the creator? You're not watching a movie - you are simply looking at symbolic notations, but a great creative process is happening inside you. Those symbols are automatically, without any lag in time, converted into images. So, there's definitive proof of that verse, "Aham Brahmasmi. I am the creator." That deepens your understanding a little more. Continue to read. Most people find it hard to read for extended periods because they fall asleep. If you're practicing meditation while reading, you can stay awake easily because you're not only reading, you're not only watching the text in the book, you're also watching the one who's watching. You're also aware of the entire process.

Meditation is never opposed to action. Meditation is not even opposed to mental action. You can be in a relaxed, meditative state, and your thoughts can pass through in front of you without any problem. The only condition is you have to be in the present moment. You have to either watch your breath or your heart center. Pick any center on your body and continue to read. Initially, you will find it hard. You would rather simply read, forgetting about the body because you can drift more. You might see meditation as a disturbance for reading, and you might see reading as a disturbance for meditation. But it is only temporary. After a while, meditation settles by itself, and reading settles by itself. And once you're able to get to a point where you're able to be in the present moment and read, magically, every time you are reading, your meditation is deepening. You don't have to study the scriptures separately and go into meditation separately. You can study the scriptures and go into meditation. The deeper you go into meditation, the deeper your understanding of the scriptures. The deeper your understanding of the scriptures, the deeper your meditation. The learning becomes two-dimensional. You have to try this to know how magically it works.

This has not been a traditional meditation technique because books and reading are a modern phenomenon. Meditation was always taught orally by teachers, so there was no necessity to combine reading and meditation. We don't find reading meditation in ancient scriptures because there was always a teacher. Now, for the modern man and the future, reading would become a fantastic meditation because you have to study the scriptures to understand meditation. Because they both are so deeply connected, you can bring them together. It's just like mindfulness. When you are taking a walk, your mindfulness is not opposed to walking. You can walk and be mindful. It's the same while you're reading. You can read and be mindful, but because you're sitting still, your mindfulness becomes meditation because you can go deeper.

What is the distinction between mindfulness and meditation? Mindfulness is about being in the present moment, but meditation is about starting from the present moment and going deeper. If you want to go deeper, you cannot be walking. You cannot be cooking. You cannot be talking. You have to sit quietly. Your body has to be totally relaxed, and reading offers you that perfect posture and the perfect opportunity and time to simply sit, connect with that center, and continue to read. Once your meditation deepens, you will not even know the difference between normal reading and meditative reading. Your reading itself will become meditative. Once you touch a certain depth in your being, once you know how to be there, then you can be there for as long as you want. You can be there while you're reading. Words become ideas; ideas become knowledge; knowledge becomes experience; eventually, experience becomes your ultimate truth. This is the only process of going deeper and higher. The rest are going in circles. When the entire process is right there: Human language, your mind to decipher that language, your heart to rejoice in that language, your body to sync all that knowledge and information into experience, and then ultimately your beautiful self to turn it all into a transcendental experience. - what more could you want for meditation? The entire process is right there.

Dancing with Shadows

SHIVA'S THIRD-EYE MEDITATION

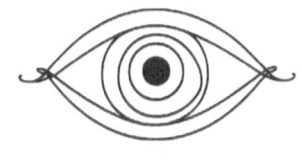

The third eye is usually identified as the seat of consciousness, awareness, intelligence, and intuition. The third eye is our true eye, through which we see things. The eyes with which we see the world are only an outer layer of observation. When we look at something, our eyes aid us in the process of observation. But the real observation, the real watchfulness, is happening somewhere deeper. So, third-eye meditation is a way of starting from the outermost layer of sense perception and going deeper.

TRANSCENDING THE HEAD

The third eye is normally identified as the spot between the two eyebrows. In the meditation tradition, that is where you identify the third eye and start watching. You close your eyes, sit in a comfortable posture, and start focusing in between your eyebrows. The third eye meditation is unusual in a way that it tries to remove your head by focusing on the head. The objective of meditation is to move you away from your head center to the actual center of your being. Before understanding the method, and the technique, it is important to understand why to move away from the head. What is the problem with the head? The head is the seat of the brain - supposed to be the most important part of the human body, through which we perceive the world. Almost all the main senses are located on the face, so why this insistence that we have to move away from the head? There's not a single authentic meditation technique that doesn't talk about how to go beyond the head, or how to move away from the center of the head. There's not a single meditation technique that puts you there, that puts your focus on the head and keeps it there. The whole objective of meditation is to transcend the head. Why? This is important to understand.

Once, a Zen master was asked, "What is the most invaluable thing in the world?" He said it was the head of a dead cat. Why? Because you cannot put a price on it. If you were to ask me what is the most useless thing in the world, which has no place in meditation, bliss, or joy, it is your head. In fact, the head is the single biggest obstacle between us and our unlimited perception of life. Because we have emphasized thinking so much and become addicted to the process of thinking - assuming that all this thinking happens inside our brains - every time we try to understand ourselves we go straight to the head. That's why when you're stressed or worried, your hand automatically moves to your head. Headache isn't just a physical symptom of your head aching. If you ponder it, more often than not, a headache occurs when you are overly stressed, anxious, or worried. You say, "My head is splitting." In a way, we assume that all the stress, all the strife, is happening in the head, in our brain. That's why when we sit in meditation, the hardest thing to deal with is the incessant noise, which we assume is coming from our heads.

When you sit and close your eyes, without even realizing it, you are trying to see from inside the head. This might sound a little silly, but deeper layers of meditation will take you completely away from the head, putting you in a totally different space. In fact, you might not even believe that it's possible to live without thinking about the head at all. Throughout the day, you can perform all the activities you're doing now, being vibrantly involved in life without thinking about your head or worrying about the stress within it because your center has shifted. There's so much addiction to the head because of how we have categorized the human body. For convenience's sake, we've divided the human body into different parts and assigned each part a function. When explaining the human body to a child, the easiest way is to divide it into parts: That's my eye, it helps me see. That's my nose, it helps me smell. There are the ears, that's the tongue, and this is the body. For each, you assign a function.

What often gets overlooked is that a human being can perceive the same thing through multiple senses. They cannot only see through their eyes but also perceive through their skin, smell, and taste. Seeing isn't just about colors and movement; it's about perception. You can recognize the same movements and the same perceptions using your other senses. The reason we don't think in these terms is that we aren't introduced to this idea. We're not familiar with the notion that our entire body can perceive things - every point of our body is a center of perception. What you think you're doing through your head, you can actually do by shifting to the heart center or the naval center. This concept might be entirely alien to the Western mind, but in the yogic tradition, it's embraced without trouble. Through exploring yoga and going deeper into meditation, individuals can connect with existence from multiple centers. It's then that they realize there's something else inside them that's perceiving things, independent of the body. They understand they aren't solely confined to the body - they're closest to it, perceiving things through it, but they aren't defined by it.

Shiva's Third-Eye Meditation

Due to our classification of the human body and the insistence that all our thinking occurs solely in the brain and nowhere else, when we sit in meditation, we feel confined within the head. This feeling of being trapped in the head makes meditation challenging. Ultimately, breaking through that barrier grants a glimpse of bliss. Interestingly, a similar experience occurs when consuming alcohol, smoking pot, or using substances like psilocybin mushrooms that induce a high. These substances redirect your awareness away from the head and toward your true center, your being. Essentially, all drugs inducing a sense of high shift your focus from the head to this true center, bringing a feeling of openness and shattering the confines, leading to a sense of freedom that translates into blissful experiences, as you're no longer confined or limited to the head.

Another reason for our fixation on the head is the modern language concerning intelligence. We've extensively discussed the brain's power, complexity, and intelligence, leading to an overemphasis on the brain. The term "brain" has been so heavily used that we've assumed thinking solely occurs within it. If all thoughts are presumed to be stored in the brain, then everything known about oneself comes from those thoughts, implying a separation from the brain.

Logically, this implies one is nothing but the brain, which is the false knowledge to overcome. It's not true - there's more to an individual than the brain or the body, and there's a way to experience this. Moving away from the head, assumed as the seat of intelligence and thinking, is crucial. Additionally, it's also the center of the ego. When referring to the ego, pay close attention to which part of the body is implied. If one were to somehow extract the ego and present it, it would point to the head, where the ego resides. The ego represents a blend of self-images a person has constructed - how they look, how they talk, their perceived intelligence, their wealth - all rooted in thinking, which primarily resides in the head.

Ken Robinson, in one of his TED talks, talks about professors. He says, "I like professors, but they're kind of disembodied in a literal way. Professors look upon their bodies as a form of transport for their heads. It is a way of getting their heads to meetings." When you think about it, although it is a humorous way of describing a professor, it is not only a professor. Most human beings are disembodied. They tend to look upon their bodies as simply a vehicle to move their heads from one place to another. The most important thing is their head and what's in their head, and wherever they go, they have forgotten their bodies - the body doesn't even exist - it's all about the head. You might be taking a walk in a beautiful garden, clouds above, greenery all around, beautiful flowers, honey bees, but where are you? Pay close attention. If you're in the body, you can experience all that. You can experience the vibration. You can experience the sensation. You can experience the changes in temperature and all that. But you are completely stuck in your head. You might be in that garden, but you're thinking about something else.

Every time we are in one place but thinking about something else, we are literally disembodied. What is the necessity for meditation? What is the necessity for a technique like third-eye meditation? The necessity is because we are disembodied beings. We are living like ghosts, where one part of us - the mind - is doing its own thing, and with every given opportunity, it wants to fly away. Then there is the body that wants to be in the present moment, that wants to experience life, that wants to enjoy life. And the body knows that the only way to enjoy life is to be in the present moment. The mind has no conception of the present moment. On top of this, we have attributed all our intelligence, smartness, and everything that satisfies the ego, to the head. And we insist on staying there. The same thing happens when you sit in meditation. You don't want to move away from the head center.

SHIVA

The third eye meditation is a powerful ancient meditation that comes from the Hindu scriptures. It is also part of Buddhism, but mainly the third-eye meditation is recognized with Shiva. In Hindu mythology, Shiva is part of the trinity of gods. There is Brahma, there is Vishnu, and there is Shiva, who is also known as Maheshvara. Brahma is the creator, Vishnu is the sustainer of life, and Shiva is the destroyer. Of the three, Shiva is regarded as the ultimate, as the pinnacle. Surprisingly, the destroyer is recognized as the ultimate; he is recognized as the ultimate yogi, the ultimate meditator, the one who's eternally in meditation - whose every inch, every body part is in meditation all the time for eternity. He's looked upon as a symbol of meditativeness and also worshipped as the God of destruction. What does he destroy? That is the most important thing. Shiva is the destroyer of your head. Shiva is the destroyer of your ego. That is why if you look at statues of Shiva or if you look at his pictures, he's wearing a garland made of human skulls. Most people don't even know what that means.

It is assumed that because Shiva lived in the graveyard, he used to eat out of skulls - the skull was his bowl, the begging bowl. And because the skull symbolizes death and he has conquered death symbolically, he's shown to be wearing a garland of skulls. But the actual definition is, he is the one who cuts your head off, not literally but figuratively. Because he understands the single biggest obstacle between you and your ultimate realization - the unconscious you and the conscious you, the limited you and the limitless you - is basically your head. This doesn't mean that you are completely removing your thoughts or completely removing your head. It only means that you're shifting your center. When the center shifts, your ego disappears. Remember, ego is purely imagined; it has no real existence. Its power comes from you assuming that it is real, and it is a part of your thinking. What is ego if not for thinking?

THE TECHNIQUE

Shiva is identified as a yogi who destroys your ego. This meditation technique of watching the third eye is, in a way, a derivative of his desire to take off your head, his desire to shift you away from your head center to your true center. So the technique begins with keeping your focus between your two eyebrows, which is the seat of the third eye. Even now in India, the space between your eyebrows is considered one of the most sacred. That's why when you're getting married, only the husband is allowed to touch the spot between the two eyebrows. He touches that spot and puts a spot of what in Hindu tradition is called "kumkum." It's a spiritual recognition by the husband that, "I have permission to touch your third eye because that is the most sacred part of you." Of course, it's all symbolic. It comes from a certain degeneration of meditative culture. Because India has always been a culture steeped in the yogic tradition, steeped in meditative tradition, a lot of the rituals and customs that they observe now are simply degenerated forms of meditation practices. So the third eye is regarded as the seat of intelligence, the seat of consciousness, the seat of the ego, and it's also your center of disturbance.

When you sit, close your eyes, and keep your focus on the third eye, it doesn't relax you. This is one meditation that pushes you into more disturbance, that pushes you into more chaos. This is not an easy meditation; it is much more difficult than watching your breath because watching your breath is gentle and you have a little more space to move around. Breath is moving in and out, and breath is the seat of relaxation. But your head is the seat of stress. It's the seat of your ego. When you try to keep your focus between the eyebrows, you cannot easily relax, and that is the objective of the meditation. You have to keep watching that spot with utmost focus, not just awareness. Your entire focus should be between the eyebrows, so much so that you should forget the eyebrows, forget the forehead, forget the head, forget where you're sitting, forget your surroundings, everything. Your focus should be one-pointed until your disturbance reaches its peak. You have to continue to watch the third eye until it is unbearable to watch. It will happen when you continue to watch. Even during a one-hour meditation, there will come a point when you feel like just opening your eyes and running away. Only when you practice this will you know how much a third eye meditation can stress. But the key here is this is all only for someone who's just beginning the practice. For a seasoned meditator or an experienced meditator, it doesn't stress them because they have already shifted a little bit away from the head center. They can watch the spot with a little bit of distance.

When you are beginning meditation for the first time, nothing can disturb you as much as keeping your focus between the eyebrows. That is the objective of the meditation - to keep watching it so that a day will come when the very thought of going anywhere near the third eye, going anywhere near the head, scares you. Automatically, something shifts inside you. Every time you go near the head, something pulls you back to the center because there is another real center where there is no danger; you don't have to go to the head. You come back to the original center. The practice of watching the third eye would intensify pain, stress, and pressure so much that when you realize there is a way to step away from the head, there is a way to step away from this third eye without losing your sense of aliveness, your consciousness, and your ability to be in action, you would automatically choose the other center. That is why after about one month of regular rigorous practice of third eye meditation, something shifts inside you fundamentally. You will understand the difference between relaxed and stressed, and you will understand the head is the seat of all stress, and there is another center. It could be your heart center, it could be your breath center - any center other than the head. If you're able to shift there, there's natural relaxation. Only when that center shifts, your journey truly begins.

As long as you're stuck in the head, you're only moving around in the world of your thoughts. There is no relaxation, no enjoyment of meditation. Meditation has multiple layers. The first layer is the shift from the head to your true center. Of course, you have to continue to practice to be rooted in your true center, but at least you know that a true center exists. As of now, there is no center that you are operating from other than your head. Your body is literally nonexistent. You become aware of your body once in a while - when the body demands, when there is a necessity. Otherwise, you are always in the head, and that is how you perceive yourself as well. Watch yourself when you're sitting, when you're getting up, when you wake up from bed, when you're eating. Just notice: Which experience are you most rooted in? Is it in the experience of the body or is it in the experience of the mind? You'll be surprised - "Do I really have a body? And what is the necessity of the body?" That's when you realize your life has become stressful, chaotic, and limiting because you have pushed yourself to one corner of your being, and you are so much more.

You can step away from the head. You can be at your breath center. You can be at your heart center. You can move in and around the body; that itself will give you that sense of freedom, that feeling that yes, I can move around a little bit. And then you can go outside - your perception can shift outside your body. You can sit in meditation. In deep meditation, you can become that tree that is outside. You can become the sky, or you can become the bird flying in the sky. For those brief moments, you can totally forget your body. This might sound like an impossible thing because you are stuck in the head. If you step away from the head, you will see all kinds of possibilities open up. You will have so much more freedom to move around. That is what you experience in meditation as unwinding, as relaxation, as bliss.

Your head has to go. Third-eye meditation is an indirect way of getting rid of the head. It is a beautiful technique that focuses on the seat of the problem. By focusing on the center of all your anguish and troubles, you are trying to go beyond it. Yoga understands meditation, and understanding that when you focus on something, understanding deepens, and as understanding deepens, the illusion breaks. A simple shift happens - "Why am I stuck in the head? I can be somewhere else, I can keep my focus on my breath. I can be in an imaginary center and still use my head, still use my brain." What a great feeling that is, to know that you are something more than your head.

This meditation is for those who want a much more forceful, more aggressive approach to meditation. Third-eye meditation is not gentle - it will disturb you. In fact, the disturbance will extend a little bit throughout the day because if you're sitting and focusing so much, if you're practicing it correctly, if you're insisting on focusing between your eyebrows and you're not shifting your awareness here and there, you will have a headache and that will continue throughout the day. But because it puts you in that state of disturbance, it also takes you out of that disturbance sooner than other meditation techniques. So, if you're looking for a more aggressive way of shifting your center from the head to your body, then this is a wonderful meditation. Be prepared to go through the disturbance, go through the pain. But on the other hand, all that you are searching for is waiting, just on the other side.

Shavasana

Shavasana, or playing dead meditation, should be the easiest of meditations. How hard can it be to play dead? Well, it is hard. Let's try to understand a few things before diving into the practice of Shavasana. Death is a very enigmatic idea. We fear death, and yet we go on living as if we're going to be here forever. Death is never far away; it is very close to life. Death is simply the other side of life. Life has no meaning without death. In fact, it is death that adds all the meaning to life.

Imagine for a moment if there were no such thing as death. Imagine you were to live forever and ever and ever. Life would lose all its meaning. What is the purpose of living? Somewhere, the end is what gives meaning to the journey. Would you undertake a journey without any end to it, without any destination? And what would such a journey be like? How would you experience that journey? What would be the qualitative difference of that journey when compared to a journey that has an end?

This experience of life, this way of living, whatever you are doing now, someday is going to come to an end. How would your journey of life be different if there was no end in sight? It would be totally different. The way you look at things would be different. You would become more self-centered and more greedy if there was no contemplation of the end. If you were to live here forever, experiencing life as you currently do, with nothing that you are being taken away from you, with your body and mind existing eternally, you would become the worst possible person to be around because there would be no meaning for love and compassion.

There would be no meaning for sharing. There would be no meaning for living moment-to-moment because it all becomes a question of accumulation. That is how Man is living now.

Contemplation on Death

Although death is an absolute reality, deep down somewhere, Man thinks that he's going to be here forever. Although he knows his mind and body are going to die, because he believes in something immortal within him, he saves for the future. He thinks about after his death. He thinks about his children and his grandchildren. He thinks about his family lineage. If death were to be the reality of your life, then why should your thought process extend beyond your death? It's because there is a part of us - the most important part of us - that does not know the meaning of death. The self within us, the consciousness within us, the aliveness within us has no death. In fact, death is a silly idea for the self because how can the self experience death? If death is an experience, it has to happen to the self, and if the self is experiencing death, then it is not dead. There is something still alive. By the very definition, experience can happen only to something alive, not to something dead.

This deep-down awareness and knowledge of our immortal self is what translates into a misunderstanding, blocking our contemplation on death. We don't think about death. We don't accept it because deep down, we know that we're going to die. But all that we are doing in life is restricted to the mind and the body and there is a death to that. This lack of understanding is one of the biggest causes of conflict. Why? Because contemplation of death, understanding the ephemeral nature of life, knowing that someday you will have to leave all this and you cannot carry anything you've accumulated - that is what gives you that single most important reason, that impetus, to be in the present moment and experience life and enjoy life. That is the only thing that stops you from postponing all your joys and pleasures of life. You take away that thing, you take away contemplation of death, and then the whole of life becomes an accumulation process.

There is a disconnection, a misunderstanding of not fully seeing that the body belongs to death: There is something other than the body inside me. There's an aliveness, the consciousness that can never know death. There are two completely different dimensions to my reality; I am not just one. I am these two different entities. Somewhere, I have to make a conscious choice to bring awareness of death and also to forget about death. I need to do both if I am to understand life fully. There are moments when I need to be with the self, I need to connect with my true self and live as if there's no death - that helps me live without any fear, enjoy each moment, and just go through the experience of the self. Then at the same time, I should look at my body, I should look at all my activities, whatever it is that I'm doing, and see that someday all this is going to come to an end because it is the body through which I'm experiencing life.

When the body is gone, there is absolutely no meaning to this life I'm experiencing. There's no meaning to these trees. There's no meaning to birds, human beings. or society without my body being there through which I can experience all these things.

Without this dual way of looking at things, it is easy to live thinking that we're going to be here forever so let's do whatever we want - let's keep on accumulating things. Death is such a big reality, such a constant reality, that you live in fear. You think about it all the time. You worry all the time; wherever you go, you see death in one form or the other. Small changes in the landscape of reality, small changes in your social structure, in your economic status, in your health immediately remind you of death. Then how can you enjoy life? How can you experience this moment fully?

This is where meditation comes in. This is where the practice of watching death comes in. Shavasana is a beautiful method of consciously moving closer to death. It is important to understand death is only in the idea. The closer you move toward death, the more pointless, more silly it will become, because at the center of all experiences is not death, but life. The deeper you go into your being, even with the desire to die - "I want to go away from this body. I want to go away from this mind. Let me lie down as if I'm dead. Let me pretend that I'm dead." - the deeper your pretension, the more authentic your pretension, the more alive you feel. That is the strangeness of the death meditation. For those who are observing on the outside, this might seem to be a very negative approach to meditation because most meditations are usually about relaxation, about connecting with your inner silence, your inner stillness. They are about life, how to be more peaceful, more joyful, more loving, more kind, and compassionate. Here, what the hell are you doing trying to die?

Nothingness

In meditation, death is a beautiful experience. In fact, it is the most beautiful of all experiences. There cannot be a grander experience than death. Buddha called it "nothingness." The ultimate experience of enlightenment, awakening, he called it nothingness. If nothingness is not a form of death, then what is it? Everything is gone. Your mind is gone. Your body is gone. Your self-identity is gone. Your name and form are gone. Isn't that a kind of death? And yet, look at the beauty of it. Buddha came back from there. He did not die. We did not lose him, although he went in search of death. He said, "This is the day I am not going to get up until I become enlightened." In a way, he was telling himself, "I am ready to die. I am ready to give up my mind. I'm ready to give up my body." The only thing you need to remember is this is Buddha saying it, not some suicidal lunatic. Buddha is suicidal in a different way. He is suicidal in an existential way. He knows the value and meaning of surrender. He knows the art of surrender. So for a Buddha, marching toward death is the ultimate thing he can move toward.

For someone who does not understand death, who has not contemplated death, who has not gone inward connecting with himself, contemplation on death, thinking about death can only lead to one logical conclusion - that is suicide. He does not understand death. That individual, that fool who commits suicide knows nothing about death because the very moment he tried to end his life, he gave birth to another one - that is not how you experience death. There's only one death that is possible, and that is conscious death. Death is a reality only when you experience it consciously. When you transcend your mind by understanding it, when you transcend your body by understanding it, when you become the aliveness and you drop your body consciousness, that is the only way you can experience death. Only for the one who has experienced that nothingness, that meditative nothingness, there is no rebirth. In one sense, there is no necessity to die again. That death is enough.

Suicide has to be one of the most violent things an individual can do, even more violent than killing someone else. Ending your own life has to be one of the most brutal and violent actions. The very object, the very purpose with which one does it, is defeated because you cannot experience death like that. It's only a momentary blip. Tagore says it beautifully: "Death is not extinguishing the light; it is only putting out the lamp because the dawn has come." It is just like sleep. You've gone to sleep and you wake up again with a new life. Death is the ultimate of experiences. It takes practice and effort. It takes a method to experience it. It is not a cheap experience that you can have just by ending your life. Death is too grand a phenomenon to become available so cheaply. It is only the misunderstanding of death that makes it seem like it's so easy to die. The single biggest quest of Man from the beginning has been learning the art of dying. What is meditation? What is mindfulness? What is awakening, if not for the art of dying, consciously moving toward death?

But look at the irony - the one who goes in search of death never experiences it. For the one who's courageous enough to walk toward it, death has disappeared. But for the one who's clinging to life, afraid of letting go, afraid of understanding death, who's living in constant fear of death, he dies many times before the actual death. In fact, for him, the actual death never comes, but he keeps dying day by day. That has to be understood at multiple levels. Understanding at an intellectual level will help you to navigate it, but then it has to be understood at an experiential level. Many philosophers, as well as scientists, have intellectually understood that. At least that gave them a little bit of that inner intelligence necessary to live without fearing death. For example, Einstein, at the age of about seventy-five, had a burst nerve or something, and the doctor told him that if this was not operated on, he would die - an operation was the only way to save his life. Einstein refused to undergo the operation. He said, "It is tasteless to prolong life. I have done my part. Now, I will go elegantly." It takes courage to say this. Most people cannot say this. They want to cling to life until the last moment. They want to torture the body and push it to its absolute limits because of a simple lack of understanding of death. Nothing scares a human being like death. For him, death is the end of all things, the end of all experiences.

Knowing That You Don't Know

If you truly understand, it's nothing but ignorance. You don't know what death is. If you knew what death is, then what is there to fear? Socrates was about to be given the poison hemlock for his crimes against humanity - poisoning the youth was the accusation - and what was his crime? He tried to awaken individuals. He tried to illuminate their lives. He tried to teach them to be themselves. That was his crime. He said, "To fear death is nothing other than to think oneself wise when one is not; for it is to think one knows what one does not know. No man knows whether death may not even turn out to be the greatest blessing for a human being; and yet people fear it as if they knew for certain that it is the greatest of evil." The fear of death comes only because of ignorance - because we don't understand death. For all you know, that might be the most beautiful of experiences. Death might be the grandest of all experiences. How do you know? Look at the beauty of this. Socrates was not a meditator. He was not a Buddha. He was not awakened. He didn't know what death is and yet just using his mind, his intellect, his philosophical abilities, he came to the point of, "Why should I fear something that I know nothing about?"

Fear rooted in ignorance is pointless because if I know what death is, then I can make a distinction - should I be afraid of it? I would have no idea what happens after my death except for what people have told me, except for what I've been listening to. Socrates' intellect, his intelligence was sharp enough to reject all the ideas, theories, and concepts of life, and that itself helped him to embrace them. He moved toward death, not in fear, but with full awareness that he was going to die, and yet it did not scare him. Why? Because he had made it his life to embrace ignorance. He was the one who said, "What you know and what you don't know are two very different things. When you know something, you know it. When you don't know something, you have to know that you don't know it." Awareness of ignorance is knowledge. When you know that you don't know something, you at least know that much - that you don't know.

Many live in utter ignorance and continue to believe that they know. They have substituted their knowing for information, for knowledge that they've accumulated from outside. Most of humanity is filled with borrowed knowledge, borrowed ideas, and borrowed concepts, and that is what is keeping individuals in bondage. That is what is keeping them in pain because their experience is telling them something else. The ideas they are picking up from the world are telling them something else. That conflict is what is keeping them agitated and disturbed.

A man who lives by his own individuality, by his own experiences, has very little to fear in life. Even when he's in ignorance, he is not afraid because he knows what ignorance is. He has tasted that ignorance. It is not an idea or a concept. Anything you have experientially understood and you have touched liberates you. What you know liberates you. What you don't know also liberates you because you did not just pick up the idea from outside. This is where religions took perfect advantage of this ignorance of death. Because Man feared death, because he did not understand death, religions were able to take advantage of this, filling his mind with all kinds of nonsensical ideas of heaven and hell. And look at the way a person lives who believes in heaven and hell. He's trembling. He's living in fear. Whatever he does, he's living in fear. If he does something wrong, fear of hell. If he does something right - have I done it right? Is this the perfect way of doing it? How can you be sure? You are subscribing to a totally arbitrary idea of heaven and hell because those are not your experiences. You've not experienced heaven. You've not experienced hell. You've just been listening to such idiotic concepts. Naturally, you have no understanding of death so you live in fear. Even a philosopher or a scientist who has not gone deep into meditation - just by experientially connecting with their knowledge, with their wisdom, rejects blind authority and dogmatic beliefs. That is a given. Socrates was not religious in the traditional sense, nor was Einstein. That is why they didn't have to fear an imaginary idea.

IMAGINATIONS GONE WILD

Most of humanity is living in fear of imaginary concepts, imaginary ideas. The soul is trembling. First, death has to be understood philosophically. Many other things in meditation don't have to be understood philosophically; you can just dive in. But death - you have to understand it philosophically because the word is where we are stuck. We use the words "life" and "death" very interchangeably. We talk about the death of the body, the birth of the spirit; we talk about aliveness. The words "living" and "death" have created a lot of confusion. We don't know what is living or what is dying because there are multiple entities here. There is the self, the mind, the body, my desires, and then there's this concept of coming back, reincarnation, and death being a momentary experience; then there is Nirvana, enlightenment - it's all confusing.

Philosophically, you have to make a separation, a distinction between the deathless part of you and the part of you that, no matter what you do, will die. A simple distinction: your spirit, your self, your true being has no death. It cannot die. That is what you experience as "I want to be here forever" or "I will be here forever." It has nothing to do with your body. It has nothing to do with your mind. And then there is your body, which is already in the grave. The grave is already dug. The body is already placed in the grave. The only thing left to be done is for the soil to be added and covered up. We are already in the grave. Look at the body. Every day it's moving closer and closer. It is constantly reminding us, but we refuse to accept it.

There's one interesting story that comes to mind. During one of the Christian death ceremonies, the body is placed in the grave and they're about to cover it up. Relatives are standing around, there's great mourning, and there is a priest who is offering his prayers, doing whatever he does to send the body wherever he wants to send it. This one old lady comes running, and she throws an orange into the grave. This priest immediately picks up the orange and says, "What are you doing? When do you think the departed will come to eat this orange?" There's an old Indian chief standing there; he leans forward and says, "When the spirit comes to smell the flowers." Nobody said anything after that. See, right there, we put the flowers, we do all this, somewhere deep down believing that that spirit is going to experience that. Otherwise, who are you laying the flowers for? It's not for you - you are giving it as an offering to the body. If you can give flowers, why not an orange?

Apart from that, every year, once a year, you offer all these things that the person enjoyed. Now, where is this coming from? It's coming from the belief that he's still alive, he's still watching, and he still has these expectations. Otherwise, why are you doing it? But at the same time, we cannot stretch this idea beyond the rituals. If you are offering flowers, flowers are fine, but if you start offering fruits, pizzas, and drinks, it will look stupid, but some cultures offer such things. If you look at the whole of humanity, most of our rituals and traditions are surrounding death - not life.

The world's largest religion has nothing to do with life. Christianity is all about death. It's all about crucifixion. It's all about celebrating the death of that one man - not even the death - the sacrifice. We are celebrating the fact that he decided to become suicidal for the sake of his God. In a way, in Christianity, we are worshipping suicide. Think about it. According to the stories, Jesus knew that he was going to die. He's talking about it in the Last Supper, so that means he's knowingly, willingly marching toward death. Isn't suicide a crime? But that's where our understanding of death proves to be so shallow, so pointless, so meaningless. On the one hand, we have glorified a man to a point of unimaginable status where every day we worship him - the idea of a man sacrificing his life. On the other hand, we tremble at the very thought of our death, at the very thought of the death of our loved ones. Such a big dichotomy. All that can be reconciled within your own being by making a conscious effort to understand it.

The Technique

Without bringing in theories, without bringing in religious concepts, decide for yourself - I want to know death. I want to taste it at a different level. Let me intellectually taste it. So every day, let me make it a habit to contemplate on it. Let me think about it. Let me make it my meditation practice.

There's already a meditation practice in the yogic tradition designated for death, Shavasana. Lie down as if you are dead. There is the practice. You can do this after your other meditations. This could be the ending meditation of all your other meditations. Let's say you're doing your breathing meditation, watching the candle meditation, or whatever meditation you're doing. At the end of it, just completely let go, completely surrender, lie down on the floor on your back, put your arms out, let your palms face upwards, and just close your eyes and pretend that you're dead. But pretension should be real. You cannot just imagine that you're dead. Every thought that crosses your mind, every sensation you feel, everything you experience - you should not even pay any attention to it. Of course, you need to be aware, you need to watch it, and you need to let it go as if it's not happening to you. How can it happen to you? You're dead.

You have to be serious while practicing Shavasana. You have to take it seriously that "I am dead now." Shavasana is very different from regular meditation. In regular meditation, you can move around a bit. You can adjust yourself if there is a real urge to scratch. If there's an itch, you can scratch. But in Shavasana, that defeats the whole purpose - you're dead. It is hard because you have to suspend all your mental and physical impulses to act. You need to just accept the fact fully that you're dead.

Initially, it will seem silly because you're very much alive, you're watching everything, and you're also thinking about it. Am I doing it right? Am I dead enough? Your mind does not understand death. Your mind simply uses the word "death" as another word and starts adding more ideas to it. But this reveals something beautiful. Damn, it's hard to die. It's not easy. Even in the idea, it is so hard to die because there's something so vibrant inside, so alive that no matter what I try to do, it is watching. However, I instruct this creature that's inside me to stop watching, it won't stop watching, and that should tell you something - maybe watchfulness is my nature. Maybe it is impossible to die. There, you're going deeper. And let this not just be an intellectual exercise - let it seep into your body.

Every day, when you lie down and surrender yourself, go a little deeper. Hold onto the idea of death a little longer. A day will come when something magical happens. You will begin to notice that you are succeeding. Something is dying. All your pretension is helping you to move away from the sensations of your body, away from the sensations of the mind. In a way, you are detaching from the pure unconscious intensity of the mind and the body.

Up until then, your aliveness was totally intertwined with your mind and body, with no possibility of separation. Now, for the first time, you are experiencing your aliveness as something a little disconnected from your mind and body. You're able to see that something is dying. Yes. My mind is dying.

My body is dying. But at the same time, something is becoming more alive. The fewer sensations of the body, the fewer sensations of the mind, the more alive I feel. How is it?

The deeper you go into Shavasana, the fewer the influences of your mind and body, but the greater your experience of aliveness. That will create the pathway for you. Now you have seen the path, so the deeper you go into death, the more alive you become. There's only one conclusion to that: Maybe I am the center of it. If I continue on this path, I will experience total aliveness with no experience of the mind and the body. I would have experienced Buddha, nothingness. I would have died only for the mind and the body. I would have become aliveness itself. That is the only moment you will truly know what death is. That is the only moment when you can truly transcend all the ideas and concepts of death and know it as an experience.

Once you know death as an experience, you will just laugh at the whole idea. You will conclude that death is the silliest of ideas. It is not real; it is purely imagined. An imagined idea is tormenting us. Think about it. Something that is not even real is what troubles us all our life. Throughout our lives, we fear death in one form or another. In all our minor fears, the ultimate fear is always about death. And death is not even a real thing. This should make you question -

"If I can be afraid of something that isn't even real, then what is real? Am I really real? Is my body real? Is my mind real?"

It's just like that Upanishad story where a man is walking in the dark and he sees something. He's almost scared to death. It looks like a snake, and he jumps out in fear. And then when there's enough light and he looks at it, he realizes that it was not a snake; it was just a rope. But think about it. The fear that he experienced was real. He could have had a heart attack. But the triggering point of that fear was purely imagined. There was no snake there. That means we can scare ourselves to death by using our imagination. Nothing has to be real there, and death is exactly that.

Our fear of death is purely imagined. We are freaking out every moment because we are unable to understand it. Of course, just an intellectual understanding isn't enough when your loved one dies. You need something more because in those moments your emotion takes over and completely submerges your intellect. You cannot be intelligent when you're engulfed by an emotion. That is why no matter how deep your intellectual contemplation of death is, in those moments when your loved one is dying, you will feel the pain.

It is very much possible that Socrates could have accepted his death, but if he had a child, wife, mother, or father who was dying, I am sure his heart would have trembled because he had not gone all the way into experiencing deathlessness. He knew it as an idea. Buddha, on the other hand, would not tremble. Buddha can smile at not only his death but the death of his loved ones because he knows death is an illusion. He knows that they are not going anywhere. Yes, they are disappearing from his experience, but their experiences are continuing. And he knows that in their experiences, "I am there. If I have given any love, if I occupy an important place in their minds, I will be nagging them even after death because I'm a part of their aliveness. I'm a part of their consciousness."

Buddha doesn't even go that far because he knows death is an illusion. That fear has no basis in reality. So to truly transcend the fear of death, you need to go toward it. You need to go into it meditatively. You need to go into it consciously, one step at a time. And Shavasana can be the door through which you can experience death.

Sit Down and be Quiet

I don't want to sit quiet. I don't want to sit still. What is the point of all this? How long will it take for me to get adjusted to the idea of sitting still?

It's the conversation the mind is having with itself, once in a while putting it out as a question. Meditation is hard on the mind because, in a way, you are trying to erase the mind, but not permanently. You are making a conscious decision to create a space for yourself where the mind cannot enter. If you can do that much, if you can stay in that space where the mind cannot interfere, you have found the door. Then how deep you go from there, how much bliss you experience, entirely depends on you and your willingness, because now "you" are choosing to experience something. It's not your mind. As long as it's your mind, there will always be that conflict. Apart from the disturbance of the mind, your body also experiences discomfort when it is made to sit in one position for extended periods. That is easy to deal with. We'll get to that.

Mind is a Filter

First, let's address the mind. By its very nature, the mind exaggerates pain, especially when you remove external distractions and simply let it focus on one thing. The reason we don't experience this directly is that we are not aware of this nature of the mind - we are distracted throughout the day. We move from one thought process to another, from one activity to another. We don't watch the mind. We don't watch how the mind is interpreting events and experiences for us. We are so busy moving around that we don't have any time to inquire into the nature of the mind. When you do inquire into the nature of the mind, you will see that the mind is filtering everything. The mind is not presenting you with a direct experience. The mind is the filtering mechanism of experience. If it is the filtering mechanism, then the question is, how is it filtering? What kind of filtering is happening?

An experiment was conducted that gives an idea of how the mind exaggerates pain. The study involved gathering a group of people, inflicting some sort of pain, and studying their response. They studied the generation of pain, the exaggeration of pain, and how the mind responds to that pain. Two groups were created. One is what you call the study group who were given certain specific instructions, and the other group had no specific instructions. Both groups were told to dip their hands into freezing cold water. The study group was given the instruction that they needed to distract themselves from the pain. They have to do something - think about something else, try to suppress the pain however they can. To the other group, no such instruction was given. They were just told to go through the experience, and we'll record the pain response.

When they finished the study, surprisingly, they found that the first group, the study group that was instructed to suppress pain, experienced significantly higher levels of pain compared to the other group. That was surprising because normally you would tend to think they had been warned of the pain and also instructed to distract themselves. So naturally, when they began to experience pain, they'd either sing a song or think about something else. Thus, naturally, the body would experience less pain, and that's what we should notice.

That is not what happened. What occurred was exactly the opposite, and that is important to understand. It's significant to comprehend because of the mind, and what the mind is doing there. In the first instance with the study group, the mind was instructed. In the second group, there was no such instruction. So, in the first group that experienced more pain, you have involved the mind more. That is the significant point. It doesn't matter whether you gave the instructions to suppress the pain or to exaggerate it, the most important thing is you drew the attention of the mind to the pain. So, in an attempt to suppress the pain, the mind started experiencing the pain more. That's when they realized this is the psychology of the mind. When it tries to avoid something, it has to watch it more closely, and the way it does this is by exaggerating it. Because you have given it the instructions, "Watch this pain. Don't let it reach certain levels. Divert your attention away from it; suppress it," the mind is waiting for the pain. Even when there are moderate levels of pain, it exaggerates it. The mind adds its own layers of pain so that it can observe the pain clearly.

The same thing happens in meditation. It's not that your body isn't used to sitting still. If you pay careful attention, you'll see that your body is still most of the time. When you're sitting in front of the computer, your body is still. When you're in your car, your body is still. When you're asleep or eating, your body is still. Your body knows what it is to be still. It's the mind that is the problem.

Sitting Still

When you sit in meditation, the change, the difference between meditation and any other regular activity, is only that you are telling the mind to watch the body. You're telling the mind to watch the breath, not to get distracted, not to drift away. So, here you are instructing the mind to watch the pain. Just as in that experiment where the subjects were told to suppress their pain, here in meditation, you are telling the mind to watch it. Although you're simply telling the mind to watch the body, there is nothing else to watch in the body other than pain. It exaggerates every small discomfort: an itching sensation, a bit of circulation problem in certain parts of your legs, the wind blowing on your skin. Your mind completely exaggerates even the sensation of a hair moving to a point where it feels like pure torture.

The mind either wants to escape, open its eyes, start running and doing things, or it has to scream in pain. It has no other option. This is the part of meditation that is the hardest. This is where you are taming the mind. You are controlling the mind without actually controlling it. You are understanding the nature of the mind for the first time.

Something interesting happens when you start watching pain. There are, of course, real physical pains, and no matter how much you watch that pain, it only increases. Let's say you have a cut or an infection, an actual physical disturbance to your body.

Those pains, when you watch them, get amplified. But all other transitory pains that come and go when you watch them while you're sitting in meditation, you can see they move like a wave. The pain starts at its lowest level, moves higher to the peak, tries to push you into action, wants you to move your legs, wants you to scratch. But if you don't give in, if you continue to watch it, the pain subsides. The sensation magically subsides. You've not done anything to remove the pain. Then where did it go? Why did it subside? It was not a real pain. It was a pain exaggerated by the mind - that is why it moves in waves. A pain that moves in waves is really the pain that the mind is exaggerating, and the body is okay with that pain. The body is okay with that discomfort. It is the mind that wants you to act.

STILLNESS OF THE MIND

When you continue to watch this movement, these sensations coming and going, it will be a little hard at first. But at the end of one or two months of regular practice of meditation, you will understand the difference between the pain arising in the mind and that arising in the body. Once you see that all the discomfort you're experiencing is only from the mind, you won't bother about it. You will let it subside.

Sitting Still

Having said this, there is no rule in meditation that you should not move. This is another big misconception of meditation because we have seen statues of Buddha, and in the statues, he never moves. We have somehow assumed that we cannot move. "Maybe he reached those deepest states of meditation because he never moved." You can move, but with one condition: when you decide to move - first, as much as possible, try not to move - because the mind is exaggerating, it will want you to act every few seconds. Give yourself at least fifteen to twenty minutes where you make a conscious effort not to move. Even if your legs begin to fall asleep, in ten minutes, they aren't going to rot and fall off. At least you know that scientifically; your mind is exaggerating it to that point where you're afraid you won't be able to stand up. That's it. You're gone. Somebody has tricked you. Look what's happening to your legs, but give yourself fifteen minutes. More often than not, the urge subsides. But if you still have the urge to move, be mindful of the body - watch your body and then move a little. Don't get up and move around. Don't move too much. Just the way you would adjust when you are sitting in front of your computer or when you're sitting in the car, you make that adjustment. Your body shifts, the weight shifts. You can do that. That does not disturb your meditation.

You don't have to equate the stillness of the body to the stillness of your mind. Stillness of the mind is the objective in meditation, not the stillness of the body.

The stillness of the body is only a useful prop to attain the stillness of the mind. Once you attain the stillness of the mind, the stillness of the body becomes irrelevant. That's why, once you reach deeper levels of meditation, you can be in that meditative state and even walk and move around, while maintaining that state.

For instance, imagine your nose starts itching uncontrollably. There's no hard and fast rule that you should not scratch. You can, but do it mindfully so that your meditation is not disturbed. If you scratch it without being mindful, you allow the mind to enter, allowing thoughts to disturb your meditation. That is the only condition you need to impose on yourself.

Meditation is a simple phenomenon. It isn't very rigid, not a "This is the only way to meditate" scenario where doing one thing wrong disrupts your meditation. That's not how meditation works. It's a flow, a beautiful dance where you are adjusting. The mind adapts itself to the new environment, as does the body. It's like taking your mind and body to a new place. Everything is different - the light, temperature, people, conversations - it's a new experience.

Meditation is a new phenomenon for both the mind and the body; they're utterly confused. "What's happening here? What are you trying to do? Okay, you're sitting still. My memory says after this, you should go to sleep because normally, when you sit still or lie down, you fall asleep. But you're not falling asleep; you're fighting sleep. Okay, are you solving a math problem? Building something? Designing? What are you trying to do?" No, I'm not doing any of that.

Doing nothing is a totally alien concept for the mind or the body to understand. The body knows action and movement, while the mind knows dreaming and desiring. You're asking them to do something different, so naturally, there will be discomfort. Expect it, and expect the mind to exaggerate the problem - that, too, should be anticipated.

The more the disturbance, the more your understanding that meditation is happening. If there's no disturbance when you sit in meditation, there's a good chance that you are either drifting in thoughts or just falling asleep. If you're truly watching the breath or focusing on whatever meditation technique you're practicing, there will be discomfort. It's perfectly alright and natural to experience this disturbance.

Create a little bit of balance. Don't heed everything the mind tells you and move around too much, but don't be so rigid that you decide to sit stone-like. Somewhere in the middle, it's okay to shift. Allow the mind a little bit of space so it doesn't panic. Allow the body a little space because that's what prevents panic.

If you sit still and say, "Okay, I want to sit still. I don't want to move an inch," the body goes into panic mode. But when it has the urge to move, if you just shift a little bit and continue to meditate mindfully, the body relaxes thinking, "Oh, good. He's not dead." That's all the body needs - confirmation that you're alive. Once it knows that, it will let you be in that posture for a while.

Meditation is an art, a beautiful dance. It cannot be too rigid, yet at the same time, it cannot be boundless. You need to have some basic rules, and the fundamental one is to try and be still but also allow for a little movement. Then you can experience what Patanjali calls "sthira sukha asana" - a firm, pleasant posture.

Sound of Silence

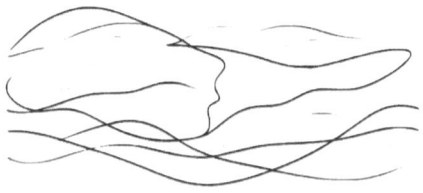

A Zen master was asked, "I've heard that there is one thing that cannot be named. It has not been born. It will not die when the body dies. When the universe burns up, it will not be affected. What is that one thing?" The master answered, "A sesame bun." The Zen master was joking - the actual answer to the question is "silence."

There are very few things in the human experience that are unchanging. Experience itself is part of the changing landscape - it comes and goes. But once in a while, if you're watchful, if you pay attention, you will connect with something real - something that is there, was there, will always be there, and is not separate from you. Once you touch it, it is yours. Once you figure out a way to get to it, once you know how to travel through that landscape, once you have learned how to read the signposts and you know how to get to that space, you can go there whenever you want, however many times you want, and you can stay there for as long as you want. Nobody is stopping you from going there. There are no restrictions on how much time you should spend there.

Missing Silence

One such thing is silence. The idea of silence has been mostly misunderstood. That is only natural because how can the mind understand silence? It can, at most, imagine silence. When it tries to imagine silence, because it does not know the quality, the sensation, or the depth of silence, it imagines it as an absence of something. It imagines it as emptiness. That is why the mind is never enthusiastic or excited about pursuing silence. It is more interested in pursuing all kinds of desires that don't add anything to your being, that simply take you from one part of your mind to another, keeping you just on the surface. It can drag you along these endless desires for a lifetime, knowing well that it's not changing you as a person, it's not adding to you as a being, nor is it transforming you from the inside. And yet, it never understands that if it can pursue silence - which is right there, which is a part of your very being - it can find all that it is searching for in those desires.

The mind simply cannot put these things together: happiness, peace, bliss, contentment, certainty, and silence. It does not understand that silence contains all this. Silence is not emptiness. Silence is also fullness. Silence is that one thing that doesn't need anything else. Silence is complete by itself, so there's no way for the mind to really understand its value. Throughout human history, cultures have used different methods and devices to trick the mind into falling into silence. You cannot present silence as an argument to the mind and expect it to understand.

Cultures that have only been concerned with the philosophical understanding of life, with a mere objective understanding of life, have totally missed silence because silence can't be brought inside the boundaries of philosophy or science. Western civilization has been dominated by science and philosophy. The Greeks were mostly interested in philosophy. They worshipped logos. Logos is where we get the word "logic" from. A culture that worships logic, how can it understand silence? Most philosophers completely missed silence. There were only a few rare philosophers, like Socrates, who were also mystical, involved in trying to have a direct experience of life. They didn't just want to talk about life - they also wanted to become a part of it. Only a few philosophers have understood the value of silence. Most others don't even include it in their philosophical discussions.

Similarly, with scientists, there are no scientific experiments worthy of mentioning that are dedicated to understanding silence. It is baffling when you think about it - the amount of time, the amount of resources we have spent in trying to understand sense perceptions. We see something and we want to study it. But true science is about going beyond our own sense perceptions and looking into the nature of reality. You have to assume a few things that are not directly in your perception. For example, how would your scientific experiments change if human beings were born blind? Then your entire language of inquiry should change. You should inquire more into the nature of sounds, the nature of silence because silence is more real than sound. Sound comes and goes, and you need an organism to capture sound. But silence can be there by itself. You don't need a machine or a bio-mechanism to capture silence. That right there should tell us that silence is more of an existential quality than simply a perception.

If I see the sun moving in the sky, if I see the clouds moving - as real as they are to me - if I'm truly scientific, I would also be skeptical about what I am seeing because I'm seeing it through my body, through my eyes. Ask a simple question: If I am trying to investigate into the nature of reality, why am I so stuck with human perception? The way I see things is most certainly different from how other creatures see things, how other creatures experience things. Let me try and investigate those things that we all experience - sleep, silence, stillness, consciousness, and aliveness. Not a single creature can be separate from these experiences. If there is an animal somewhere, it should have some sense of itself. It should have some level of awareness. Otherwise, how can it interact with its environment? How can it make decisions without awareness? Somehow we have become too preoccupied with human sense perceptions, so neither science nor philosophy has taken much note of silence, has given much importance to silence.

Emptiness

The mystical branch of life, the meditative branch of life, the experiential branch of life - those individuals who wanted to truly understand life, truly connect with life, not as a concept, not as a theory, but as an actual experience - have all spoken about silence. Not only have they spoken about it, but they have also sung and danced about it; they have spoken about it in ways that only a mystic can understand. Because silence is you. That's your ultimate nature. And it is not just the absence of something. It is not just the absence of thoughts, the absence of desires, because the absence of something is still negative. It's like saying, "Here is a cup." What is a cup? Either it can be filled with something or it's empty. When it's filled with something, it has more value. Let's say a cup filled with good coffee is more valuable when compared to an empty cup. What do you do with an empty cup? What we do not understand is that an empty cup is infinitely more valuable than a cup filled with coffee. Have you ever gone into a store to buy a cup filled with coffee? You always buy an empty cup because you know that is its true value, that emptiness is its true value. You can add coffee to it. You can add tea to it. You can add water to it. You can add wine to it. Whatever you want, you can add to it, and it allows for all kinds of experiences as long as it's within the limitation of that cup. So the possibilities and potentiality of that cup are infinite. But where is its true value coming from? It is not coming from the cup. It's not coming from the material the cup is made of. The cup could be made of porcelain, metal, or wood. It doesn't matter.

What is the true value of a cup? In fact, what is the definition of a cup? When does it stop being a cup? When does a cup lose its "cupness"? It's when it does not have any empty space. If the whole thing is filled with something and if you cannot take it out of the cup, then it's no longer a cup. The true value is its emptiness. All that we can hear, all that we can see, all that we can perceive, all our sense pleasures - when compared to the emptiness that is inside us, the silence that is inside us - are nothing. Our true value comes from silence because it is silence that allows for other experiences to happen. Without inner silence, there is no way to empty our experiences.

Once an experience happens, you cannot take it out. It just sits there. So how can you have another experience? The reason you can have multiple experiences, and listen to multiple things, is because knowingly or unknowingly something inside you is making that space. But because you are unaware, because you are unconscious, as soon as you make that space, something else is filling it. Your own mind is filling it with new ideas, new dreams, and new thoughts. Once you see that silence is the greatest thing that can add value to your being and it is the greatest of all things that are part of your nature, you will approach it differently. You will look at silence differently. You won't just think about it. You know that the experience of silence would be different. But because there's no way to argue with the mind and convince it, you need a method. You need a technique.

One of the oldest and simplest techniques that the three major religions that have sprung from India - Buddhism, Jainism, and Hinduism - have used is Om Chanting. Om Chanting is central to all three major religions. It is repeated before every worship session and chanted before uttering the name of any deity. For example, when you say "Om Namah Shivaya," you are talking about Shiva but starting with "Om."

"Om" is the starting mantra. It is the first sound of any mantra. And what is a mantra? "Man" is mind and "tra" is technique or method. Anything you use as a technique to calm the mind down, to move away from the noise and chaos of the mind, is a mantra. Similarly, if the body is a technique, any technique you use to quieten the body and move away from the sense pleasures of the body is Tantra. Similarly, there's Yantra. "Yan" is anything outside of you, and "tra" is technique. So if you're using any device, let's say you're looking at a candle flame and trying to withdraw your senses from that, that would be called "Yantra." If you're wearing a metal bracelet or anything that you believe anchors you to the outside and reminds you of the inside, that is "Yantra." So "Om" falls into the category of mantra. It is specifically used to calm the mind down.

How does chanting Om calm the mind? And what is this "Om?" Let's dive a little deeper. Although Om is recognized as a monosyllable sound, it comprises three parts. You can spell "Om" as "Aum." There's the sound. If you dissect the "Aum" sound, you'll find three distinct sounds: "ah," "ooh," and "ma." Although they occupy only a fraction of a moment, they're present if you listen closely. Now, where does the sound originate? If you close your eyes and say "Aum," feeling the vibration in your body, which part vibrates the most? You'll notice it's primarily your belly. The sound emerges from a certain depth within;

it originates from your belly. Then, as the sound continues, it seems to emanate from the heart center. When you say "oh," it doesn't reach your belly but vibrates around the heart. However, for the "m" sound, you need to go a bit deeper. Sounds aren't just symbolic notations. In ancient Hindu culture, sounds were understood as derivatives of vibrations, with each letter or word designated for the specific vibration occurring within the body.

There's "ah," there's "ooh," and there's "mmm." Now, when you pronounce "mmm" and pay attention, you'll notice it vibrates primarily in your head. So, what exactly is sound? Sound needs to resonate somewhere. For you to hear a sound as you're making it, it must resonate within a chamber; otherwise, there's no way for you to hear it. If the sound just goes straight out without coming back, there's no resonance, and you can't hear it. Vibration is essentially something that resonates within a certain space. The fact that Om chanting demonstrates there's emptiness inside you, that you're not just a solid block of muscle, is proof of this principle.

When you do chanting, it's almost like your belly is hollow inside. Inside doesn't mean inside of your body. You have to imagine an inside dimension. Similarly, when you say, "oh," it's almost like there is emptiness near your heart center, and similarly, "ma." So when you chant "Om," you're literally vibrating your entire upper body. You're not just reciting a mantra; you are vibrating with the mantra. Now, what does this do? Because the vibration is real, because you can actually feel the vibration, it takes your attention away from the mind, and that is the method. That is the technique.

MADNESS OF THE MIND

"Om" chanting is always the first thing that is prescribed in meditation. In fact, it is almost given as a medical prescription. You go to a teacher and say, "I want to learn meditation. I want to become enlightened." He'll say, "First, you are sick. First, heal your sickness. Do Om chanting. Then you can think about enlightenment. Then you can think about deeper meditation." Because your mind is so noisy. - not only noisy, but the mind is mad - it has no sense of what it is doing. It is simply regurgitating the same things. That is why they say the mind is a graveyard. There's nothing alive there. It is only showing dead things, dead experiences that are a part of your past, but your obsession is with that past. Before you can go deeper into your being, you have to first recognize the madness that is the mind, and that is the hardest part because who is there to remind the mind that it is mad?

Sound of Silence

A pair of cows were talking in the field. One says, "Have you heard about the mad cow disease that's going around?" "Yeah," the other cow says, "Makes me glad I'm a penguin."

That's the nature of the mind. It is madness. It sees the madness all around it. It talks about it. But somehow it thinks it is different. Isn't that how you treat your mind? The disease is right there. You can see it. You can see it in all others. You can see how it's driving everybody crazy. But somehow you think your mind is different, the nature of your mind is different. There's no need to control your mind. There's no need to approach it cautiously. There's no need to watch it because it's your own mind. The whole world is suffering from the Mad Cow disease, and everybody is thinking they are not that cow - "I'm not that. I'm something different." No. You're the same. You also have the same mind. You also have the same body. Maybe you have a little more awareness of what's happening and that is why you're thinking about it. That is why you're trying to get to the bottom of it. Apart from that, the madness is there. So the first thing that is prescribed is Om chanting because it shifts your awareness from the thinking dimension to the feeling dimension.

Many schools of meditation have forgotten the right way of chanting "Om" because they are not taught about the vibration. They're not told to watch the vibration. They just keep on chanting it as a verbal mantra. They think that the word "Om" itself is something significant. They don't realize the word has nothing significant in it. It is just a word. You can write it as "O m," you can write it as "A u m." You can write it with a symbol. It doesn't matter. It's the vibration it creates within you that is significant.

There was an interesting study conducted to try and understand the effect of mantras on the body - different kinds of chanting. They discovered that Om chanting affects your body. It affects your biochemistry. It affects your autonomous nervous system, including your digestion. There's something that happens when you're doing Om chanting which does not happen when you're doing any other kind of chanting. That is why chanting is not meditation. You cannot replace watchfulness and awareness with chanting, and that is what most people inadvertently do. When they start reciting a mantra, they forget that the objective of a mantra is to feel the vibration inside, and they start repeating different kinds of mantras which eventually become wish fulfillment. They start asking for things. When your mantra degenerates, that is when it becomes a prayer. When your prayer degenerates, that is when it becomes begging. You are just begging for things. You're not scientifically going deeper into the sounds and vibration. You are beginning to look at those words themselves as something significant. Scientists have not taken any of these things seriously because surrounding the science of meditation, surrounding the science of silence, there's so much stupidity, misunderstanding, mental noise, and clutter that they don't want to come anywhere near.

Scientists, however, seek uniformity. They look for the singular essence of phenomena, the definitive "one thing" that defines an experience or concept. Yet, if ten people were to describe gravity, each from their own emotional perspective, such diversity holds little appeal for a scientist. They aim to explore phenomena that stand independent of human experience. This mindset leads to a disconnect between meditation and mindfulness; the varied and often contradictory nature of individual experiences leads to the premature conclusion that participants are merely hallucinating, that there is nothing "inner" to discover. Consequently, the entirety of spiritual pursuit - be it religiousness, the quest for spirituality, awakening, or enlightenment - is dismissed. They reject figures like the Buddha, not because of a lack of validity in his experiences, which mirror those of Jesus, but because the language used to express these experiences varies greatly. For a scientist to reconcile Buddha's and Jesus's teachings - merging the concepts of the kingdom of heaven with that of nothingness - is a monumental challenge. Without direct experience of this nothingness, without personally encountering that kingdom of heaven, such reconciliation remains elusive.

This is where he simply concludes that these people were just mad. They're talking about some internal experience. There's nothing for me to explore. There's nothing for me to investigate because I want to explore those things that we all are seeing and we all agree upon so I can try and understand the nature of stuff. Because we all see the stars in pretty much the same way, I can study stars. Because we all look at plants the same way, I can investigate why plants are green because we all see the green color. Imagine if each one of us were to see a different color, then he would not inquire into that color because it's a subjective experience. That is how such simple and beautiful techniques like Om Chanting have not been a part of any scientific inquiry. But when they do conduct research, once in a while, they can see that it does something to your body because it is not just the sound, it is the vibration. And why should any vibration affect your body? Your body is not a fixed entity; it is also a part of the changing landscape of life.

Your body is a rhythm that is holding itself together, and most of your body is actually empty. It's a hollow chamber where things can resonate within, and that's it. When a vibration happens, your body heals itself. Your body relaxes. And most importantly, you are stepping away from the mind. That is the relaxation the body experiences. If you were to have a conversation with your body in private - although it is next to impossible because your mind will not allow it - if you can somehow throw the mind out and have a private conversation with the body and ask, "What is your one wish? What is that one thing you want?" The body would say, "I want to get rid of this guy, the mind. That is all I want. I am bliss. I can give you all the relaxation, all the certainty, all the bliss you're looking for. It's all right here. But this mind is the problem because he is constantly talking. He is glorifying your ego, not allowing you to come to the body.

The body is a reality but the ego is purely imagined. How does the mind nourish the ego? By constantly embellishing it, by constantly enhancing it. Every time you tell yourself something nice about yourself, without your realization, you are building your ego. "I'm smart. I'm intelligent. I am capable of this. I am this. I am that." Every time you say something like "I am this," the mind picks it up and keeps it - "Oh, this is what this creature likes." Once in a while, when you are trying to drift away from the mind onto something more existential like the body, the mind comes back with those words. "You are smart. You need to achieve this. You need to go there. What are you doing with the body?" We don't realize it, but it is that simple voice in our mind that we have to go beyond because that is our addiction.

A man walks into a bar and orders a drink. As he sits there, he hears a high-pitched voice say, "Hey, those jeans look really great on you." The man looks around but sees nothing. He then returns to his drink, thinking nothing more of it. But then a moment later, he hears the same voice again. "I really like what you have done with your hair." The man again glances around but sees nothing. Now he wonders if he should visit a doctor as he clearly seems to be hallucinating. He calms himself down, but then as he believes the voice is gone, he hears again. "You seem like an awesome person." He puts his drink down, completely scared, and looks around wildly. Still unable to find the source of the voice, he calls over to the bartender. "Hey, what's that voice I keep hearing?" The bartender replies "Those are the peanuts. They are complimentary."

That's what the mind is. It is as useless and unimportant as the free peanuts you get when you go and sit in a restaurant. We get it as a compliment. We don't want it, but it's there as a part of our mechanism. And what is its job? To compliment us - "You are this. You are that. You can do this. You can do that." And once you start entertaining those thoughts, you are naturally taken away from the simple things - silence, stillness, the vibrations of the body, the sensations of the body, enlightenment, and awakening, which are your very nature. Because the mind does not see these things and you trust the mind, you trust the compliments of the mind, you are chasing all that your mind wants you to chase. How is it that we can miss such a simple thing as silence? It's because of the mind.

Om chanting shuts the mind down. The moment you start vibrating with the sound, you cannot think about it. You are either vibrating with Om or thinking about Om or something else, so there's no way for both to be together. Hence, the student is introduced to Om chanting first. You can use it as your anchoring point for your meditation. Om chanting is one of the best ways to begin your meditation, but after a while, it is not necessary. Initially, you have to pronounce the words, you have to intone from inside, you have to connect with the vibration, and you have to do it loudly. And then slowly, you can reduce the volume, and it can become quieter and quieter. Then a day will come when you can shift it inside, and you can just intone the words inside; you don't even have to pronounce them. You can just feel the vibration in your belly, in your heart, and in your head, because the vibration is always there. You are simply using sounds to connect with it.

Once you connect with the natural vibration that's happening there, you don't need the sound. Then eventually, the chanting of Om will connect you to the real Om, the primordial sound, the first sound of the universe, the only sound of the universe, which is silence. Once you connect to that inner silence, you have found something eternal. It can never be taken away from you. It is hard to imagine the feeling of finding something that you can never lose. That would be the first thing you would have ever found in your entire experience of life that cannot be taken away from you. Everything else, all other experiences can be taken away from you, including your body. All that care, all that love, everything that you've poured into that body, and all the experiences it has given - in one moment, death can take it away. But silence can never be taken away from you. Even death cannot take silence away from you, because silence is silence. It is the sesame bun. It cannot be destroyed. It cannot be burnt. It is eternal. You can call it whatever you want, you can give it any name, but once you touch it, you know that is what you've been searching for.

Of course, there is still the journey, but at least you know you have found that first undeniable signpost that you're moving closer to yourself. Silence is the first authentic indication that you are not the body or the mind, because how can the body listen to silence? How can the mind listen to silence? The mind can only listen to noise. If you can listen to silence, then you have to be something subtler than even the silence. The body is grosser than silence. The mind is grosser than silence. So just by simple logical deduction, you can understand that you are something different. Anything subtle has to also be eternal, has to be permanent, has to be a part of you. And initially, when you touch that silence, you will not be able to recognize it as silence. When you first touch it, it just feels like another sound. Once you start connecting with it more and more, it almost feels like you're listening to a totally different kind of sound. You can hear silence like the sound of a waterfall. After a while, it is not even subtle. You can hear it with the same intensity - in fact, with even more intensity than sound. But how do you know that it's silence? Because the quality is totally different. When you touch it, you realize nothing is holding it there. There's nothing that is supporting it, and this sound is not coming from outside. It is coming from inside. Only when you experience it, you will know the qualitative difference from Om to silence and then to deeper layers of your being. But this doesn't mean that if you have not done Om chanting, if you have not connected to silence, you cannot become enlightened. Silence is an important step, but you can even bypass silence. There are meditation techniques where you don't go into the listening dimension at all. You can watch your breath and go deeper and deeper and go all the way to enlightenment without even hearing the sound of silence. Even the sound of silence has to be heard. It is still restricted to one dimension of your being. The real silence, the ultimate silence, is not just the absence of sound. It is the silence of everything. It is the silence of seeing, the silence of smelling, the silence of tasting, the silence of touching. Your whole being has become silent, including the "I" thought. That is the ultimate silence.

Om chanting is there to connect with the silence, which is the first layer beyond the mind, where you can rest without the disturbance of the mind. That is your first base camp. If you are climbing Mount Everest and you are taking the path that goes through Om chanting, that goes through listening, then the first base camp is silence. If you're doing any kind of hearing meditation or listening meditation, continue that meditation until you hear the sound of silence. So how long do I do Om chanting? Until you can hear the sound of silence. The day you're able to hear silence, then you can drop Om chanting, you can drop all chanting, and that silence itself will become the chanting. That silence itself is your mantra, and that itself is your anchoring point. From there, allow your being to take you as deep as it wants to take you without external devices. The device has done its job. You can drop it now.

WHIRLING YOUR WAY TO BLISS

The whirling dance or "sema" has to be an unusual kind of meditation because it doesn't look anything like meditation. It seems like a meditation technique that was invented by a child. He was just playing and decided to rotate, and he felt something. And that became a technique. People love to get exact steps of what to do in meditation, but what's more useful is understanding the overall atmosphere of the technique. Why was it created? Where was it created? Who created it? That is more important than just the mechanics of the technique because mechanics can be altered. Meditation allows for flexibility and individuality; you can bring your own flavor to it. If a teacher has recommended that you take ten deep breaths before going into, let's say, a dancing meditation, you can take five deep breaths. You can take fifteen deep breaths. If he says to stand still for ten minutes and then move for five minutes, then stand still again for five minutes - what is more important than the actual number is the method that he is offering: the alternation between movement and stillness. The duration is flexible. The duration is always flexible in meditation. You can meditate for thirty minutes, an hour, or one whole day.

Rumi

Meditation is too vast of a phenomenon to be restricted inside the human dimension of time. It also depends on your level of understanding of the method and your experience. The deeper your experience, the more you can play with the method, and the longer you can stay with it. Initially, when you are beginning, of course, you can stick to the guidelines. Understanding the overall context of a meditation technique is very important, and it is more so in the case of the Sufi whirling meditation. The entire essence of the meditation is in the man who created it. It is impossible to understand the Sufi whirling meditation without understanding the Sufi master Jalāl al-Dīn Muḥammad. Rumi was a mystic, a poet, and more importantly, he called himself a lover. His entire poetry is about that longing to connect with the divine. It is about transcendence, but transcendence without a method. Love itself is the method. The longing itself is the method.

When you read Rumi's poetry, even if you know nothing about meditation, if you have not been introduced to any technique, when you start reading his work, something happens in your body, something happens in your mind. That longing, that cry, that silent, primordial desire to connect with something beyond touches you. Although he's speaking from his experience, looking at the world through his eyes, the longing is so deep that you see yourself in him. That is what a poet is. He's not trying to impress you or get the attention of your mind. He's not being clever or manipulative. Just like when a child cries, you know there is no manipulation there. That is why you respond. There's no sophisticated language. There's no clear articulation of what the child wants. Yet, just the genuine longing draws your attention. That cry is a language of its own. It tells everything you have to know about the state of the child, so you go to its aid. Rumi's poems are like that. They're not structured; they move in all kinds of different dimensions, from worldly to the otherworldly, from the mind to the body, and he doesn't even care to hold a certain structure. Yet, you cannot miss the longing in his heart.

Rumi met a wandering dervish by the name of Shams, Shams of Tabrizi. He was a mystic, a meditator. Rumi was so intoxicated by this man's level of understanding of life, and his connectedness with existence, that Rumi decided to become a mystic himself, and he dedicated all his poems to Shams of Tabrizi. In fact, his love for existence is sometimes dwarfed by his love for Shams. Now and then, he comes back and talks about Shams of Tabrizi and how he's dedicating these songs to him. Longing is a prerequisite for meditation. A method is useful. Without longing, a method is useless. You can be given the perfect technique and the exact structure, but if you don't understand the overall context of the meditation and how to see it like the one who created it, you will be missing something because all meditation techniques come from a certain depth, from a certain understanding. They're not just arrangements; they belong. Let us start with a few of Rumi's words because that's where the essence of whirling meditation lies. Once you understand the man, once you understand his poetry, once you get the taste of what he is speaking about - what is this longing, why don't I have this longing, and why is his longing so deep and so intoxicating - then you will understand his method, his meditation.

Rumi says, "What is the body? That shadow of a shadow of your love, that somehow contains the entire universe. Language and music are possible only because we are empty, hollow, and separate from the source. All language is a longing for home." He has laid it out. He has condensed the entire human experience, which is intricately connected to language, to longing. Psychologists, scientists, and archaeologists have all tried to understand: What is language? Where does it come from? What is the purpose of language? Who created language? There are all kinds of interpretations.

Music and Language

There's an interpretation that I particularly like, which says there was a time before civilization as we identify it now. People were mostly hunter-gatherers, living a nomadic lifestyle, but they were not always moving. They moved and settled in a place, and as long as there were resources for them to consume, such as animals to hunt, they stayed there for as long as they could.

There is a reason for this. Although we often look at human history purely from a man's perspective, if you consider it from a woman's point of view, staying in one place makes much more sense for her when she's carrying a baby or nursing a baby. It does not make sense for her to always be moving. She has to be in one place. It is dangerous for her to keep on moving. So, it is more than likely that even nomadic tribes settled for a while. During these settlements, men would go out to hunt, and women were left behind at the dwelling to take care of the children and other members of the community.

There's a theory that language was created by women because men were away hunting, and they had to remain silent during the hunt. They did not have to create words, language, or sophisticated expressions. Human history suggests that men remained a little more primitive than women for a longer time. Jewelry, art, and other creative endeavors are first associated with women. That is why you can trace the source of almost all creative endeavors back to women. Then why not language?

It is very much possible that women started experiencing something inside them because they were alone. Even though they were with their kids, they were not out hunting, allowing them to relax. They didn't have to be as tense as men, who were taking care of crucial aspects like food and safety. Women had the opportunity to connect with themselves more, and in that connection, love and longing came naturally to them. Existence is feminine, so somewhere, women would have seen the connection between themselves and existence. When they wanted to express that connection, they would have created symbols.

Of course, initially, it's all verbal. Written text comes much, much later in human civilization, so she would have started either singing or identifying certain things that she's experiencing inside through unique words. And from there, human language evolved. In a way, Rumi's interpretation supports the idea that language is not a social activity. It wasn't created to enhance communication between individuals or to improve hunting or building. It had nothing to do with civilization or expressing intentions and desires to each other. It makes sense only when you bring that deep spiritual longing. That is what gives rise to the sophistication of language because the deeper the longing, the stronger the longing, the more words you need. Otherwise, you don't need so many words.

It is only when there is pain of separation that the mind explodes in all kinds of ways of trying to connect with what it is missing. Rumi says, "We are away from home, and we are longing for home. We're longing to come back," and that is what poetry is. That is what music is. That is what language is. And, more importantly, the human body has to be empty. It has to be hollow inside. It has to be missing something to accommodate music and language.

Language is what reminds you of the longing. Language is what helps you communicate that longing to someone. Language is what carries forward that desire, so the one who has forgotten, the one who is living totally oblivious to what he's missing, is given the taste of what he's missing. Without language, it is impossible to communicate, in any meaningful way, that something is stirring inside me, something is missing - I want to experience it. Normal emotions are not enough. Normal expressions are not enough, because normal expressions are to express emotions that are happening here and now - experiencing pain, happiness, and hunger. That's about it. But poetry immediately transports you to a different time and realm. That is why poetry has very little to do with daily activities. That is boring poetry. If poetry is about what you eat, what you hunted today, what was your daily activity like, it would be missing all that deep longing.

The purpose of poetry is to momentarily take you out of your ego. As Rumi says, "When the grape skin of the ego breaks, the pouring begins." Fermentation is one of the oldest symbols of human transformation. Throughout this poetry, you hear references to a tavern and wine intoxication, and he refers to the body itself as a grape, and the ego as the grape skin. That is how thin - that is how flimsy the ego is. But unless the skin breaks, fermentation cannot happen. You can have all kinds of grapes together. You can put them in the cellar and wait for them to ferment, but the fermentation does not begin until the skin breaks. The skin is what keeps all that intoxication inside.

So, in a way, it is our ego that makes us dry, dull, and boring in our interactions with people because it's not the interaction of the intoxicated selves, but the interaction of egos. That is why we find it hard to understand someone, to go deep into them, and connect with them. Mostly, it's the conversation between two minds. That is why it seems there's nothing useful, nothing meaningful, or deep to explore.

When you can transcend that ego, when your longing becomes strong enough, then the fermentation begins. There's something beautiful about the reference to fermentation. When you drink, you wobble. Your mind and body are intoxicated - they're disoriented. But at the same time, you're also reminded of something deeper. Everybody who has become intoxicated knows something happens in intoxication that they cannot explain. They keep going back to it again and again. They don't understand what it is that they've experienced that they want to experience again and again. Rumi says, that for that brief moment, when you were intoxicated, your ego was transcended and you had an opportunity to get a glimpse of your deeper self, although momentarily.

In fact, for Rumi, a tavern is almost like a temple. You go there to dissolve your ego to connect with something higher. For the one who knows the art of intoxication, he does not need wine. He can turn the very air around him into wine. He does not even need water. In fact, this is the meaning of Jesus' words of turning water into wine. Water is a reference to something ordinary, a daily routine - there's nothing special about it. It's just water. You can turn even simple, dull, boring momentary existence into an intoxication, into a deep intoxication. That is what is the reference to wine. Well, Christians got it wrong. If they had seen the symbolic meaning, if only they had asked, "Wait a minute. Turning water into wine. Could it be poetry?" If it is poetry, then it makes perfect sense. In poetry, we use similes, metaphors, and allegories to compare one thing to another, to explain something that we cannot readily explain. Maybe that is what he's talking about. Maybe this man was a poet. Let us read his verses as if it is coming from a poet. Every word will make sense then.

All your interpretations will be proven wrong because a poet's words can never be interpreted literally. He's drunk. He's intoxicated. How can he speak straight? But you can connect with his longing, so when he says you can turn water into wine, in a simple poetic way, he's saying you can turn your ordinary life into an intoxication. You can turn pain and suffering into ecstasy just by understanding your body, understanding your mind, going deeper, and connecting with yourself. If you do this without any fear of losing the body, if this longing is deep enough, and if you connect to that inner child within you, you won't just step out of your house. You'll run into the street. You will start whirling. You won't speak because you're a child. You won't explain. You'll say, "Let me just rotate." It is a natural outflowing of that longing and, more importantly, of surrender.

To understand the whirling devilish meditation, to practice it - the word "practice" is not the right word for the whirling dervish meditation - to dissolve in it, to merge in it, to lose yourself in it - you have to get into it with that surge of longing inside. Then you can understand the movement. You can understand how to rotate. You can understand why the body assumes that posture.

If you look at a whirling dervish, there are a few things that you can notice, which will be present in all the variations of the whirling meditation. One is the movement. There is no hurry. There is no counting of steps. There is no keeping track of how many times you've rotated. There's no method, nothing. You only see a rotation - initially slowly, and then it becomes faster and faster. And then it reaches a point where it becomes pure poetry. There's no effort. There's no force. The rotation is just happening by itself. And they usually wear long gowns that whirl in the air, giving you that impression of waves. It's almost like more than the body that is moving. It is the clothes that create that beautiful, mesmerizing waving motion.

Even the clothes they wore for that meditation reflected their inner state. They didn't wear something tight and restricting. They wore something that could freely flow in the air because as that cloth moved in the air, it gave them that sense of the body also moving. The body is not rigid. It's not fixed.

Rumi himself says the body is just the longing for love. It's empty. It's hollow. You're just allowing the body to wave without any conscious effort. The head is always tilted to one side. The head is not straight. It's almost like "I am in surrender." When you surrender, your head tilts. You don't keep it straight and stiff. You have to look at a whirling dervish to understand what I'm talking about. The hands fling out or they keep it on their chest, and they rotate. None of this is a method, but when the longing is deep, the body automatically assumes a certain posture. There's no point in trying to imitate the body movements from the outside. If you try to just copy the movement without understanding the inner process, you will be stuck in a certain posture. And when your body wants to release and wants to move in a certain different way, you will not allow it because you will fear that you're moving away from the method - you're moving away from the technique. But when you understand the inner state the body is in, you will understand why they're always silent.

When the whirling dervish comes to the stage, he's accompanied by only two things: Music and silence. Music for the body, silence for his spirit. He wants to be silent throughout the practice. Throughout that longing, how can you long using words? Words are inadequate. Words can only express your longing, but when you're actually longing, words are useless. You have to be silent, but the body needs the cues to move. How much to move? How to move? That is synchronized by the music, and Sufi music is beautifully integrated with the whirling meditation. The kind of instruments they use: a reed flute and a simple one-stringed instrument with simple rhythmic tones, nothing harsh, nothing discordant - just simple rhythmic longing. Over some time, your body gets tuned to the music, and then it automatically moves in its own rhythmic way. But you have to be silent and still inside.

WHIRLING

A Sufi, a dervish, can whirl for as long as he wants without getting dizzy. Now, something is interesting here. If you try to rotate, the first thing that you will experience is dizziness. If you rotate for any longer than, let's say, two minutes or three minutes, you will fall. Now, how is it that a dervish can whirl without getting dizzy? It's a form of dance, and they can whirl for hours together if they want. And at the end of that whirling, they can just stop whenever they want, and without wobbling, without shaking, they can just walk away. How is this possible?

Scientists say that the dizziness happens because of the loss of balance. The explanation is that the mechanism that controls the balance of the human body is inside our ears. There are canals inside the ear filled with liquid lined by tiny hairs which send a signal to the brain about the posture of the body. So when you rotate, you are sending conflicting signals to the brain, and the liquid is moving, creating disorientation. But this is only one explanation of balance. This does not explain why after repeating the process to make yourself dizzy many times, the dizziness disappears. The explanation is that eventually, the mind gets adjusted. The brain gets adjusted to all this movement and it stops getting dizzy. But that isn't a satisfactory explanation. Why should the brain get adjusted? There is a deeper spiritual understanding.

When you start rotating, you initially feel dizzy because there is no separation between you and the body. You are fully identified with the body. You have not gone deeper into the meditation of whirling to separate yourself from the body. That's what meditation is. You go deeper where there is some distance between your body and your self, and your self is always still. Because you have not gone through the journey, you are your body. So when your body rotates, your identification with the body is so strong that you feel that sense of dizziness. The body is experiencing dizziness, but you will also experience it.

Why does this disappear? Once you start practicing, it disappears because slowly over some time, you can move to the center of your being. And eventually, there will come a point where you are totally disconnected from the body. You don't feel any dizziness because you are always still. It is the body that is moving. It is the body that is rotating. Only when you experience that moment from inside, a moment where everything disappears, the whirling disappears. The music disappears. If someone is sitting and watching you whirling, they disappear. The whole universe disappears. What remains when everything is gone?

When all the movement is gone, including the movement of the mind, something remains. That something cannot be spoken about. That something cannot be put into words. That something can only be experienced. In fact, the only way to experience it is to simply be it or become it. That is the part of you that experiences everything. So you are at the very source of experiencing. You have finally come home. That was your longing.

If you understand Rumi's words, you will understand the whirling meditation. The whirling is the silent cry of the heart. It is almost like looking up to the sky and saying, "Take me away. Release me from this body. I'm not going to do anything that I do during my normal day. I'm going to just rotate. I'm going to lose all my orientation. I'm going to lose my sense of up and down, left and right. I am willing to disorient my body. Take me to the other realm. What more can I do to prove to you that I'm not interested in the body? Everything else I do somehow shows that I'm only interested in the body. Even if I walk to the edge of the cliff and jump off, I am still doing something with the body. It is still me who's choosing to go stand at the edge of the cliff and jump off."

In whirling, you are at that perfect balance where you just don't care for the body. You don't think about it. You don't look at it as the vehicle to take you to a higher realm nor as an obstacle. You simply are in a mode of surrender. And why whirling? Why not sleeping? Because if you sleep, you are in a deeper surrender. But the problem is, who's there to watch when the awakening happens? You are asleep. That is why the whirling. That is why it is meditation. Whirling meditation is just pure poetry in motion. You have to approach it like a poet. Method, technique, and structure should be as minimal as possible. And it should all be set before you begin your meditation. Once you begin your meditation, you should forget all about the structures that the mind has created and simply dive into the practice.

THE TECHNIQUE

Make sure initially, even if you fall, you don't hurt yourself much. Start whirling in a place where you know you are safe, and make sure there are not many things around you that you can bump into. Because initially when you begin practicing, you will feel dizzy. You will fall. You will sway and swing. So accommodate for all that. But over a period of time, the dizziness disappears. Then begins the true enjoyment of meditation. Now you're not getting disoriented; now you're able to watch.

Imagine every day, every time you go into this meditation, you're watching the body move, you're watching the body rotate. And then slowly the energy starts moving toward the watcher. Initially, you are too interested in watching the body, so all your awareness is on the body. After a while, the awareness shifts to the watching itself. Now slowly, day by day, the watcher is becoming more and more primary. The watching and the watched are moving to the periphery until that day comes when the whirler is somewhere far away on the edges of your consciousness. The one who's whirling, the one who's watching the whirling, is right at the center, and that center is filling a vast landscape. It is not a single point. That point has expanded to being an entire realm. Outside this realm, somewhere someone is rotating. You can see the shadows of the body. That is when you'll understand Rumi's words, "What is the body, if not for the shadow of the shadow of your love." And what is love? That entire realm is love. You are love. Stillness is love. Silence is love. When there are no words, nothing to express, nothing to long for, that is love. All that you recognize as human is far away on the periphery. You are love.

And then one moment will come when even that periphery will disappear. For somebody sitting and watching, there is the whirling - there's the one who's whirling. But for the one who's inside, everything has disappeared. He has transcended the human plane just by rotating. A simple method filled with deep longing transcended him from the limited plane of human experiences to a higher realm of pure bliss and joy.

TANTRIC SEX

If there can be any meditation that can be regarded as important, as simple, and as scientific as Buddha's watching the breath meditation, it has to be tantric sexual meditation. Sex is as natural to the human body as breathing. It is one other dimension through which the human mind, the human body finds its release. The body is a closed entity. A few things are very important to understand about the body. The body is not open to the experiences happening either inside or outside by its own will. If you leave the body by itself without the intervention of your awareness, without bringing your thoughts and desires into the picture, the body simply shuts down. It revolves around a few very basic processes and even then, it goes on withdrawing its energies. It starts consuming less and less; it starts moving less and less. It loses the desire to repair itself. Eventually, it just becomes useless. When I say the body is a closed entity, what I mean is by itself, the body is closed.

There is something else, some other energy that interacts with the body that makes it open. And again, it's not open all the time - it's open during certain experiences. It is most open during an orgasm. Why? Because orgasm is not an experience. There is a lot of misunderstanding about sex and orgasm, which is what has completely perverted our understanding of these two most basic processes of life.

First, anything natural that is not forced on you, that is not added on to you, has to serve some purpose. And it has to be useful to your being in some way. Nothing is unnecessary in the body. All the biological processes aid the body in performing at its optimal level, repairing itself, taking care of itself. If something is rejected, it can only be done artificially from the outside, unnaturally. And forceful repression of sex is an outside phenomenon that tries to suppress the energies that want to find a natural outlet from the body. Repression never works because you are damaging the body, you're damaging the mind in the process by closing the doors of a body that is already closed.

Orgasm

Sex is one of those rare methods through which the body finds a release. If you don't allow that release, if you don't understand it, you are damaging the body, and more importantly, you're damaging your mind. There have been innumerable psychological studies conducted. Sigmund Freud, in particular, did extensive studies on the influence of sex, the symbolisms of sex, the desire for sex, and how it manifests in the mind and the body. One very important thing he discovered was that repression of sex leads to all kinds of psychological problems. In fact, right from childhood, through the interpretation of dreams, he was able to see some of the most painful parts of the human mind, around which the entire personality of that being revolved, was centered around the repression of sex.

Why is it? Why should sex be such an important outlet? When it is messed with, when it is meddled with, when it is not understood, it can lead to all kinds of psychological problems. Because sex is not only one of the outlets through which the body finds its release, it is the only outlet through which it finds the ultimate release, and we have termed this a "moment of orgasm." You experience something. It's pleasurable. It's blissful. At least you know that it is an experience you want to have again and again, hence the craving for sex. But if you understand orgasm, you will see that it is not an experience at all. Now why isn't it an experience? What is an experience in the first place?

For something to be regarded as an experience, it has to pass through one of our five senses. You have to either see, hear, touch, smell, or taste it. Everything we experience in the world is experienced through our five senses. Orgasm is the only such thing that we experience without the help of any of our senses. You cannot see an orgasm. You cannot hear an orgasm. What you are seeing and hearing is the organism, not the orgasm. You cannot touch it. You cannot smell it. You cannot taste it. All five senses are totally incapable of experiencing orgasm. Then what is it that you are experiencing?

You are a physical body completely bound by the limitations of the senses. Everything you experience in life, you know how you're experiencing - you know through which sense it is passing. Now here is something that is totally beyond your understanding, beyond your explanation, and you simply call it an experience because you don't know what else to call it. In fact, orgasm is that moment when all experiencing ceases. One step ahead, even the experiencer ceases to be in that moment. It is not something that is happening to your body. It is not that you're touching one pleasure center in your body. It is the complete release of the body. It is the complete release of the ego, the complete release of the mind. It is that only moment when you are not there.

In all other moments, there is you interfering with the experience, and that is why no other experience can come anywhere close to giving you that experience that you have during an orgasm. There is not even a comparison. You can try all kinds of things to try to replicate that experience. You can use drugs. You can use alcohol. You can jump out of a plane. You can do whatever you want, but you will never experience orgasmic ecstasy because you are striving to experience it, and your senses are acting as mediators between you and what you're experiencing. In a way, orgasm is that pure experience, the purity of which is a testimony to the fact that you are not interfering with that process. That is why it is so pure.

Now, what do I mean by pure? By pure, I mean it has nothing to do with you, your mind, or your body. You have accidentally fallen into a realm. You've been given a glimpse of the beyond. Orgasm is that moment when you are touching a dimension other than the three-dimensional world that you're experiencing. Yes, you are experiencing it inside you, but you're not experiencing it inside your body, and your mind is nowhere there. Your mind freaks out, and about the time you're getting close to orgasm, it just disappears. Your body shivers in that moment.

If you pay closer attention, you will see that they both know something that you don't know. That is why they are trembling. That is why they're trying to run away from the experience. There is something else that is pushing you toward the experience, but your mind and body fear the experience. Why? Because orgasm is the only moment in your worldly experience where your mind and body both die. It is the death of the mind. It is the death of the body. After that, the mind comes back. The body comes back, but they're not the same. An individual before orgasm and after orgasm are two completely different individuals. Something has given way to the natural flow of the mind and body. Something has suddenly stopped it, reminding it of its transient, ephemeral, fleeting nature, and it is only a glimpse. It is a glimpse of the beyond. It is a glimpse of your true self. It is a glimpse of your awakened nature. It is a glimpse of enlightenment. Orgasm is that moment when without meditation, without going through years of meditative self-transformation - if there's any shortcut through which you can be given a glimpse of the beyond - it is orgasm. It is right there within us. It is too powerful of a phenomenon. That is why it has been subjected to all kinds of misunderstanding, all kinds of suppression because it is the seat of religiousness. It is the seat of the search of Man. All that religions have been preaching against, orgasm nullifies in a single moment. How can an experience of heaven be any more blissful than the experience of orgasm? Imagine if you were to tell someone, "I'll take you to heaven, but you can never have sex. You will never experience this orgasmic ecstasy. You will experience all kinds of other things." You would say, "I don't want it." If you truly understand bliss and the nature of bliss, they cannot be two different things.

There can only be one type of bliss. Bliss cannot be graded. Other emotions can be graded because there's a filtering process happening. Either you know bliss or you don't. You know bliss through sex. Then how is it that someone can promise you a greater bliss? No. They can't promise that to you. They can only guide you to that place where that one single momentary bliss can be extended beyond a single moment. That is what meditation is. That's what mindfulness is. That is what awakening is, where what you're searching for is the same orgasmic bliss, but you're searching for it consciously. You're creating conscious pathways to get to it so that you can go there whenever you want, and you can stay there for as long as you want. You can find the ultimate release that is not dependent on either your body or another body, but what you're searching for is hidden in sex. By understanding sex, by understanding orgasm, you can find one other way of getting to that bliss. You can turn sex into meditation.

Marriage

If you go back in time and look at the entire ritual of marriage, the union of male and female, all the ceremonies connected to that union, the very purpose of two individuals coming together in a relationship was to stay together, explore each other so that they both can attain spiritual liberation. Otherwise, think about it, there is no necessity for marriage. Why do you have to get married for sex? Animals don't get married and they have sex. They find a natural outlet through the body. So what was the necessity for two human beings to stay together longer than the duration of sex? It's because you have to stay together longer to understand each other. You have to explore each other to be able to transcend this plane of existence. Marriage was a pure form of meditation. Of course, over time, that whole idea completely degenerated into just a ritual. "Oh, everybody is getting married. We have to get married." And then, because sex was repressed from the outside, marriage became the only way through which you can have sex. Then the whole meaning of marriage and sex completely changed. What was supposed to be a spiritual endeavor of knowing each other, understanding each other, helping each other connect with that unlimited bliss that exists inside both of you, became just a means to have sex because it was prohibited on the outside. The whole idea was twisted and turned, and it became so confusing that after a point, people stopped inquiring into the nature of sexual union. Because what is there to inquire? "I want to get married so that I can have sex. And I know what sex is. It is pleasurable, and I'm going back to it again and again."

After a while, it gets boring, and then you get disinterested. It's the same process everybody goes through. What is there to inquire here? There is a lot to inquire. First, the idea that marriage is social has to be dropped. Socially, marriage has no value whatsoever. It is an agreement. It is a contract. It is meant for a certain external purpose. Two individuals don't have to get married to experience the social comforts, but two people have to come together and stay longer than the desires of sex. When the pleasures are satisfied, you have to stay longer for an understanding as a way of transcending the mind and the body - to look at sex as a meditation. So when we move away from marriage as a social activity and look at the union of the male and the female purely as an interplay of energies, we can understand a lot about the necessity for two human beings to come together, and the right way of coming together, the right way of understanding each other. This alone can totally renew the understanding of marriage. This is the only understanding through which marriage makes sense. Because literally, the word "marriage" means something is getting combined. It's a union.

That is why we don't use the word "arrangement." Socially, it has become an arrangement, but the word "marriage" still retains its authentic meaning - that is, it is a union. So the man is using the energies of the female, and the female is using the energies of the man in a way, to neutralize each other's energies to a point where they can completely disappear. If you can look at sex as purely a play of energies, then you are just looking at the masculine energy and the feminine energy. Let's say we call the feminine energy positive, and the masculine energy negative. For whatever reason, that is how I chose to describe it. Let's say they come together, and just like any two forces in nature, when the positive and the negative come, there's an explosion. First, they are drawn to each other - they're attracted to each other. Let's not go into other kinds of sexual unions. As of now, let's talk about the general understanding that a male is attracted to a female and a female is attracted to a male. Now, why a male is attracted to a male and why is a female attracted to a female, is another topic of discussion. So there is the positive and there is the negative, and there is an attraction, and they come together. And then there is the play of energies - there's the exploration of energies. Sex has very little to do with the body. Bodies are only being utilized. There's something else that has taken over that process. Looking at sex purely as a bodily function, it is a way of deriving pleasure out of each other's bodies and is what leads to all kinds of perversion in sex. Misunderstanding of sex is what leads to clinging to the body.

Let me make it very clear: sex is not porn. Porn is a complete deviation and perversion of sex. If sex is divine, if sex is sacred, porn is useless because the first assumption in porn is there's no love. There's no union. There is no marriage. There is no intermingling of hearts or spirits. Only two bodies are doing whatever they are doing. It is ugly because something very sacred is missing.

Why is a union between a man and a female - when there is love - why is it so beautiful? Why is it so soft? Why is it so rhythmic? It's almost like listening to a song. Two people in love, making love to each other, it's just like listening to a nice melodious song. There's rhythm. There's waving. There's vibration. There's connection, there's embrace, there's so much happening there. But on the other hand, in porn, there is nothing but aggression. In every move, in every action, one is trying to gobble up the other. And senselessly for what? Because your entire idea of sexuality has moved to your mind. Now in your mind, whatever you're doing to that other body, you are possessing it. The more you're able to do, in different ways, it is satisfying your ego, which is an opposite process.

In sexual union, in tantric sexual union, the entire objective is to go beyond your egos. But in porn, it is about satisfying the ego. That is what makes these two things totally different. Sex is divine; it has to be approached with a certain reverence. You cannot be in a hurry, and you cannot approach it without love. If there is no love, then sex is equivalent to porn. And the love has to be on both sides. For it not to be possessive, it is not enough for the man to say, "I love the woman. So if I'm having sex with her, then it is sexual union." No. You are an idiot. There is no sexual union happening there. For union, both energies have to come together. There has to be consent, an agreement, an arrangement, and a deep understanding that we are not just interested in each other's bodies. We are interested in something deeper. In a way, you're going to the woman and asking, "Can you help me to connect with myself? And I'll help you to connect with yourself." The moment you approach sex as a meditation to help each other connect with your inner selves, the entire quality of it changes. How can you be in a hurry to help each other? "Let's do it quickly. I want to help you as quickly as possible." It just doesn't make sense. Everything slows down. You prepare for the experience. You make arrangements. It could be lighting incense, a candlelight, or using flowers.

If you look into ancient Hindu scriptures discussing sexual union, the elaborate preparation that goes into it may amaze the modern man, wondering why so much time is spent. "Ultimately, I just want to experience that release. I want to touch that orgasmic zone. That's about it. I'm just using another body." This is a completely modern way of looking at sex. The authentic spiritual perspective is that it is your meditation time. Therefore, you cannot be in a hurry, possessive, or aggressive. Once that approach is clarified, you don't have to go into the details of positions or what is allowed and what is not allowed. All these considerations come into play when the basic approach is missed, when the fundamental purpose of entering sexual union is overlooked. That is when rules and restrictions are deemed necessary. Perversion starts when you deviate from the ultimate purpose that sex is sacred and you're helping each other transcend your egos. It is about expanding your consciousness, awareness, being in the present moment, and forgetting your past and who you are as a person.

Love is that moment when your ego is gone. This is why we call it "love." Something has captivated you so much, drawn your energies so much toward it that you are no longer important. Your mind, body, thoughts, and desires have been pushed to the side. True love clears out the pathway for something else. In sexual union, love clears out the ego, creating the necessary space for the union to happen. The union cannot occur in a cluttered mind, and certainly not in a mind filled with various ideas about sex. If the mind is attempting to satisfy itself through sex, that is a deviation and perversion of sex. The mind has no place in sex; it is the first thing, like Indian slippers, that you leave outside the house before entering. This is when it becomes a sacred experience. When you drop your mind, the way you look at the other person, touch them, and make yourself available to them, - everything changes. There is no clashing of two minds; there is just a flow of energies. At the end of the day, what is the body? It is just an extension of existential energy, an accumulation of energy in a recognizable form. Otherwise, the body is pure energy. This is why two different types of energies can come together, annihilate each other, and experience orgasmic bliss, as the body is just energy. The mind is also energy, but it is a manipulative energy that can turn and twist things to create its own world of thoughts.

Dr. Parker, the biology instructor at a posh suburban girl's junior college said during class, "Miss Smith, would you please name the organ of the human body which under the appropriate conditions expands to six times its normal size and define the conditions."

Miss Smith gasped, blushed deeply, then said, freezingly, "Doctor Parker, I do not think that this is a proper question to ask me. You should be asking a boy and I assure you my parents will hear of this."

With that, she sat down very red-faced. Unperturbed, doctor Parker called on Miss Johnson and asked the same question. Miss Johnson, with composure, replied, "The pupil of the eye, in dim light."

"Correct," said Dr. Parker. "And now, Miss Smith, I have three things to say to you. One, you have not studied your lesson. Two, you have a dirty mind, and three, you will someday be faced with a dreadful disappointment."

SEX ON THE MIND

Sex cannot be on the mind; you cannot be thinking about sex all the time. The reason sex has moved to the mind is because we have totally misunderstood it. It is such a fundamental force, such a fundamental energy that is meant to give you a glimpse of the beyond. It is too powerful a phenomenon. When you try to suppress it, curb that energy, it finds outlets in ways you cannot even imagine. This is what we see in the world - the repression of sex leading to the sexualization of society.

Osho says that the mind of Man is brimming with sex. Wherever he goes, whatever he sees, is reminding him of sex. He is right. This is because he has forgotten the entire process, forgotten that it is a meditation. You cannot think or dwell on your meditation when you're not actively meditating. You might love your meditation, be addicted to it, and have gone so deep that when you sit in meditation, you don't feel like getting up at all. Despite all that, in your natural life, when interacting with people and engaging with the world, you're not constantly thinking about meditation. You're not looking at everything around you and saying, "How do I turn that into meditation?" This is because it is not a possessive desire; you know how to go there when necessary and there's no need to think about it all the time. When you want to go into meditation, you can go as deep as you want.

Only when sex is looked at as a meditation can it drop from the mind. There is no other possibility of ridding the human mind of sex other than turning the entire practice, the entire ritual of sex, into a meditation. The possibilities are there because the desire is there, and you also know that something spectacular is waiting for you to experience at the end. Unlike most meditations where you have to spend years before getting the first glimpse, here you get the glimpse in the first session itself. So you don't need external justifications to pursue the path; it's already there. All you have to do is approach it in the right way - use each other's bodies to connect with that center. Orgasm is not an experience; it is just a moment when you are touching a zone where your mind, body, and everything happening in the world are pushed out. In that zone, there is only pure existence, and that is what you experience as bliss. It is a moment of pure perception of life with nothing obstructing you.

Once you start moving consciously into sex, once you become watchful and aware of the process, slowly it starts dropping from your mind. Now you understand that whatever you're thinking about sex is not what sex is. Sex is not possession, dominance, control, or an ego-defying endeavor. The reason sex is in the mind is that it is an ego-satisfying endeavor. For most people, they find justifications for their existence, for the existence of their egos, through sex. If you were to take away the possibility of sex from their lives, their whole purpose, the meaning of life, disappears. Why are you working hard? Why are you earning money? Why do you want to be famous? At the center of it, at the base of it, is sex. The whole of humanity is driven by the desire for sex. It is the energy of sex that we see manifested in so many different ways, and yet, we have not gone any deeper into understanding this force, hence the state of the world.

Hence, the root - if I have to use the word "root" - of all evil in the world is the perversion of sex. In one form or another, Man becomes violent when he does not understand sex. Repressed sexual desires make him violent. A man or a woman who has found sex as a doorway to bliss and has learned how to enter the process consciously would be the most beautiful, most loving, most compassionate, genuine, childlike creatures. There is no reason now for all the mental perversions. There is no reason for the ego because you have found the ultimate. Once you have found the ultimate, once you know how to go to that ultimate, then the whole world will simply look like small bypasses to get to the same thing.

It is a misunderstanding that has taken Man on ambitious journeys, on unwanted trails. The simple understanding is that what you are searching for is right here within you, and you have experienced it. You only have to understand it. That alone can remove almost all negativity, violence, hatred, jealousy, and frustration from the world. That's where it starts. Repression of sex is the seed of violence. That is what weaves and becomes something else. If you study violence, if you study violent groups and their behaviors, you can always trace it back to repressing sex. One of the most violent institutions of Man is religion, and there is a connection between religion and the repression of sex. We don't have to go too far. Religions have been the most violent, and they have been most repressive toward sex. Right there is proof that the more perverted your understanding of sex, the more you try to curb it, the more you try to build walls around it, it will find an outlet in some other way. And that is what has happened.

As a method, as a practice, the only thing you should be bringing in apart from the reverence, the sacredness to sex, is not being in a hurry to jump into orgasm. If you are in a hurry, you are not creating the pathways. You are running so fast, not looking at the signposts. You won't know next time if you want to experience the same thing. You won't know where to go because you have just rushed to it blindly. Conscious movement, conscious journey into the exploration of sexuality is what tantra is all about. And look at the beauty of the word. "Tan" is body, "tra" is technique. Tantra is just a way of using your body as a technique to transcend the body. It is a simple, beautiful, scientific method of getting to your ultimate nature, experiencing that ultimate, which is beyond your mind, beyond your body - your true self.

Dancing with Shadows

Taranga Meditation

Move your head and connect with your inner stillness. It is a meditation technique that gives you enough room to play with the idea of movement and stillness. It is a technique that dispels one of the biggest myths - that you're sitting in your head, that you are your head. The head is not the head of your being. It is not the pinnacle of your being; it has never been, except in your imagination, your books, concepts, and theories. In reality, you have always been somewhere else. Moving away from the head is, in a way, moving away from death and toward life. There are two kinds of death: One is the absolute annihilation of something, the end of something, and the other is when something is hidden. It can be so hidden from you that it is as good as dead. If your life is hidden from you, if the source of your life is hidden from you, you can have it, but still, it is as good as being dead to it because you don't know where it is. There cannot be a bigger travesty than to think that everything you are - your aliveness, your ability to perceive the world, your emotions, your love, your connection with existence, and everything that you see around you - is somehow happening inside a meatball inside that tiny head. For an individual, this is a tragedy.

Don't Compromise on Truth

When an individual is everything, everywhere, when they are the very pulsating heartbeat of the universe, to think that they're stuck in their head has to be the biggest of tragedies. What does being stuck in the head do? You can be a universal phenomenon. You can see the connection between everything. But that simple idea that you're stuck in your head disconnects you from everything. I would love to quote a line from "Atlas Shrugged" by Ayn Rand. She says, "In any compromise between food and poison, it is only death that can win. In any compromise between good and evil, it is only evil that can profit." I say that in any compromise between death and life, it is always death that wins. There cannot be any compromise in your understanding of yourself. If you compromise even a bit, if you don't search for your ultimate self, your true self, if you decide to stay somewhere in the middle - "I'm okay with this much understanding. I'm okay with the idea that I'm just stuck in my head. I'm okay with the idea that I'm just a limited body because that is all I experience. There's nothing more to it" - any compromise in your search for truth, death wins.

The search for truth is a matter of life and death. Either you will find life, or you will die. There is no compromise there. Either you will get to your ultimate being, live as consciousness, as aliveness, as an eternal being, or you will die as a body, limited in darkness. And death is not the end of the mind. Your body dies, but that unconsciousness, that unawareness continues as another life, more darkly, because at least with the body, there was an opportunity for you to search for the light. You were searching for it. But now that you don't have the body, you might have to resume your search again. Yes, if you have continued your search, the tendency of searching stays with you, and your search continues. Death is not the absolute end of your misery. When death wins, it does not just win by ending things; it wins by taking you right back to the beginning of your search. You have to start your search again. You have to find yourself again.

If you have never meditated, if you have never turned inward, then you are starting right from scratch. For all you know, you might never find that guide. You might never find a teacher. You might never find the pathway again. But if you have started your search and for whatever reason your search was cut short in this lifetime, the tendencies of searching, the memory of searching, identifying the landscape of meditation will continue. That is the only thing that continues after death. That little bit of silence that has seeped inside you. That little bit of stillness that has seeped inside you. That is your only possession. That is the only thing you can carry forward after death. All your accomplishments, whatever it is you've achieved in this life, mean nothing. When the body goes, everything goes with it. Only that which is not restricted to the body continues. And what is that one thing that does not belong to the body, that belongs to you, that continues after your death? It is stillness. Stillness cannot be a part of the body. Why? What is your human body if not for movement, if not for change? When the body is perfectly still, when nothing is moving there, when there is no search, when there is no agitation or disturbance, where is the body? If you were to just sit, close your eyes, and connect to that inner stillness, notice how your body just disappears. There is no necessity for the body to be there.

Playing with Stillness

When you learn to play with these ideas, you can break the boundaries. When you start doing things like sitting in meditation and suddenly start moving your head, it might seem totally nonsensical. If somebody is sitting and watching you, they might wonder what you are doing. Have you lost it? It will seem very unscientific. In fact, if you were to tell a scientist, "I'm actually trying to connect with my inner stillness by shaking my head," they'd say, "Are you crazy? Go do something else." A scientist does not understand what's happening on the inside. Their business is outside. Even when they try to go inside things, they're still going inside the outside of things. They're never going inside the inside. They're never connecting with the inner dimension because they don't even believe that it exists. For them, outside is everything. That is why Immanuel Kant says, "Science is organized knowledge, and wisdom is organized life." How true a statement! Even our greatest scientific understanding of life is nothing more than organized knowledge. But wisdom comes from knowing life from the inside.

When you organize life - your experiences, your true authentic taste of life - that is when you touch the zone of wisdom. Although these practices may seem nonsensical from the outside for the one who is experiencing them, they are adding a little bit of intelligence to that reservoir of wisdom. You would be able to see it for yourself. I would say you need to be a little less smart than a scientist. You don't need to be sophisticated; you don't need to be as smart or as objective as they are - you should be a little more playful in your approach. A scientist is a little too serious in their exploration. So, you don't need as much intelligence as a scientist, but you definitely need a little more intelligence than a politician. If you were to pick one group of human beings who would be the hardest to teach meditation to, it has to be the politicians because they are so up there in the ideas of life. First, they need to step back from concepts to experience to be able to see what's happening. At least a scientist is familiar with experience and experimentation. Although they're experimenting on the outside, they know what it is to experiment. They at least have the possibility of doubt - maybe something is happening here that I don't understand. At least they approach it with that much open-mindedness. As a meditator, you need to be somewhere in the middle, a little more intuitive, a little more intelligent. Then you will be able to see what appears to be nonsensical on the outside is actually making a lot of sense: "I can enjoy movement because I am stillness. I can enjoy change because I am the unchanging. I'm able to enjoy all the experiences of life because I am the one who's experiencing it. I am not lost in my experiences. There is something inside me that is still and silent."

When you start connecting with your inner stillness and provide a contrast, such as the shaking of the head, it becomes easier to observe the stillness. Let me share a small story from my own experience with this. When I started my meditation, I went into it with ferocious intensity. I wanted to sit in meditation all the time, for as long as I could, as many times as I could. The first month of my meditation, my whole world was meditation. Whatever other things I did, I did reluctantly - not because I was enjoying meditation, not because meditation was joyful; it was a challenge, something new I was trying to understand. So, I labored hard for a month, trying to connect with my breath, trying to connect with my inner stillness. Deep down, I had this feeling that I had not progressed much at all. I had not experienced anything that the books I had been reading were alluding to - inner silence, inner stillness - none of those things. I was only trying to connect with the stillness.

Then it so happened one day, at the end of, I would say, maybe a month or even a couple of months, I was traveling from one city to another to deliver a training program. I was sitting in the back of a bus. There were only a couple of people sitting in the bus along with me; they were sitting in the front. And then there was a screen dividing the driver part of the bus from the rest of the bus, so you could not see the driver. So, for all practical purposes, I was alone. As usual, wherever I was, when there was an opportunity for me to go into meditation, I used to go into meditation. I never cared whether I was sitting on a bus, riding a motorcycle, or sitting in a post office or a bank. It just didn't matter to me. The landscape outside didn't matter. I just wanted to be in meditation. So naturally, I just sat cross-legged on the seat and went into my meditation. I was trying to keep my focus on the breath. Then I noticed that the bus had stopped. Of course, you can feel it when the bus stops. The bus stopped, and one person got off, so there was only one other person left. We journeyed a little further, and even this person got off. The journey was supposed to be long, about eight hours, and within a matter of one hour, both these passengers had gotten off because they were not going all the way.

Now here I am sitting in this bus all alone. I can't see the driver, so I'm sitting in this empty box that is moving. I didn't pay much attention to it. I noticed it, and then I went back into my meditation. I closed my eyes and went in. As usual, at the end of one hour, I opened my eyes. Something strange happened - because I had gone so deep into my meditation I had completely forgotten that I was sitting on the bus. Then, I didn't even realize that when you go inward, you can connect to a stillness where you don't even experience the movement. So, for all practical purposes, I was still, I was not moving. But when I opened my eyes, something strange happened. My body and mind began registering that I was moving. I could see out the window that things were moving.

The vehicle was moving, but there was something inside me that was totally still - that was not moving at all. That was the first time I authentically connected with my inner stillness - not in any flimsy way - as an experience that jolted me out of meditation. It's like, "I am still. The bus is moving. Something is moving. My body is moving, but where am I moving?" I could not tell the difference between sitting on that bus and sitting in my room and meditating. It felt exactly the same. And the connection with that silence, connection with that stillness was very deep.

For the rest of the journey, I thoroughly enjoyed this contrast. I enjoyed every small movement. I enjoyed every tree moving away from me, every house moving away from me. I enjoyed watching all things pass by me. I had never enjoyed movement that much in my entire life. Throughout my life, I was always a boisterous kid, always jumping around, but never in my life had I enjoyed movement that much. Why is that? What was happening there? The movement provided the contrast for me to enjoy my stillness. It is not the movement I was enjoying but the stillness. That is when I realized when you move the body, when you are connected inside to your meditative silence, that movement embellishes, that movement augments your stillness. And what it does in the process is deepen your connection with your stillness. While these things were happening, I couldn't put it all together to make the connection.

It took me a long time - several years - before I understood what was happening. That is how I was able to understand all these movement meditation techniques and what there is in movement meditation. For me, meditation has always been about sitting still. The moment you move, you're shaking yourself out of meditation - you're disturbing your meditation. That's when I realized that "No, the disturbance is for the body. The disturbance is for the mind. But as far as you are concerned, there is no disturbance." Of course, you cannot start with movement. If you start with movement, then you will be stuck with the movement. You need to start with stillness.

THE TECHNIQUE

So, let me give you the technique. Divide your shaking-the-head meditation into parts. For the first five minutes, sit still. Don't move. Do your regular breathing meditation, watch the candle meditation, or listen to the music meditation - whatever meditation you are comfortable with and have picked up as a technique. Connect with that stillness. Connect with that silence. Then, for the next thirty seconds, start moving your head without losing the connection with your inner stillness and see if you can enjoy the movement. Do it for half a minute and then stop. Again, go back to your regular meditation. Start watching your breath, stop the movements, and connect with your inner stillness. After another two and one-half to three minutes, move again. Repeat this stillness and movement three times. Then, during the next cycle of three movements, move your head with a little more intensity, rotate it, and see if you can enjoy that experience of stillness more. Do this for thirty seconds, then connect with the stillness. Repeat the same process three times.

You can also move your entire upper body. You don't have to restrict it to just the head. For the last set of three movements, start swaying from left to right, but keep moving your head. The objective is that "you" are sitting still, connecting with your stillness. Although your body is moving, there is something inside you that is not moving. That is what you're trying to connect to. So, sway your body from left to right, rock it from left to right, then front to back, and then rotate your upper body. You can swing your arms out and even hold on to something for support, then rotate your body, sway your body. Do it slowly initially, and then do it faster and faster. All the time, connect to your inner stillness. Again, alternate between thirty seconds of movement and two to three minutes of stillness. After completing all three movements, simply sit still for fifteen minutes.

Now, why is this stillness for just a few minutes important? If you just started shaking your head without connecting to your inner silence or inner stillness, it is possible that you can't see and appreciate the contrast because you're too much in the body. When you allow yourself to relax and then shake, the contrast becomes clear. You don't have to do this in every sitting. You don't have to do this meditation all the time. Keep your sitting still meditation primary and play with the movement whenever you have the desire to connect with that inner stillness a little more. As long as your meditation is not disturbed, you can continue to move your head.

Enjoy the process. Just play with the whole idea. This will do two things: One, it will help you to understand your level of connectedness with yourself and measure your progress in meditation. If you have sat in your regular meditation, watched your breath, for let's say three or four months, and then when you do the movement and if the disturbance is not much, that is an indication that your meditation is deepening. So, the first thing is it helps you to measure your level of meditation. And the second thing is it helps you to disconnect yourself from the regular activities of the body, which extend throughout the day. Once you know how to be still and allow the body to move, you can do the same thing when you're not sitting in meditation. You have learned how to be in meditation even amidst movement.

When you're taking a walk or going about your daily activities, you can try to connect with the same stillness inside. Just pause for a moment, get in touch with your stillness, and then slowly move without losing the connection with your stillness. There, you are extending your meditation beyond just one hour. Play with the whole idea and see how much more you can enjoy movement. This practice will extend to all movements. You can even enjoy it while you're driving. Suddenly, while driving, if you become aware of yourself, you will notice the contrast. A moment will come when you can see that yes, the car is moving, your body is moving, registering the movement, but there's something inside that is still. That will be your first introduction to your true self. After that experience, nobody has to convince you that there is something inside you. You can listen to all the arguments of a scientist or a philosopher; they can deny the self, they can deny the inner, but your experience has shown you that the inner exists. Then there is no arguing and debating. It is just about going deeper and experiencing as much of that inner stillness as you can, to eventually, ultimately, become that stillness itself. On the inside, you are silent. You are still. You've transcended all disturbance. You've become the stillness itself.

Dancing with Shadows

VIPASSANA

The most important and simplest of meditation techniques is Buddha's watching the breath technique. In my opinion, all other meditation techniques are deviations from this. If you were to ask me to name that one meditation technique that I would recommend for everybody - young, old, man, woman, sick, healthy - and if I could choose only one, I would pick watching the breath meditation.

In the words of Zen master Cheng-tao Ke, "Like the empty sky, it has no boundaries, yet it is right in this place, ever profound and clear. When you seek to know it, you cannot see it. You cannot take hold of it, but you cannot lose it.

In not being able to get it, you get it. When you are silent, it speaks. When you speak, it is silent. The great gate is wide open to bestow alms and no crowd is blocking the way."

The first thing to remember about any meditation technique is why you are meditating. What is the objective of meditation? What is the purpose of meditation? And you should never forget the ultimate that you are searching for. It has to be the ultimate that you are searching for - it cannot be something in the middle. If you get something in the middle, it's fine. If you get relaxation, peace, or joy, it's fine - but don't look for them. Don't go in search of them. You go in search of the ultimate because the ultimate is the easiest thing to find - it's your very nature, and you're not going anywhere to find it. The ultimate is within you. It is outside of you. It is all around you. You are in it. What are you doing when you're sitting and watching your breath? The simplicity of the process has to be understood. Once you know what you're looking for, then you can keep on adjusting your meditation - keep on adjusting your technique to align with it. What is missing is only the alignment. The experience is not far away.

You could be sitting attached to the truth. You and the truth could be the closest of companions, but if you are facing in opposite directions, that closeness doesn't matter. That is exactly what has happened. As bodies and minds, we have shifted our attention, shifted our focus away from that ultimate truth, what the Zen master calls "tao," the way. It is everywhere. It's all around you. If you search for it, you will not find it. But it is right there. When you speak, it is silent. When it speaks, you have to be silent. He's talking about the very nature of how the mind and truth are different. When you're in the mind, you're not in the self. When you're in the self, you cannot be in the mind. The first realization is that whatever it is you're trying to realize, you are very close to it. So only the simplest of methods, simplest of techniques will work. The rest are all deviations and complications.

What is that rhythmic, simple, ever-flowing, natural part of you? When no effort is required on your part, it happens by itself. You wake up in the morning, it's there. You go to bed at night, it's there. When you're angry, it's there; when you're peaceful, it's there. It was there at your birth, and it will be the last thing you're going to leave when you die. What is that one thing? Your breath. The simplest of things.

Pranayama

There is a reason why watching the breath is one of the most important and popular meditation techniques. It is not an accident. It is not because,

"Oh, that was the technique Buddha gave." No. Even before Buddha, this meditation technique was popular. In yoga, we call it Pranayama. Look at the beauty of the word: "Prana" is life, "Yama" is exercise, method, technique. You're watching the breath, but the term used to describe that process is watching life itself - watching your prana. The reason why watching the breath has been so popular is that one big problem in meditation is forgetfulness. Any technique you pick, the technique is not the difficult thing. It is to hold on to it for extended periods. Let's say you're sitting in meditation for one hour - you need to be as close as possible to the technique. It involves focusing, awareness, and relaxation. But because these things are natural to the being but unnatural to the mind and the body, you keep forgetting it and you have to keep coming back. Any technique that helps you to come back quickly and easily if the distance is not too far between your technique and where you have drifted, is beautiful.

Breath gives you that perfect opportunity to be very close to your mind and body, even though the mind drifts. Of course, when your body drifts, your breath drifts with it. If you decide to take a walk, your breath is always there. You cannot leave your breath and go away somewhere. So as far as your body is concerned, the breath is always there. When you decide to bring it back - because the breath is right there, it's not an external object, it is not even an inch away from you -

it's easy to come back. It's also easy to watch the breath because the rhythm of the breath and the rhythm of the mind are connected. When the mind changes, when the emotional content of the mind changes, the breath changes. That is why your breathing changes when you are happy, when you're excited, when you're angry, or when you're frustrated. I don't have to know anything about you. I don't have to know your past. I don't have to know your medical history. Nothing. I don't even have to visually look at you. Just give me a way to measure your breath, to see the fluctuation in your breath and I can tell you what mood you are in now. Why? Because your breath perfectly mirrors your emotional state. Because it is a happening.

Just like the mind, your breath is just happening, and they are in sync. So when you're watching the breath, if you begin to drift in thoughts, if you pay closer attention, the breath will tell you first. "I'm going to drift now. Notice how my rhythm is changing." Your breathing becomes shallow when you begin to drift in thoughts. When you're in the present moment, your breathing is deep. You take deep breaths. You settle down more. You relax more. But when your mind starts getting agitated, it starts thinking about the process of breathing as opposed to just focusing on breathing, the breaths become shorter and shallower. It's a very subtle difference, but you can notice. As a meditator with a little bit of practice, you can notice.

Breath gives you a beautiful indication of what's happening inside. It's a wonderful automatic measuring tool that is available to help you measure your level of meditation, your level of relaxation, and your level of agitation. When you forget your breath altogether and drift into thoughts, then you have broken away from meditation. It's easy to see. When you want to come back, it's easy to come back. That is why watching the breath has been one of the most fundamental meditation techniques. It is the beginning of all meditation techniques. It is the beginning of all yogic practices. Even schools that have deviated away from normal meditation, that have forgotten that the ultimate purpose of meditation is to awaken, is to become enlightened, even such schools start their practice with watching the breath. In yoga, at least in modern terms, Pranayama is not recommended as a method for enlightenment but rather as a way of reducing stress, and reducing unwanted thought processes. Still, it starts with the breath. Why are we still holding on to the breath? Because everything starts with the breath. Your mind is linked to the breath. So people figured out that "Even if I'm not searching for the ultimate, if I want to relax a bit, if I want to be mindful, then watching the breath is the best way to do it." And your breath is always there with you wherever you go.

The Technique

Let's look at how to approach this. What is the method? What is the technique? First, you need to assume a comfortable posture, a relaxing posture that keeps you alert and awake. Any posture that keeps you both alert and awake is a good meditation posture. You have assumed the meditation posture, and you have closed your eyes. You know what you're searching for. You're not imagining it, but you know that there is something right here, a sensation, a feeling, a center - "I want to touch, and I can touch that center only when I'm relaxed. I'm going to use my breath as an anchor to relax deeper and deeper into myself. I'm going to shift from my mind center to my body center, which is the breath." Literally, breath is the body center, and you begin to watch.

You watch the breath moving in. You watch how it fills you up. Watch the subtle changes in sensations as you take the breath in. You will experience tiny tingling sensations in your body as the breath goes in because breath is not air; it is life itself. It is prana. You take the breath in; it almost gives you a sense that you are expanding a bit. That is what is happening. That is what breathing is. Breathing is not just the exchange of gases. It is an interaction with the aliveness that is around you. As you take the breath in, you're taking the life force in. Observe how deep the breath goes. What centers does it touch? How long does it stay there? But you stay only with the flow. Then the breath stops; it circulates, turns around, and exits.

When you're exhaling again, watch the entire flow. Notice how something has changed now. The feeling is different when you are exhaling compared to inhaling. You can sense this in the body. You can sense this in your mind. Sometimes, you can just watch how the body and mind are reacting to the breath coming in and going out. The mind sees the breath as something very important. When you're taking the breath and when you're aware of the incoming breath, notice how your thoughts stop. You can't watch the breath and think about it at the same time. Impossible. Right there, that should tell you that you're operating on two different levels. Two different centers are operating. The mind center and the life center. Breath is the life center. When your focus is on the life center, your mind center disappears. It is that simple. You're not trying to change the content of the mind. You're not going deep into analyzing the mind; you are simply shifting the center. It takes a little bit of effort. It takes practice.

Once the center shifts, you have shifted away from the center of chaos and confusion. The mind is the center of all chaos, all confusion. People keep wondering how meditation works. It is my mind, it is my body, it is my breath. What can change by simply sitting and watching the breath? This is the change that happens. Yes, you are one. Your mind is one. Your body is one. It's all right there, but your focus and awareness can be on different things at different times. As of now, your focus and awareness are completely on the mind. You're obsessed with thinking. That is what has taken you away from the center. That is what is causing the disturbance and agitation that you're experiencing, and that is the longing to come back to the center. That is the longing to come back to meditation because you have shifted away from the true center.

That is how meditation works. Meditation does not try to change the content or the nature of your mind. What it does is shift the identification. It just says, "You are way too attached to your mind. Your mind is one small part of your being. If you are the whole body, your mind is the tip of one of your fingers. You have forgotten the whole body and you have become obsessed with the tip of that one finger, that is why you're disturbed." Somewhere deep down, something is reminding you that you are more. You are something more. But your mind constantly keeps pushing you into that corner - "No. There's nothing more to you. You are just this problem and you need to solve it. That's it."

The mind is just a problem solver and it looks at your whole life as a problem that you've got to solve. It does not realize that life is not a problem. Life is an experience. Life is swimming in the vast, undivided ocean with nothing to obstruct you. But the mind doesn't understand that. That is why a small shift from the mind to the breath is the shortest of distances to travel. But in terms of transformation, it is the grandest. It is the biggest. Nothing can transform you from inside as much as that small distance you have traveled from the mind to the breath. How far is the mind from the breath? One blink away. It is one breath away. You take the breath in, and when the breath is going out, if you forget to watch it, you're in the mind. In fact, I would say you're not even one breath away from the mind; you are half a breath away. You take the breath in, that's half the breath. And then if you forget to watch it, your mind has entered. That is how close you are to truth and also that is how far you are. And how easily you can forget the life center and shift into a purely imaginary center. It is important to remember that the mind is an imaginary center. No matter how enticing it is, no matter how powerful and entertaining it is, you should know that the mind is not your true center. Your true center is your breath. The true center is your body. Come back to it. Watch the flow.

Every time your mind drifts, gently bring it back. Yes, there are times when you will completely forget the breath. It will happen when you begin your practice. It'll happen again and again. You want to keep your focus on the breath, but the mind keeps on interfering. It starts with thinking about the breath. It appears as if I am doing the right thing. I'm thinking about the breath. I am watching it because watching can also be done by the mind. But the watching of the mind is done through thoughts. That is what thinking is. That is what drifting is.

It takes some time for you to understand the nuances, to understand the difference between watching through your being and watching through the mind. Watching through the mind is always a qualification. Yes, it's relaxing. Yes, it's good. It's been five minutes. You are watching the breath. You are inspired now. You've drifted from watching; you're thinking. That's how subtle the difference is. But once you start recognizing it, you will know how not to entertain the mind - "Okay. You go on talking. Let me watch the breath." After a while, you will stop listening to the mind because you know it is repeating the same thing. There's nothing new in the mind. It's the same old repetition. And then you would enjoy being with the breath more. Although breath is also repetition, it's the same thing, but it's never boring because it's not a mental loop. It is happening very close to existence so there's no boredom. You can sit and watch your breath for as long as you want. This whole idea of boredom comes from the mind. It does not come from the body. Bodily processes are never boring. The mind can become boring because it uses language, it uses images.

Imagine if I'm showing you the same photograph a hundred times a day. That is boring. But if you are in the zone of silence and stillness, you can be in that zone for as long as you want without getting bored - those are existential qualities. It has nothing to do with the mind. So just be with the flow. Enter the body along with the breath and leave the body along with the breath. Now with each breath try and relax a little more. Use your breath as a way of relaxing your body. Invariably, because focusing is involved, when you start watching your breath, your body tenses up. It is subtle, but you can notice it's happening. You are becoming stiffer and stiffer because you don't want to let go of the breath.

That's where you add one other condition to your breathing: Yes, I want to watch my breath, but at the same time, I want to use my breath to relax more. So when you exhale, exhale deeply. Just push it a little further. I mean, when you inhale, inhale deeply. Don't exaggerate the breathing. Let it be natural. Just at that point when you think, "Yes, I've taken the breath enough, now I'm going to exhale." Just breathe in a little more. That will help you to be aware of the breath. Just take in maybe half a second more and similarly with the out-breath. Keep on extending that. In, out. In, out. Very simple technique. Your attention sometimes shifts to the mind, it sometimes shifts to the body sensations. Sometimes it starts listening to things because you don't just have one sense of watching or focus. You have five different senses. All of them are craving for attention. Sometimes your smell sensation is activated. Sometimes you feel thirsty and you start thinking about water or food.

The senses - that's how you drift. You start experiencing a sensation, and what is a sensation? A sensation is something that stems from the senses. You start thinking about it, you drift, and you come back to the breath. Breath is also a sensation, but it is a sensation that does not lead to thinking. It just keeps you right there. If you are experiencing the sensation of breath, if you get the desire to breathe more, the breath is right there. You don't have to stop and go to the kitchen to find your breath. It's right there. So this is one method - watching the flow.

You can also watch the gap between two breaths. Just a small difference in the method. Keeping everything the same - your body posture, your search for the ultimate, your desire to move away from the mind center. Instead of the flow, just watch the gaps. There are two times you can watch the gap in one breath. One is you take the breath. As you take the breath just before the breath goes out, there is a pause. There is a momentary gap, and you're waiting to experience that gap. The breath comes in - just acknowledge the gap and then let the breath go out. Before taking the breath again, there is another pause on the outside, and you take the breath in. One pause on the inside, one pause on the outside. Just keep your focus on the pause.

As you continue to practice, this one momentary pause begins to expand. As of now, it is one moment because your mind is very quick to put you back into the flow or take you away from breathing. But with enough practice, when you come to the pause - that pause itself feels like a long pause. In the pause, in the stillness, time disappears. Initially, it's just one moment. You might even be thinking, "Where is the pause here? I don't see any pause. The breath is coming in and it's immediately going out." It cannot be immediate because the breath has to change direction and a change of direction does not happen without a pause. However small, however momentary that pause might be, just watch the pause. Breath goes out again, watch it. Just stay in between those two pauses.

Now the question is, what do I watch? When I say watch the breath, that is your meditation. The natural question is, do I watch the flow of the breath? Do I watch the pause? Or do I watch the sensation of the breath? What do I watch? Two separate techniques - One is watching the flow. The other one is watching the pause. Now there's no confusion. There's not much you can do there. In fact, you should not be doing anything more than simply watching the flow or watching the gap.

You don't need complicated methods or techniques. Yes, depending on your personality, depending on certain tendencies you've accumulated throughout your life, certain meditations will appeal to you more. But in almost all of the meditations, you will see the basic process is the same as coming back and watching the breath. The foundation of meditation is the same.

It is very much possible that breathing meditation might not be for you. It might not resonate with you. You might want to find something else. Use the breathing meditation as the yardstick to measure your other meditations. Otherwise, you would not know which one is resonating with you. You need to have some basic technique to measure it against, and watching the breath is the basic technique. There is no opposition in meditation between one technique and another because all techniques lead to the same destination, so you can practice hundreds of different techniques. You are still moving toward the same center. It's not recommended to practice too many techniques in too quick of a succession. You are unable to watch the subtlety, the nuances of the technique, and adjust better because you're shifting from one to another to another. It's just like driving. When you're learning to drive, it is better to pick one vehicle and learn to drive fully in that. Once you learn how to drive that one vehicle, you can learn to drive other vehicles. But when you are beginning, you don't shift from one vehicle to another to another. Although you can, although the mechanism is the same, the subtlety and the nuances are different, and that disturbs you.

That much is the difference between one technique and another. Every technique is about driving, about learning how to drive, learning all the nuances of driving. The only difference is the scenery is a little different. Depending on which vehicle you're in, the way the mechanism moves is different, and the way you have to adjust to it is a little different. Other than that, the core technique is the same. Watching the breath is the driving school class of meditation - it is meditation 101. From here, you can explore other meditation techniques and see which one grabs hold of you, which one jumps out and says, "I am the one for you. I'm going to take you to awakening. Going to take you to enlightenment."

WATCHING THE DREAM

You're watching your dreams, whether you decide to do it consciously or not. A dream is a never-ending, continuous part of your life. At a certain level of your being, your dreams are always present; they're always there. Watching is not even a choice. Once in a while, you are thrown into watching the dream because something is happening in that dream that jolts you, wakes you up, and urges you to pause and take notice. Those are the only moments when you are conscious of your dream. Otherwise, the dream is just happening like an undercurrent, and you're not interested in watching it. The watching is happening, but it's occurring haphazardly and intermittently, intermixed with a multitude of emotions and desires, preventing you from penetrating deeper into your dreams.

Conscious watching of dreaming unravels the nature of life because your life is nothing but your dream. Just go to the center of your being and look at the world from that center. For a moment, forget concepts, ideas, opinions, and judgments of people. It takes a little bit of courage to forget what you've been taught and what you've been told, and go straight to the center of your being and look at your life from that center. Look at all your experiences as much as you can. Look at your childhood. Look at your interaction with your parents. Look at the interaction with your friends and your love interests; look at your interaction with the physical reality outside. Notice how there's always an emotional connection between you and what's happening on the outside. Nothing is just random. Even random events have a deeper emotional connection to your being. All your experiences are subjective. Why? If you are just a body, if you are just going through your experiences of life, there should be very few personal things, and you should experience them only once in a while. The rest of the time, all your experiences should be something that is happening out there. Only a few experiences should be personal. The rest should have no connection whatsoever with who you are as a person.

But watch your life. Almost every event has a deeper connection to who you are as a person. In everything, you are searching for yourself. You could be watching something that has no connection to you - a random event. For example, you're driving and you happen to see the carcass of a deer that's been hit by a car. It is a random event. It has nothing to do with your life. And yet, you cannot look at that without the stirring of your emotions, without fear of death, without connecting with the suffering of that animal in that one moment. At least for a moment, you would have thought about the suffering of that animal. You would have thought, "Oh, wish it had moved a little faster, wish it had stopped." You have no connection to that deer. You have a million other things to worry about. And yet, you're unable to pass through a single random event without bringing your personal experience to it. Why? Because life is your dream, and your dreams are symbolic.

You're Always Dreaming

There's a part of you that knows that life is a symbolic representation, a visual representation of your repressed desires. The waking state is where you are suppressing all your desires because you cannot express all your desires. There is a limitation in the physical world. In the waking state, you are consciously trying to avoid certain desires - you cannot act on every desire. In fact, there's no way to act on the majority of the desires, because it takes enormous effort to follow through on those dreams, and a lot of them affect other people. So you have to be conscious of how you're acting out your dream. This is where Sigmund Freud says something very significant. He says this is why we dream. We dream so that we can express our repressed desires.

Dreaming is a way of acting out our suppressed feelings, emotions, and desires. In a way, he is right. If you observe the nature of dreaming, one is you're always dreaming. You're dreaming during the day, you're dreaming at night, you're dreaming even when you're busy doing something - there's always that underflowing current of a dream. But there is a qualitative difference between the dreams that you have at night and the dreams that you entertain during the day. There is an intensity to your actual dream compared to your daydreaming. There is an intensity that extends to all your emotions. Every single emotion in your dream is exaggerated. Your fears and desires are exaggerated. If only you can just wake up in the middle of the night and watch your dream the way you can watch your regular waking consciousness, it'll freak you out. You won't be able to understand what's happening inside you. What are these dreams? Why are they so violent? And this is not me. Why am I behaving like this? And yet, you know it's all you.

Although there is an exaggeration, although there is manipulation of your thoughts, you know that underlying all that dreaming process, there is an individual who's not very different from you. In fact, that individual is you. You're not experiencing somebody else's dream; you're experiencing your own desires differently.

There's an interesting story from the life of Sigmund Freud, a story that became a cornerstone of psychoanalysis, which opened the doors for him to interpret the nature of the dream. Most of his psychological interpretations of dreams, his psychoanalysis of dreams, started with this one particular dream. In this dream of his, he meets a woman, a patient by the name of Irma. In fact, this whole episode is called "Irma's Injection." He's a physician, and he is trying to diagnose a problem she has. She's suffering from a lot of physical symptoms, and Freud is trying to help her out. He tries as much as he can to diagnose her problem, but he's unable to.

That leaves him with a sense of guilt that he was unable to help her. Then, after a while, he has another dream. In this dream, he is attending a party organized by his school, and he sees Irma there. Now she is showing Freud her mouth, which is swollen inside and has all kinds of white spots. This is all in his dream. He notices that she's having all these problems because his friend was unable to diagnose her problem accurately, and the medicine that he has given her has created all these other problems. He wakes up jolted from this dream, and he has this realization: "Why am I seeing this dream?" He immediately makes the connection between the previous dream and this dream. Because Freud, being Freud and having been trying to understand the nature of the dream, uses symbolisms and different psychoanalytical tools. He recognizes that this second dream was purely a manifestation of the first dream that was left incomplete. Because he was unable to diagnose her in the first dream, and he had that sense of guilt, that guilt projected itself into the second dream in a more exaggerated way, with slight variations. Now it is not him who's diagnosing, it's his friend. So in a way, in the second dream, his ego is split. But that other ego has the same personality and the same capabilities as him. So even with that other ego, which he's identifying as Otto, his friend, he is also unable to diagnose her. There is no Otto. His colleague was simply a mental projection. He's basically playing out the same episode of trying to help her and he has that same emotion of guilt. That's when he has this epiphany that dreams are a symbolic representation of repressed desires. We are playing out our dreams in the night because we did not get an opportunity to express them during the day. It's a very significant discovery, a very profound discovery.

For the first time, a psychologist - not a meditator, not a Buddha, not an awakened one, just by observing two random dreams - an individual has been able to make a connection between the waking state and the sleep state. But there's one point that he misses. He has to miss this point because he has not gone deep into understanding the nature of the mind or the nature of dreaming. Because he has only watched two dreams at random, there is still a separation between one dream and another. And still, he holds on to the dreaming process that happens during the day as consciousness, and what happens at night as unconsciousness. Throughout his psychological analysis, he differentiates human awareness into conscious dreaming and unconscious dreaming. He says a lot of the problems that we experience during our conscious dreaming process have their roots in unconscious dreaming.

If you were to ask a meditator, someone who has gone deeper into understanding dreams, who has made it his occupation to watch dreams, he would say the unconscious part, the dreams that happen during the night, are more significant. That is closer to your true nature of being than the waking state. Because the waking state is still a small part of your dreaming, and we are obsessed with this waking state, we have interacted with it so much that we have labels, names, and designations. We are invested in this dream, and we regard it highly. But in reality, your waking state is a small subset of your dreaming process.

Unless you're willing to watch your entire dreaming process, unless you're willing to dive deep into your subconscious, you won't be able to unravel the mystery of dreams and the mystery of life. How can you solve the mystery of life when you don't understand your dreams, because your life is nothing but a dream? Everything you know about yourself, everything you will ever know about yourself, comes from the process of dreaming.

This is where a psychologist and a spiritual person differ. A psychologist tries to interpret each dream independently. It started more intensely with Freud. He was so daring with the things that he spoke about the human mind. At the time when he spoke, he was running away from Nazi persecution, his writings and his teachings were condemned as Jewish teachings, and his books were being burned. He was fleeing the country, trying to protect himself and his daughter.

He dared to say that a male child, during the first five to six years of his life, develops a sexual attraction to his mother. He called it the "Oedipus Complex" - the jealousy toward the father and the repression of his physical desires. He says sexuality, the thoughts of sexuality, arises in the human body very quickly, not after the body becomes mature - the mind starts thinking sexually very early. That's what eventually filters down and becomes the sexuality of the body. It is the nature of reality that whatever we experience in the body first has to start with the mind. Even so-called physical ailments have their roots in the mind because the unconscious dreaming part is the dominant shaping force of our lives. The reason why these forces remain hidden for such a long time is that it's hard to break through the veil of thoughts and investigate into your dreaming. By its very nature, dreaming requires you to be unconscious.

You have to Wake Up

What is happening now becomes a part of your daily living. So when you wake up in the morning, immediately there is a disconnection. You don't wake up and continue to have the same dream. The moment you wake up, your dream breaks. And no matter what you do, you cannot go back and pick up the same dream. Why? More often than not, your dreams are incomplete. A lot of times, you wake up feeling frustrated that you were unable to complete that dream. And yet, you can never go back and finish that dream. Even if you were to say, "Okay, let me go back to sleep. Let me finish the dream," you cannot. Why? Because consciousness breaks the dream. Consciousness is like an absolute stop. There is no way for the dream to continue in the same way.

Put in another way, dreaming happens uninterrupted in all its vibrancy, in all its ferocity, when there is no conscious watching. The moment you watch it, your dream stops. So how do you understand your dreams? How do you interpret your dreams? This has been the biggest challenge because dreams are subjective; they are deeply connected to the individual. The true meaning of dreams can only be interpreted when you are analyzing your own dream personally, not somebody else's dream. But even Freud could not access his dreams because he was not a meditator. Only when he was randomly given access to a dream did he analyze it. Otherwise, for most of his life, he analyzed the dreams of others. So there was a severe limitation in terms of how much he could understand dreams.

There is a way to watch your dreams without disturbing them. There is a way to wake up in the middle of your dream without shattering the dream. That process is called meditation. Meditation is the only process through which you can watch your dreams without getting entangled in them. It takes practice, it takes skill, it takes learning - all that a meditator goes through as a part of learning. Reading the scriptures, understanding, interpreting them, and learning how to watch the breath, learning how to stay detached, learning how to be mindful - all this eventually contributes to that one single most important ability to watch your dreams without getting drowned in them.

How do you do this? Let us talk about the actual technique. What is the actual methodology you can apply to understand your dreams, and not just to interpret them? Interpreting is still playing on the surface. It is to understand the source of your dreams and to get to the bottom of it because understanding your dreams is not a choice. It is inevitable; sooner or later, you have to understand your dreams. Sooner or later, you have to get to the bottom of your dreams because no matter how beautiful your dream is, sooner or later, you have to wake up. That is your nature. That is why I say enlightenment is not a question of "if." It is not a question of "if I become enlightened, what am I going to experience? How am I going to experience it?" No. Enlightenment is always a question of "when." It is written, etched in the stone in your destiny that you have to be enlightened because that is your ultimate nature.

Not a single individual can escape enlightenment. Whether it happens this moment, the next moment, after an hour, after ten years, or after fifty lifetimes, it doesn't matter. If you are not actively pursuing enlightenment, you are only postponing your waking up. You might be thinking, "I don't want to bother about it." You might be hearing about it; you might be tempted to try it. But the sheer magnanimity of the effort might make you feel, "There's no way I can become enlightened."

Let me tell you something: if a thought has crossed your mind that there is no way you can become enlightened, let me say this with utmost certainty, with no doubt in my mind whatsoever - that only you can become enlightened. Let me repeat that: Only you can become enlightened. Enlightenment has meaning only when you experience it. Enlightenment is not an idea. It is not a concept. You can meet an enlightened person. You can hear all about enlightenment. You can hear all about awakening. You can know everything about Buddha's life, but you will have no conception of what enlightenment is until it happens to you. And it will happen to you because that is your existential reality.

In fact, with just one look at your life, you will see that knowingly or unknowingly, your entire journey has been toward awakening. Every moment, a small part of you has been awakening to the nature of reality. It's been happening in bits and pieces. That is what you call learning. That is what you call wisdom. That is what you call experiential learning.

Throughout your life, you have been going through experiences, and once you have played out an experience enough, the desire to play out that experience subsides, and you no longer continue to desire the same thing. To give you a simple example: the toy that you were given as a child. Just recollect that emotion when you got that toy for the first time. How did it make you feel? How much did it stir your being? Your entire universe became that toy. You played with it with full intensity, with full awareness. "This is the toy I've been waiting for." If you can be truly honest, you will see that was not even a toy. That was an extension of you. But if I were to give you that same toy now, the emotion is completely different. If you start playing with that toy and I snatch it away, would you sit and cry the same way you did when you were five? No way. So what happened to all your suffering? What happened to all that pain and anguish you experienced as a child when you were given something and it was taken away?

Conscious Watching

The same things, if they are given to you now and taken away, your pain is nowhere near as much as you experienced as a child. What does that mean? That means you have awakened enough to be detached from your pain. And nobody introduced the idea of awakening. Nobody introduced enlightenment. Nobody introduced watching your dreams and learning from them, but you were doing it. Imagine if you can do that consciously. You have been doing it, but very unconsciously, randomly, almost accidentally.

Imagine if you were to turn accidental watching into conscious watching. That is what meditation is. You are taking control of the entire process of learning.

Up until now, you have left learning to chance because you never regarded it as the most important thing. You looked at it as a distinction, as a separation between one human being and another. The more I learn, the more I understand, the better off I am when compared to someone else. It's always been a comparison.

If you look at your life in totality without comparing it with anybody else, learning is inevitable because knowingly or unknowingly, something has been pushing you toward your awakening. When you're introduced to the idea of spiritual enlightenment, you are introduced to the totality of all your experiences and how you can watch them, so that you can transcend the entire plane of dreaming. That is what a meditation technique is. When you're told, "Sit, don't move around. Don't go into the past. Don't go into the future. Just watch your dreams. Just watch your breath. Just keep your focus on the third eye." Whatever might be the technique, what is being implied here is to watch your dreams consciously.

In fact, all the methods and techniques are simply to bring you to the process of watching your dreams. When you start watching your breath, invariably, you will watch your mind because your mind will not allow you to watch your breath - it is such a strong undercurrent, and it is always there. For the first time, you start seeing how powerful the mind is, how intoxicating the mind is, and how much it wants to be in control. And for the first time, you see where you have lost control over your life. It is your dreaming process, which has totally hijacked your consciousness, hijacked your aliveness, and it has put you in a state of constant turmoil and disturbance.

So, it is not a question of if you will become enlightened. It is only a question of when. You can ignore it. You can pretend that there is no such thing called enlightenment. You can bury your head in the sand. But sooner or later, the realization will hit you that awakening is your own nature, and everything in existence has been reminding you of it. A bird flying in the sky, in a way, symbolically was reminding you of your awakening. It was telling you, "You're not free yet. See, I am more free. You cannot fly. I can fly." A flower was telling you about enlightenment. "Look at this. Can you smile like this? Can you live so momentarily without fear, without worry? See, I bloom with full joy, and I don't have fear. When I decide to bloom, I bloom fully, and I'm not afraid of dying. I carry the seeds of life in me; I'm just hoping that these seeds get scattered, and I don't mind dying, because I cannot die."

Everything in existence symbolically reminds you of your own true nature, and that is what life is. That is what nature is. The fears that you project in nature, the desires you project, the enchanting nature of nature, and the ferocious nature of nature, all come from a conversation that you have been having with yourself.

What happens when you look at the night sky, when you look at the stars? Can you look at the night sky without your emotions being stirred? You're not just looking at points of light; you're not looking at darkness. You're not looking at emptiness. There is wonder, there's pain, this frustration that you're not able to understand. There's this longing - "I want to know if someone is there." Where does that pain come from? Why are you projecting your aliveness onto the stars? There might be nothing there. There may be no one there, and yet you have a longing to see someone there. And if that longing isn't about connecting with yourself, awakening to your true nature, then what is it?

In a way, nature has been reminding you that you are not just that body; you are all this. That's what awakening is. Awakening is to realize that every single experience, everything that is happening in the universe is happening inside the dimension called you. The reason why you are unable to accept it is because you have arbitrarily restricted this dimension to just your body, and you're like, "How can stars be inside my body?" No. The stars are not inside your body, and you are not inside your body. That is the most important thing. If your body is just inside you, if your consciousness is transcendental, then there is no problem for your body to be there, and there's no problem for the stars to be there. There's no problem for a butterfly to be there. And also, there's no problem in understanding all these things. "Oh, this is my world. This is my universe. For whatever reason, I just became attached to one part of it, one corner of it which is the body. I forgot everything else. Now everything else is just coming and reminding me that I belong." That is why you feel like going into nature. That is why you feel like looking at a bird. That's why you feel like staring into the night sky because it's all you. Because you are not a physical body. You are aliveness. You are consciousness. Now what is stopping you from awakening to your true nature? This continuous dreaming process that has taken over you. And that is what you watch.

THE TECHNIQUE

This is a meditation technique best practiced before you go to bed and just after you wake up. So before you go to bed, make a conscious decision to watch the dreaming. You want to know how your dream transitions from the wakeful state to the unconscious state. At what point are you being left out of the dreaming process? It's a magical process to observe. Think about it. You're sitting, you're closing your eyes, and you're watching your thoughts. It is your own thoughts, and you are watching them. And yet there comes a moment in this watching process where somebody throws you out of the room. Something interferes and says, "I don't want you watching my dream. You are disturbing my dream," and it throws you out and continues to dream. What is that throwing out? Your sleep. Your body consciousness is thrown out. Now the dreaming can happen uninterrupted. As a practice, as a meditator, that is what you're trying to understand. Who is throwing me out? And you resist that. "No. I don't want to be thrown out. I want to be here. I want to see my dream."

The first day, you might succeed a little. You might be able to prolong your stay for one moment more. The next day, you might succeed a little more. The day after, even more. Day by day, you are adamant, you are insisting that you want to be there when the dream happens. Now look at the beauty of it. The dream is such an integral part of you, such a deep necessity of your being that eventually, the dream itself compromises and says, "Alright, I'm going to continue dreaming. I don't care whether you watch or not." The dream is not going to disappear - it distances itself. Because the force of the dream, the momentum of the dream is so strong, that just because you're watching, it cannot simply disappear.

The disappearing happens much later where the watching has engulfed the entire process. Initially, the dream just compromises. It says, "Well, I've been trying to push you out. I'm unable to. I'm okay. I will begin my dreaming, but at least I know after about ten to fifteen minutes, I can throw you out." At least for those ten to fifteen minutes, you're able to watch the dream. That will unravel your true nature like never before. For the first time, you're seeing the unconstructed, raw primordial process of creation. When a dream is happening and it has forgotten that you are there, it happens in its own vibrant intensity. It has a completely different quality. It won't be like the dream that you have during the day. It feels very different.

Although you're watching the same thoughts, the feeling is totally different. It is scary, it is shocking, and that intensity is what transforms you. That intensity is what separates you from the dream because you cannot be that dream. Something is happening in that dream which you can never identify with. The exaggerations in the dream you are unable to accept and something gets separated. Continue to watch. Slowly, a day will come when you can watch your entire dream throughout the night.

Initially, you're starting from one end. Literally, look at this process like there's a candle, and awakening is when you burn this entire candle. Watching the dream meditation is like burning a candle from both ends. Sleep is that candle that you need to burn. Sleep is the obstacle that is stopping you from becoming enlightened. Unraveling the dreaming process in your sleep is what you're trying to accomplish, so from one end, you're trying to burn it. And how do you burn a dream? By resisting sleep. You make a conscious decision to stay awake and watch your dream. So from one end, you're trying to keep the light burning. You're trying to keep the light of your awareness, the light of your consciousness, alive. "I want to watch my dream as much as possible." You will succeed a bit, and then you will fall asleep. And then you'll wake up in the morning.

When you wake up, don't just rush into activities. Just sit immediately in meditation. Start watching your thoughts and you will be able to see that twilight zone where unconscious dreaming is slowly being transformed into conscious dreaming. The quality of the dream begins to change, and the transition period between your sleep and waking is very important to understand what is happening there.

Let me give you a small example from my own experience that can illuminate this process. There was one day I distinctly remember. I had been practicing this meditation for a while. In fact, trying to stay awake during my sleep was one of my most important meditations. I was adamant not to sleep. So I had reached a point where I was sleeping maybe for an hour a day. That's about it. And even that was a choice. I had to choose to sleep. If I didn't want to, there was no necessity to sleep.

There was this one day when I started dreaming, and then I woke up from the dream. There was no difference whatsoever between that waking up and any other regular waking up. I woke up, walked up to my electric stove, and I made some tea, and I came back to the bed. That's where I used to sit and meditate.

I drank the tea. Then I tried to get up and carry on with my day. I decided to take a walk. I could not. I could not get up from my bed. And I'm thinking, "Why am I unable to get up?" One moment I'm sitting, and in the next moment I'm lying down. You have to understand the intensity of this experience because, for me, it was a real experience. One moment I'm sitting, and another moment I'm sleeping. Then I start investigating, trying to understand what is happening. Why is my body doing this? And why is there no transition between my sitting and sleeping? It's happening instantaneously.

That's when I realized that I was still sleeping. I'm not yet awake. My consciousness, my awareness had deepened so much that within the dream, I had woken up, and I was seeing the dream as if it was absolutely real. I could not make a distinction between the dream and waking up because my awareness was so deep, but I was still dreaming. I went back to sleep, and then I woke up again. This time, I'm up and I'm aware of what has happened before when I tried to wake up, but I was unable to. Then I fell back to sleep. Now I'm waking up again. This is the second time. This time I get out of bed, and I go prepare a cup of tea. That's my routine in the morning, and I come back, sit on the bed, and when I decide to get up, I'm unable to. The same thing - one moment I'm sitting, and the next moment I'm sleeping. Again, the fighting, what is happening here? Why am I unable to get up? Am I going crazy? Did I mess up something in my meditation? Did I go too far? I had all kinds of fears. And then I realized it was all a dream. I'm still asleep.

This same thing happened four times. Four times I woke up only to realize that I was still sleeping. But remember, when I wake up in the middle of my dream, it is absolute waking up. There is no way for me to tell the difference between if I am actually preparing the cup of tea, or if I am just doing it in the dream. That was the first time I had this deep, profound insight that I am always asleep. Even when

Watching the Dream

I wake up in the morning and I go and prepare the cup of tea, I am still asleep. What I call my waking consciousness is only an extension of my sleep. That is not waking up at all. And that transition period between the night and the morning is not something that just happened to me. It happens to all of us. That's when I realized we are so reluctant to shift from the sleeping state to the wakeful state, and we recollect this as our reluctance to get up. There's not a single person on this planet who hasn't hated the idea of getting up. It is the most common experience. We don't like getting up from bed, and there is a reason: it is effort. The mind has to play out this scenario, and it has to play out this scenario enough number of times before it jolts your body up.

This is the same process that happens every single day. Because you're not watching it, you just wake up, and you recollect it as some kind of disturbance. You don't worry too much about it. But if you were to actually watch the process, before you wake up from the bed you have tried and failed several times because something is pulling you back into that dream state. Something is pulling you back to sleep because somewhere deep sleep is your original nature. Waking up is only another type of dreaming. You're not waking up. It's just the language we use. But really, you're trying to enter another dream, and that is where your being is reluctant to let you go. But that is why, over a period of time, we learn how to get out of bed. We keep an alarm clock. Think about it. The amount of effort a human being has to put in to get up. He needs to have a desire to get up. He needs to have the motivation to get up. He needs to have an alarm clock, a wife, mother, or father to spank him and wake him up. Otherwise, he would be blissfully asleep for hours and hours.

This is not just the experience of a few individuals. This is the experience of the whole of humanity, including animals. If given a chance, they never want to wake up. They wake up reluctantly. Why? Because deep down, sleeping is our true nature. You have to wake up to this entire sleeping process to wake up from the dream. That is your ultimate destination. You're turning and tossing. You're struggling and striving. You are suffering. You are trying to understand. You're trying to learn about yourself. All this is happening because a part of you knows that you're still asleep and you need to wake up. So before actually waking up from the bed, I woke up four times only to realize that I was still asleep. That's when I realized if I can wake up in the middle of my dream and experience things just like the way I'm experiencing them during the day only to realize that I'm still asleep, then it is natural to conclude that whatever I experience during the day, is also sleep - it's only extended sleep. How do I know it's an extended sleep? Because it doesn't last forever. After moving around, eventually, I have to go back to sleep. Eventually, it pulls me back to it.

So your understanding of dreaming, by watching your dreaming process and practicing the watching meditation, starts where Freud's psychoanalysis stops. His interpretation of dreams - you can get to that same understanding by just recollecting two dreams and looking at the symbolism in your dreams. You don't have to go too far. But that is only the first step. After that psychoanalysis begins a meditative analysis. In fact, it's not even an analysis, but a deep meditative dive into the unconscious. Look at the beauty of the process. You're not trying to alter the dream. You're not trying to analyze it. You are only adamantly insisting, "Please let me be here. Leave me in that corner. You go on dreaming. I won't interfere. Just leave me in the corner so that I can watch what's happening because it is a matter of life and death for me. If I don't wake up from this dream, I will never know what true living is. I would not know what my true nature is, and I want to know who I am." Just insist on it every day.

Don't just go to bed and forget about yourself. Sit in meditation. Watch your dreams. Watch your thoughts. Notice how, slowly day by day, you're able to stay awake a little longer. You don't have to worry about this affecting your quality of sleep. It cannot affect your quality of sleep because you're not adding anything to your sleep. You're not agitating your sleep. You're only sitting and watching. If anything, after a while, your sleeping happens more naturally. In fact, you can practice this meditation if you are having trouble sleeping. Look at the beauty of it: If you are having trouble sleeping, watch your dreams and insist not to sleep; after a while, sleeping happens naturally. That is the mystery of life.

More than just sleeping, you are watching your dreaming process. Burn the candle from both ends so that the moment will come, that day will come when you are fully awake to the entire dreaming process. Imagine when that day comes when you're able to see an entire twenty-four hours of your life without sleep breaking it, and without all the discomfort of lack of sleep. Once your meditative awareness reaches that level, you hardly need sleep. You can watch your entire day. You can sit in bed and watch yourself sleeping. This is what Buddha did for his entire life after his awakening. This is where we get the reclining Buddha pose. When you look at that pose of Buddha when he's reclining, he's not fully asleep. It's a weird posture when you think about it. That is how he slept throughout the night. When Buddha was asked, "Why are you sleeping like this? Why don't you move around?" He said, "I don't move around because I'm aware of my sleep." What a profound statement. "You turn and toss around because you are unaware of your sleep. I don't turn and toss around because

I'm watching my sleep." Here is the most significant thing. He did not say, "I am not sleeping." He's saying, "I'm watching my sleep." This means as long as you're alive, sleep is an inseparable part of your life. That unconsciousness is an inseparable part of life, but you can wake up to that unconsciousness. It is a contradiction only in terminology. How can I be conscious of my unconsciousness? That is the mystery of meditation. That is the beauty of meditation. That is the magic of meditation. You can become conscious of your unconsciousness, and you can do it through watching your dreams.

About Nirvana

Originally from India, our teacher, Nirvana, embarked on his professional journey in the corporate sector shortly after completing his college education. However, at the age of 24, he realized there was a deep void within him that material achievements could not fill. Yearning for inner tranquility and a sense of purpose, he made the courageous decision to move away from home, leave his job, rent a modest room, and dedicate himself to the pursuit of meditation.

Devoting several years to intense meditation, Nirvana experienced a profound spiritual awakening that forever transformed his life. Motivated by this newfound understanding, he eagerly began sharing his experiences through various programs and retreats. In 2017, he traveled to the United States with one of his students, and upon arrival, he intuitively knew he had found the right place to sow the seeds of consciousness and awareness.

Nirvana Foundation is a nonprofit organization dedicated to providing individuals with opportunities to explore meditation and self-awareness through books and programs. Nirvana speaks twice a day, and his talks are recorded and transcribed by his students. These transcripts are ultimately compiled into books for publication. Currently, our teacher resides and teaches in Tennessee, where the development of the first Nirvana meditation retreat is underway.

Share Your Thoughts

If this book has touched your life, illuminated your path, or opened new avenues of thought and introspection, consider sharing your experience. Your review on Amazon will help us reach others who are searching for answers. Your reflections, insights, and experiences can light the way for fellow seekers on the path to Awakening.

Books by Nirvana

ISBN: 978-1962685009

ISBN: 979-8852311207

ISBN: 979-8392250196

ISBN: 979-8374196740

ISBN: 978-0578637068

ISBN: 978-1962685023

ISBN: 978-1-962685-04-7

www.ingramcontent.com/pod-product-compliance
Lightning Source LLC
Chambersburg PA
CBHW031248230426
43670CB00005B/83